IMAGES
of America

SACRAMENTO'S CAPITOL PARK

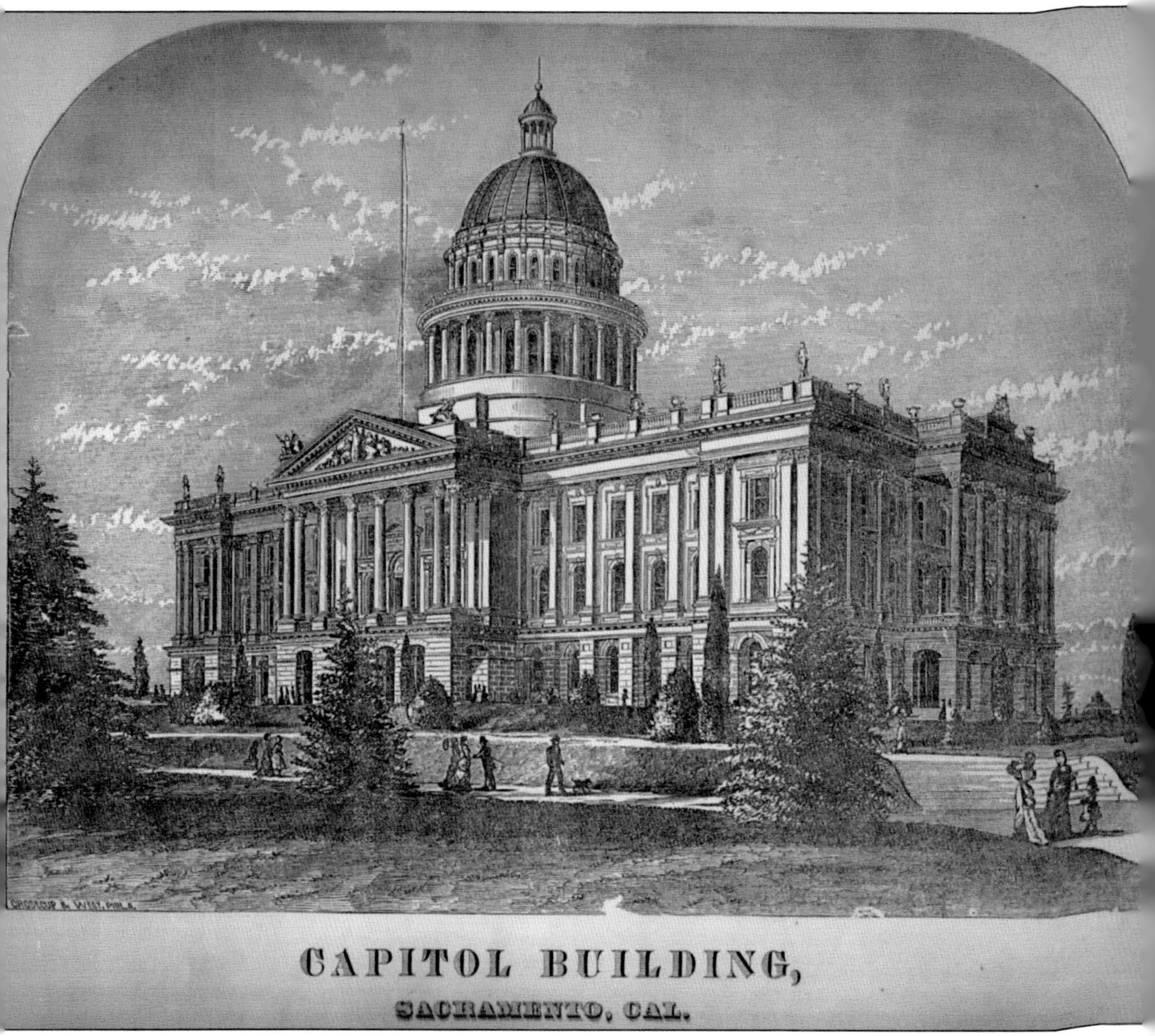

This lithograph of the California State Capitol is from the 1880 history of Sacramento County. It conveys the grandeur of the structure. At this time, the capitol building was nearly a decade old. (John E. Allen.)

ON THE COVER: Pictured is the California State Capitol seen from the northwest. The c. 1890 view includes the earliest part of Capitol Park in the foreground, the State Printing Plant to the left, and, in the near distance, the State Fair Pavilion to the center. (John E. Allen.)

IMAGES
of America

SACRAMENTO'S CAPITOL PARK

John E. Allen

ARCADIA
PUBLISHING

ISBN 978-0-7385-9688-4

Published by Arcadia Publishing
Charleston, South Carolina

Printed in the United States of America

Library of Congress Control Number: 2012941993

For all general information, please contact Arcadia Publishing:
Telephone 843-853-2070
Fax 843-853-0044
E-mail sales@arcadiapublishing.com
For customer service and orders:
Toll-Free 1-888-313-2665

Visit us on the Internet at www.arcadiapublishing.com

ad conjugi karissimi

Contents

ACKNOWLEDGMENTS

Some of my first childhood memories are of the California State Capitol and its park. Then, there are those I would just as soon forget, like getting thrown out of the building as a teenager by the California State Police for shooting "spit wads" from the inside rotunda. Yet despite some of these experiences, my love for the building and its history has only increased over the decades.

Books never write themselves. They are the product of many experiences, chance encounters, happenstance, serendipity, and so much more. There are many individuals whose knowledge, experience, and advice have proved invaluable in putting this book together: Gary Kurutz, head of Special Collections, California State Library (CSL); Koren Benoit, curator, Senate Rules Committee, California State Legislature (SRS); and Patricia Johnson, archivist, Center for Sacramento History (CSH). The following other institutions were sources as well: the California State Archives (CSA), the Department of General Services (DGS), and State Capitol Museum (SCM). The author's collection helped to round out the remainder of the material used for the book (JA).

There are also individuals, too many to list, who I wish to acknowledge. To begin with, there is my old "crew" at the State Capitol Museum—in particular, Neal Gordon, Dody Wheaton, Oscar Warner, and Bill Geach. I cannot even begin to thank all the capitol staff, volunteers, and visitors who generously shared their own experiences of the building with me while working there. Also, I want to thank the wonderful staff at the California State Library, who have patiently aided the author in his research and continue to carry on cheerfully and heroically in the face of an ever-worsening budget situation. Barry Cassidy and Mark Baker have also provided assistance. And many thanks go to my acquisitions editor, Jared Nelson. Any faults in this book are solely the author's.

I need to also recognize "Baby's" contributions in coming up with her own unique filing system. Finally, I want to thank my wife. She has made it possible for me to remain a professional historian even when Clio has been often fickle with her favors.

INTRODUCTION

The State Capitol of California, that is to endure for generations, should be a structure that the future will be proud of, and surrounded with beauty and luxuriousness that no other Capitol in the country can boast.

—Gov. Leland Stanford, 1863

The ancient Roman historian Herodian wrote, "Where the emperor is, Rome is," nearly 2,000 years ago, and it could have just as easily been said of California's state capitol. We often forget that capitols have been transitory throughout much of history. These portable governments moved as the leadership would move. Such was the case with California in its first years as a state. Where the capitol is, the capital is.

From its humble beginnings, California's capitol was located in four different cities: San Jose (1849–1851), Vallejo (1852–1853), Benicia (1853–1854), and Sacramento (1852 and 1854 to present). The seat of government made seven stops, or "removals," between 1851–1853. During its peregrinations, it covered over 400 miles, at a cost of $106,290.54 at the time. Even once settled in Sacramento, there were still numerous legal challenges and calls to relocate the capitol elsewhere in the state.

From its very beginnings in 1769, California suffered from being under-governed, whether it was under Spanish, Mexican, or American rule. Following the United States' takeover in 1846, California was placed under a short-lived military government. Following this three-year period, California was one of the few states in the Union to have never gone through a territorial phase. Statehood would finally come in 1850, but California's problem of weak and impermanent governance would remain an issue for years to come. This already troublesome situation was only compounded by the state's early years of chaotic development during the Gold Rush.

One

"Roving Vagrant"

The government of California is the most migratory civil institution known among men.

—*Sacramento Daily Union*, 1852

Californians picked the worst of all possible times—the Gold Rush—to form a new state government. Beginning in 1849, as thousands of argonauts descended on the California goldfields, few had any interest in forming a government. In fact, most had expected to already find a ready-made political system of government institutions, political parties, and laws. Instead, miners discovered a near-total political void. The quest for riches was not going to distract most from trying to find their own "pile" and heading home. Out of frustration, some miners formed 500 ad hoc self-governing mining districts while waiting for others to establish some semblance of law and order.

What California needed was a government. Eventually, some citizens stepped forward in 1849 to begin the long process of establishing an official government for California. They did so out of concern for the anarchic state of Gold Rush society. There was a pressing need to address its fluid, chaotic, lawless nature. Nowhere was this quest for social, economic, and political stability more evident than in the struggle to set up a state government and locate a permanent home for California's capital. The ongoing problem of the transience of the state capital led to the public giving it many well-deserved nicknames. Among them are "roving capital," "floating capital," "capital on wheels," "peripatetic capital," and "public vagrant."

As the seat of government, the capital was meant to be not only the location for the newly elected legislature and constitutional officers but also the home to the state archives and state library. Furthermore, the legislature met only on a part-time basis for a few months each year. So as an institution, it was anything but permanent.

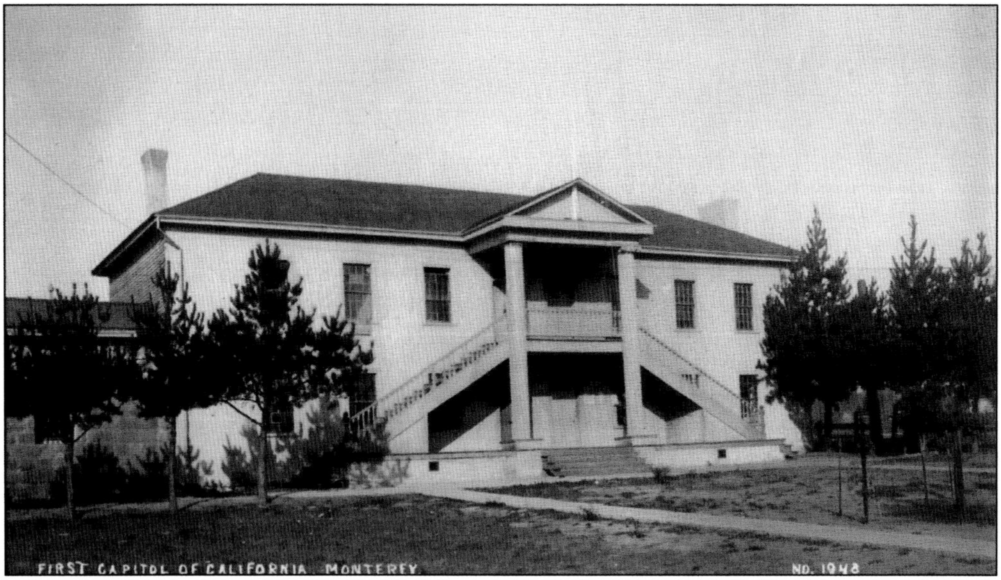

Colton Hall in Monterey served as the site for California's first constitutional convention in the fall of 1849. The 48 delegates drafted the first constitution, set up elections for state officials, established the state's boundaries, designed a state seal, and designated San Jose as the state capital. Despite popular belief, Monterey was never the capital of California. (JA.)

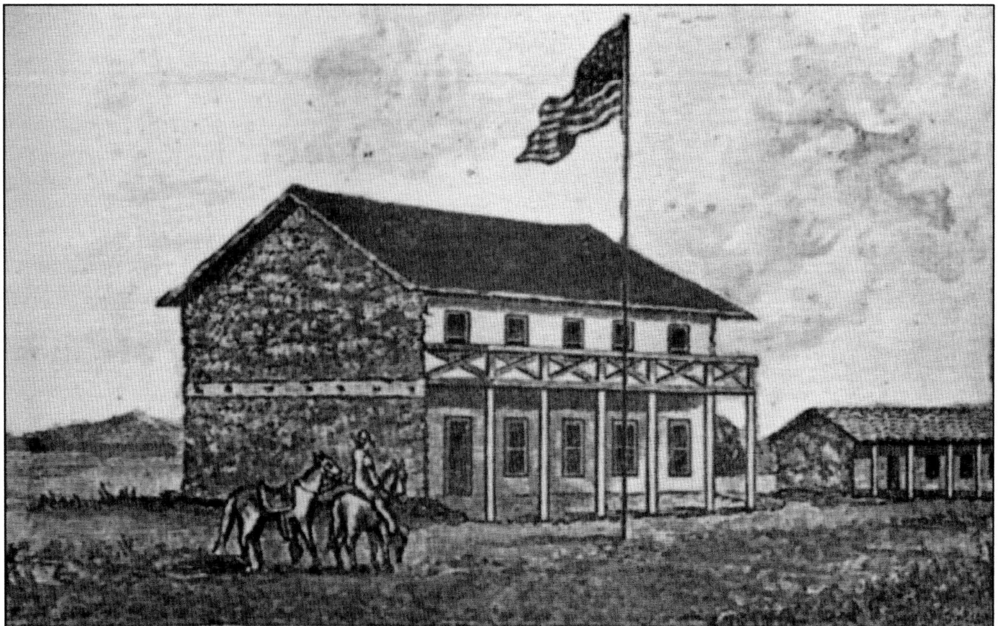

CAPITOL AT SAN JOSE--1849-1851.

San Jose, located in the San Francisco Bay area, had been selected by the members of the constitutional convention as the site for convening the first session of the legislature. The simple adobe structure served as California's capitol during the first two legislative sessions. The first session was known as the "Legislature of a Thousand Drinks," because the members retired at the end of each day to a nearby watering hole. (CSL.)

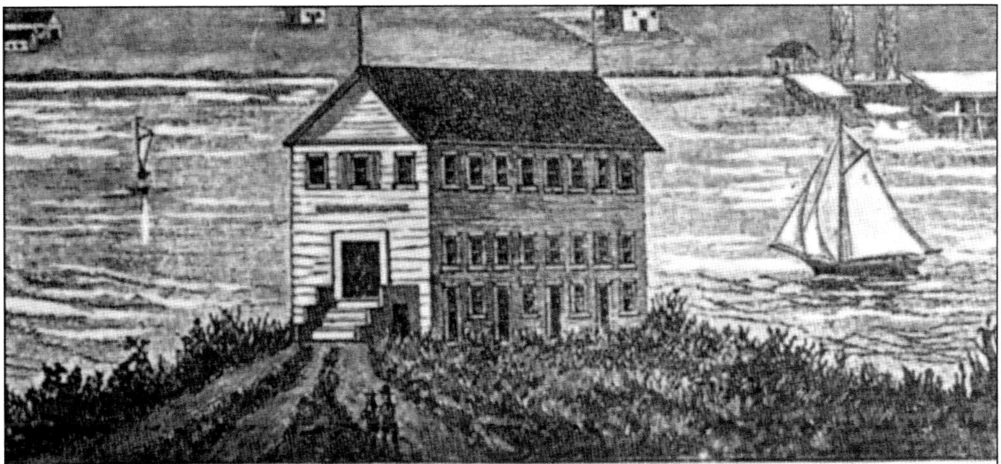

CAPITOL AT VALLEJO--1852-1853.

Prominent Californian Mariano Vallejo founded a new town named after himself and offered land to the state in an attempt to lure legislators away from San Jose. When the legislature arrived in January 1852, it found a half-completed building and few lodgings. The three-story wooden structure did have, however, one attraction. It featured a third house complete with bar and poolroom. After only a few days, legislators boarded steamers to go up the Sacramento River. (CSL.)

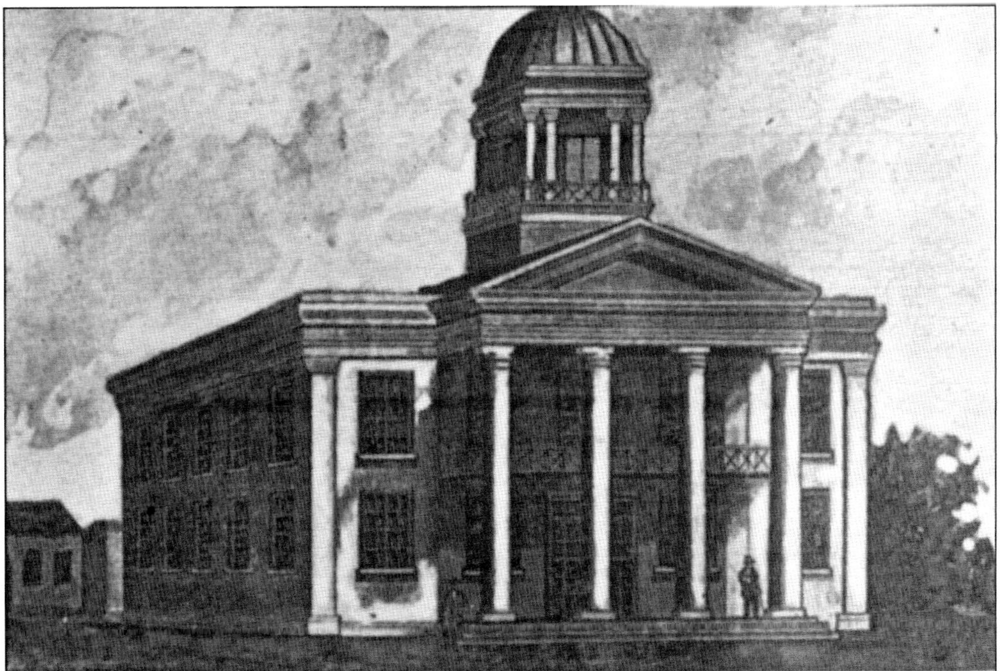

FIRST CAPITOL AT SACRAMENTO--1852-1854.

Once again, the state government was on the move to another community that would eagerly welcome California's wandering solons. Now, it was Sacramento's turn to play host. The legislature continued its third session in the Sacramento County Courthouse at Seventh and I Streets. It arrived in time for one of the periodic inundations that afflicted the flood-prone city. After completing its session in Sacramento, the legislature once more disbanded without fixing a permanent location. (CSL.)

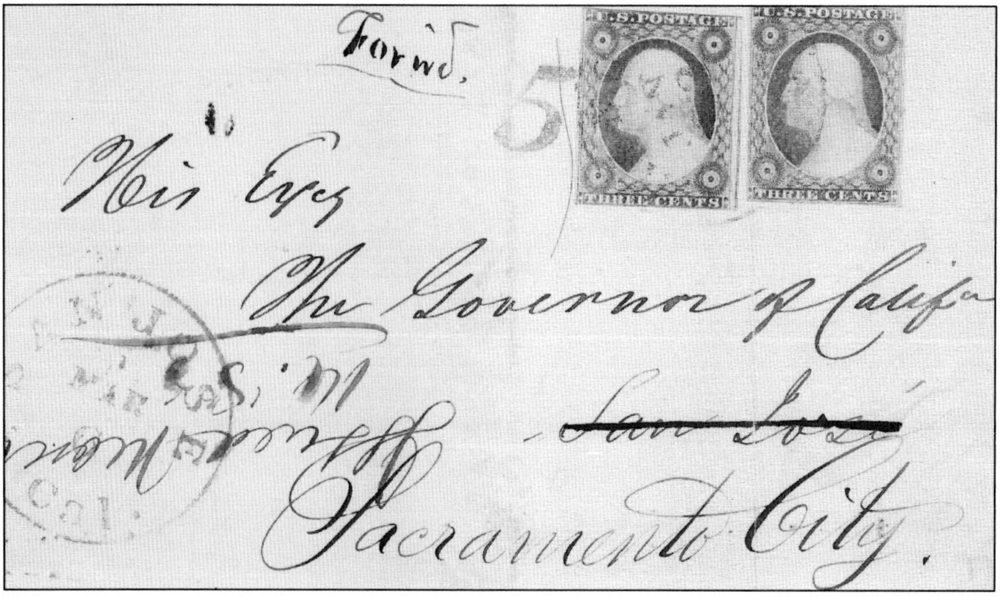

A sense of the confusion caused by the constant "removals" of the capital can be gathered from this 1852 envelope. After the letter was sent from Washington, DC, to San Jose, the postmaster had to then forward it to the governor in Sacramento, bypassing Vallejo altogether. (JA.)

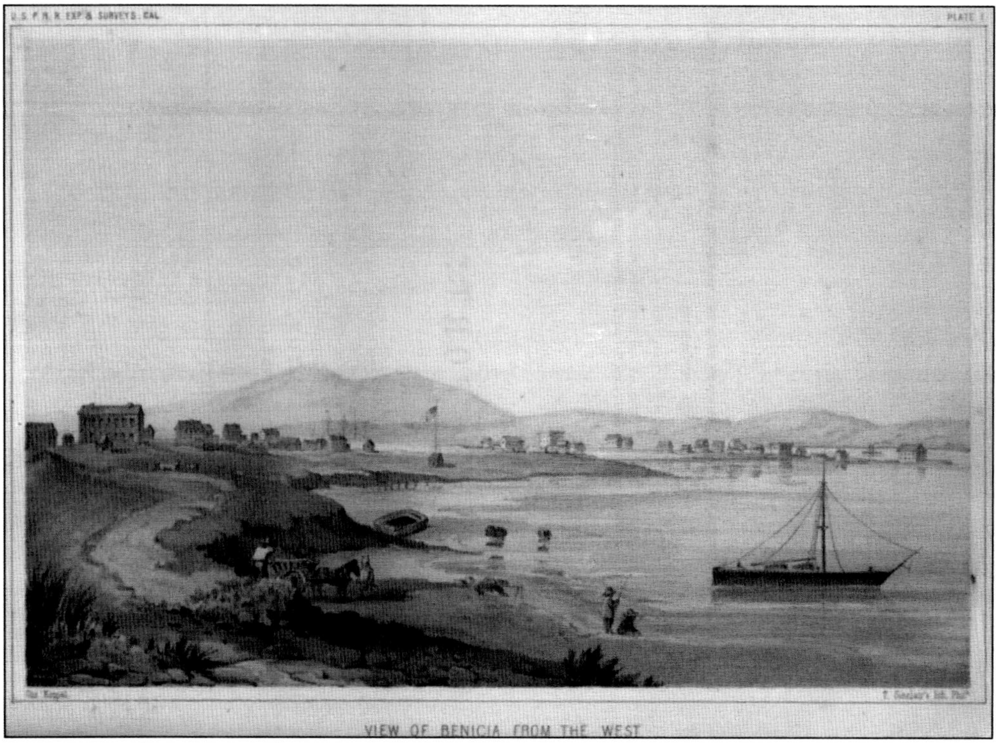

In 1853, another town in the Bay Area tried to become the home of the capitol. The citizens of Benicia (named for Vallejo's wife) offered their newly completed courthouse for the use of the state. The fourth legislative session was held in the two-story building seen at the far left of this 1855 view of the new town. (JA.)

As can be seen in this late-19th-century photograph, Benicia's courthouse was a stately brick structure with two Doric columns. For only one year before moving on— yet again—the senate met on the ground floor and the assembly on the upper floor. In later years, the building served as a courthouse, a movie theater, and is today a state historic park. (CSL.)

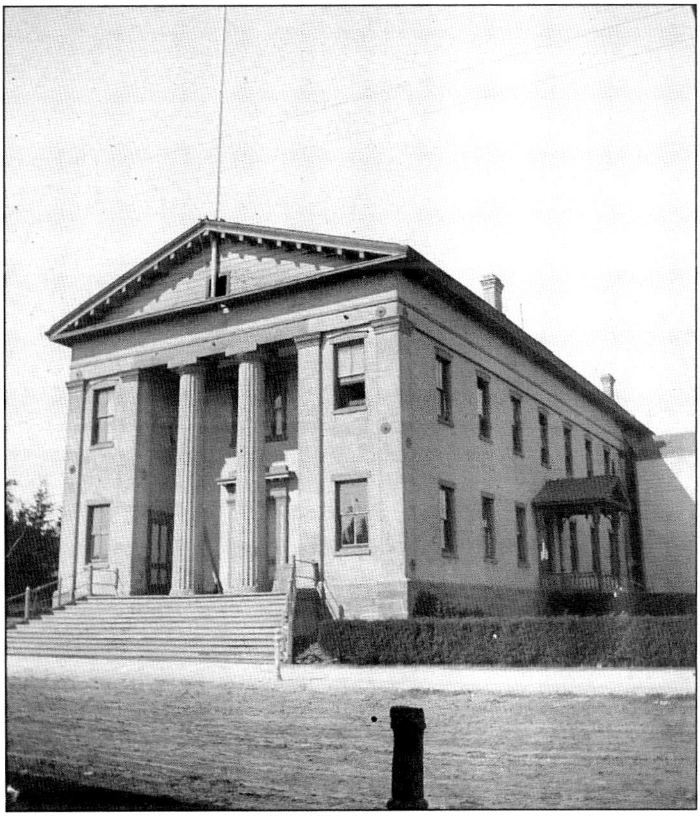

Californians, it seems, were beginning to finally run out of patience concerning their state's need for a permanent seat of government. This 1853 political cartoon, *Removal of the Capital*, reflects the popular sentiment and frustration of the time. (CSL.)

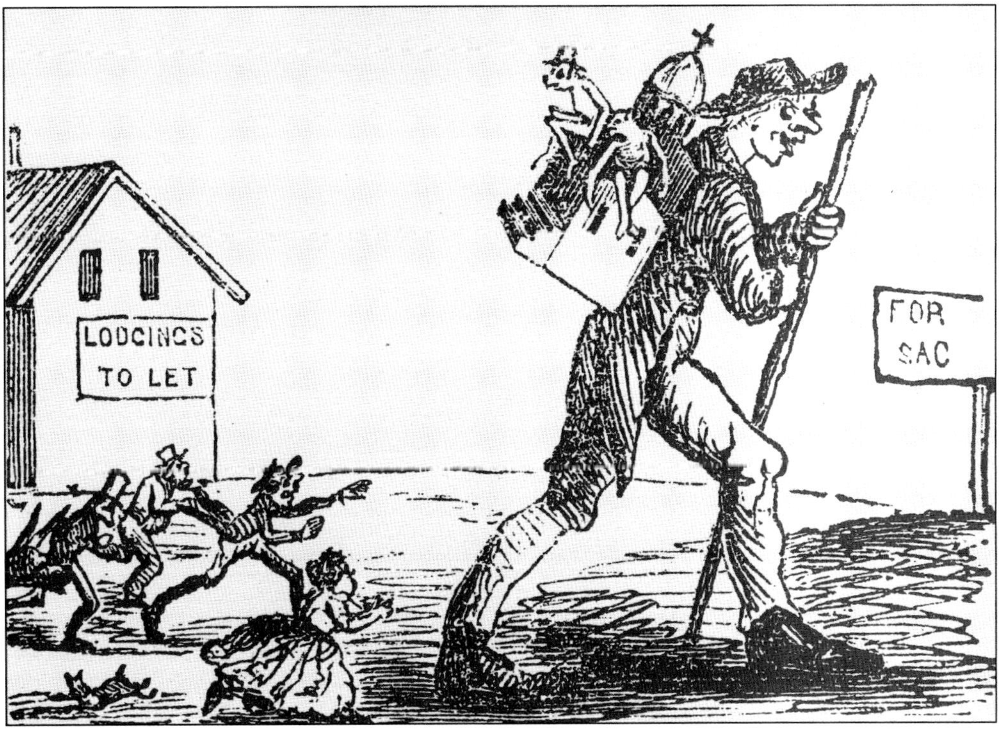

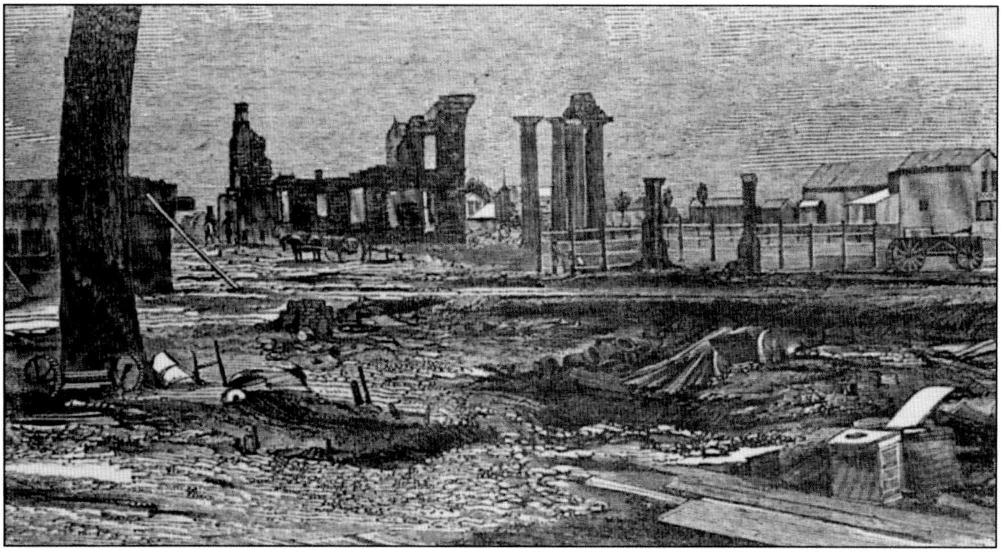

The state legislature returned to Sacramento in 1854 for a second time. Soon after the fifth session was completed in the county courthouse, tragedy struck once more. In July 1854, Sacramento suffered one of the periodic fires that plagued the city's early history. Gov. John Bigler (1853–1854) was able to rally enough bystanders to run into the burning building in order to retrieve the portrait of George Washington that hung in the assembly chamber. Little else, however, could be saved. A contemporary engraving of the burned ruins of the first courthouse is seen here. (CSL.)

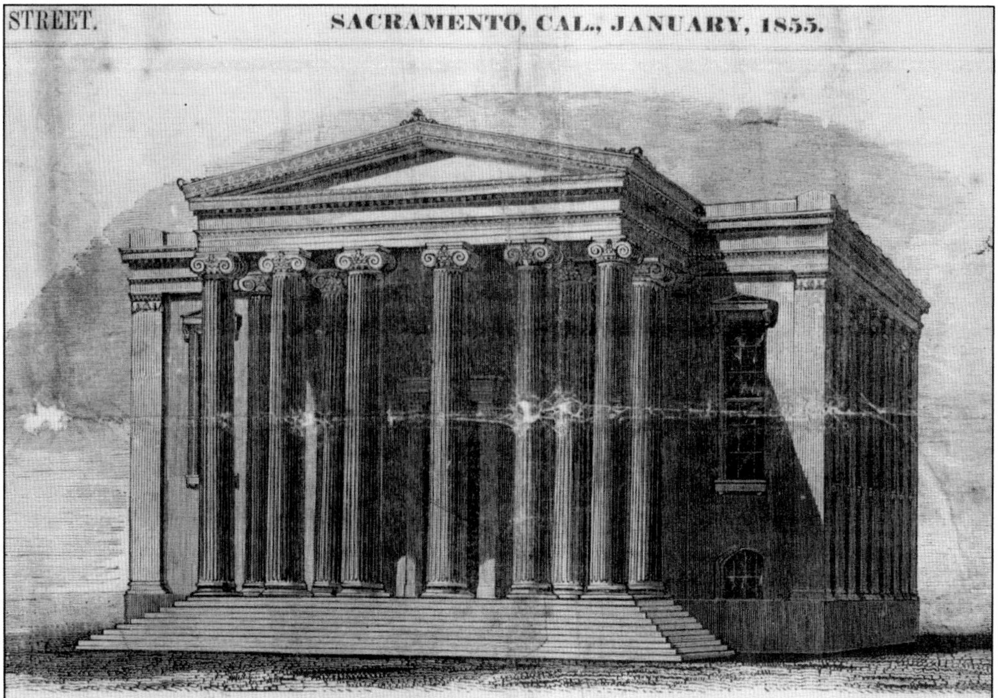

Fearful of possibly losing the capitol, Sacramentans set about constructing a new courthouse later in 1854, so as to retain the capitol for their city. Besides being the home for the capitol, the stately building would continue to be the county courthouse up until 1911. (CSL.)

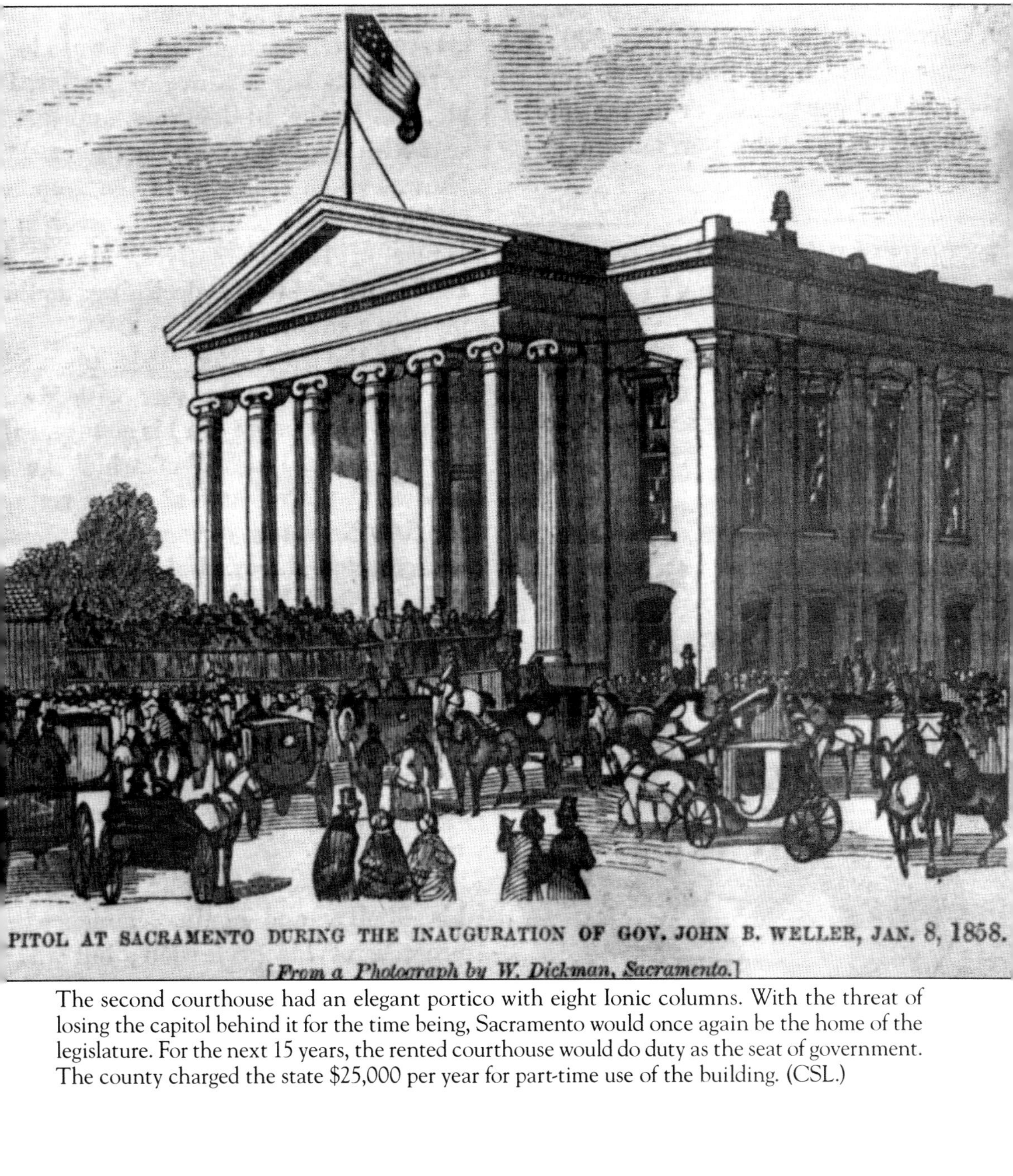

The second courthouse had an elegant portico with eight Ionic columns. With the threat of losing the capitol behind it for the time being, Sacramento would once again be the home of the legislature. For the next 15 years, the rented courthouse would do duty as the seat of government. The county charged the state $25,000 per year for part-time use of the building. (CSL.)

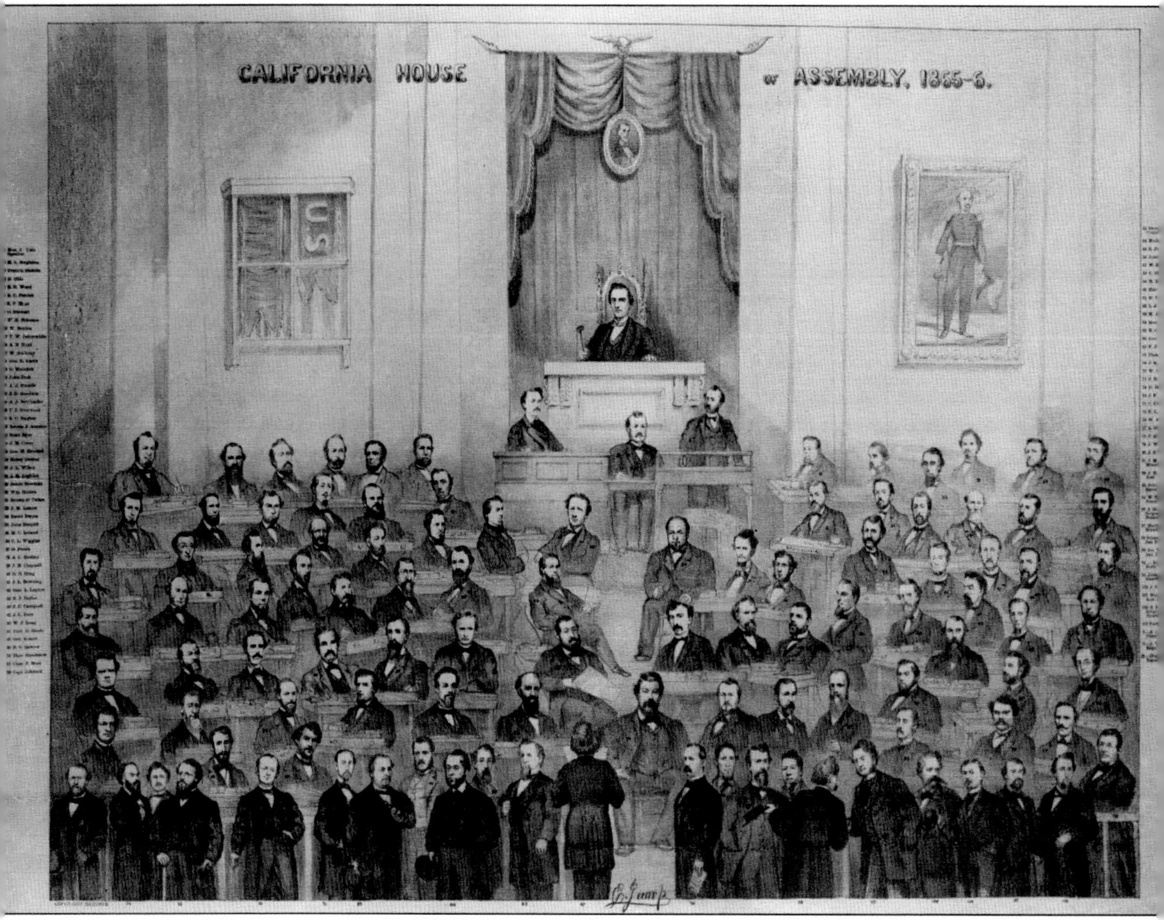

An 1866 lithograph of the courthouse interior shows members of the 16th session of the assembly, clerks, recorders, and sergeants at arms. Flanking the dais is a wall case containing two Civil War flags and a portrait of John Sutter, founder of Sacramento. The senate occupied the upper floor of the two-story courthouse, and the assembly was in the lower. (CSL.)

Two

FROM CAPITAL TO CAPITOL

May this building be speedily completed; may symmetry and order rest on each line and curve; may strength and beauty characterize each arch and pillar.

—N. Greene Curtis, 1861

Capital and *capitol* are two words that are often mistakenly used interchangeably. While it is only a question of one vowel, it makes all the difference in the world. *Capital* (from the Latin *caput*, for "head, summit, chief point, headquarters, the capital"), is defined by the *Oxford English Dictionary* as "a capital town or city; the head town of a country, province or state." *Capitol* (from *capitolium*, the ancient citadel and temple complex on the Capitoline Hill at the center of Rome), on the other hand, is, according to *Webster's* dictionary, "the statehouse or house in which the legislature holds its sessions." The problem facing the young state was to come up with a way to combine both an idea—seat of government—and a place—statehouse—into one. The struggle to make both words become synonymous with one another would take nearly 15 years.

In order for Sacramento to become California's capital, it would have to build a capitol. Sacramentans rallied to the cause by raising tax money for the purchase of land for the new building. After one failed attempt in 1859, another site was selected to the east of Sacramento's riverfront embarcadero. Design proposals were submitted and an architect selected. Miner F. Butler put forward the winning plan, with drawings by Rueben Clark. Clark would eventually take over as lead architect during the first phase of construction.

Californians picked another unsuitable time, the Civil War, to begin a massive construction project. At the time, it was the largest of its type in the American West. Construction on the capitol would be plagued by a myriad of problems: no general contractor, a rotating series of architects, lack of any complete set of architectural plans, budgetary problems, floods, shortages of materials, labor strikes, and so on. After an attempt to raise bond money failed, all construction was funded on a piecemeal basis. The unenviable job of overseeing the construction for the next 14 years was left to the Capitol Commission.

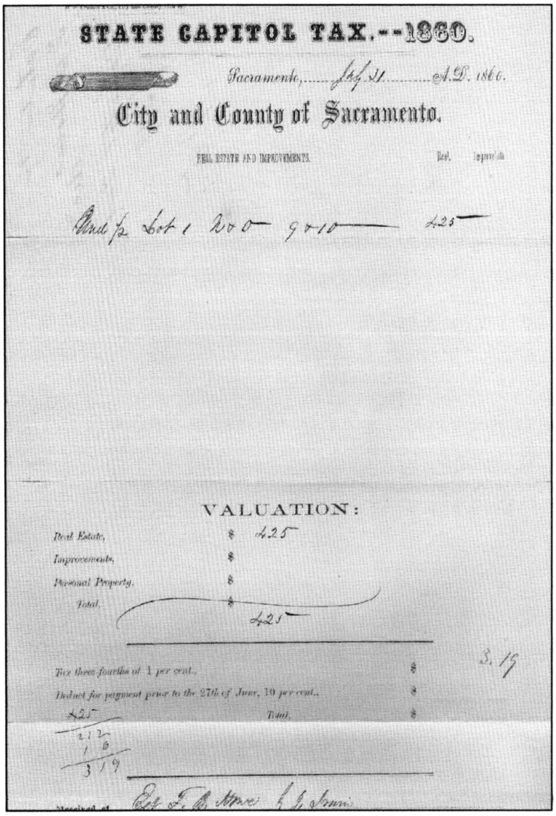

STATE CAPITOL TAX.--1860.

Sacramento, Feb 21 A.D. 1860.

City and County of Sacramento.

REAL ESTATE AND IMPROVEMENTS.

VALUATION:

Real Estate, $ 425

Improvements, $

Personal Property, $

Total, $ 425

Tax three-fourths of 1 per cent., $

Deduct for payment prior to the 27th of June, 10 per cent., $

Total, $

Here is a state capitol tax receipt from 1860. The citizens of the city and county of Sacramento agreed to levy a tax upon themselves for the purchase of land on which to erect a permanent state capitol. They made this offer of land to the state in the hopes that it would finally settle the question, once and for all time, of keeping the capitol in Sacramento. (JA.)

Here is an 1857 bird's-eye view of Sacramento. This magnificent lithograph by Sacramento artist George Baker shows how the "city on the plains" appeared just a few years prior to the construction of the capitol. The site of the future capitol will be located in the distant left part of the scene, only 10 blocks from the bustling waterfront along the Sacramento River. (CSL.)

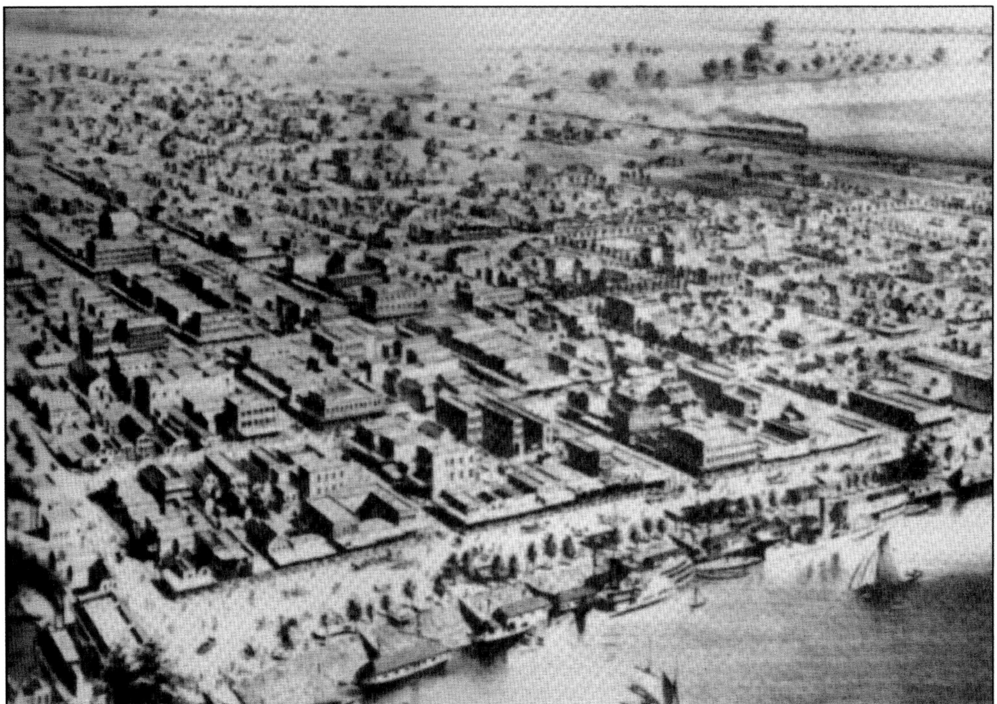

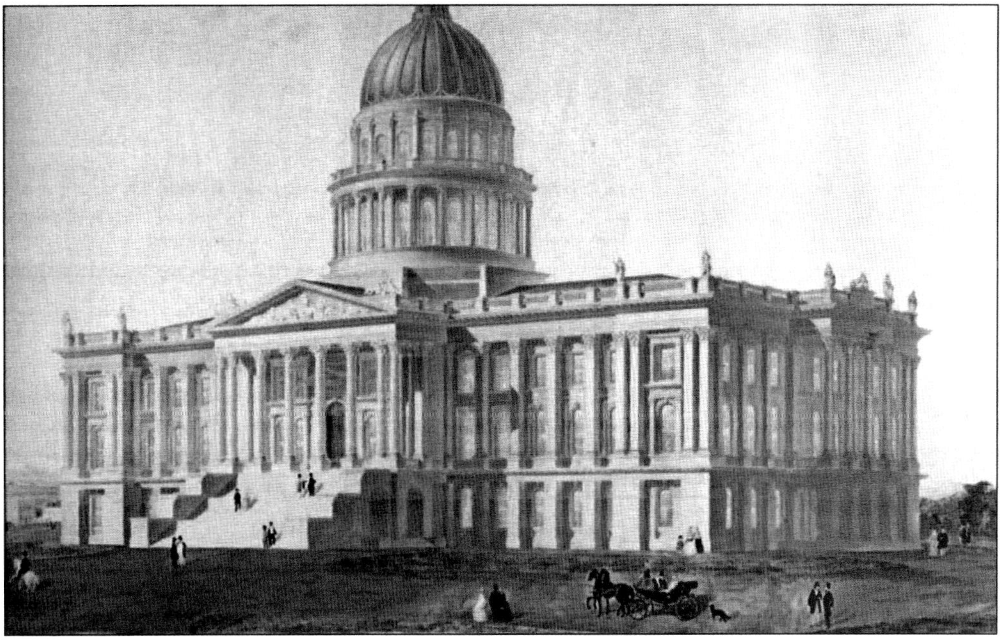

Sacramento architect Miner F. Butler won the $1,500 competition for the design of the present California State Capitol. He was the first in a succession of four architects who would oversee the major construction project, between 1860 and 1874. The winning design (pictured) was actually done by his assistant, Rueben Clark. Clark, who had experience working on Mississippi's capitol, became the first working architect on the project. The magnificent staircase leading up to the west portico in his architectural drawing was never completed due to later budget cuts. (CSA.)

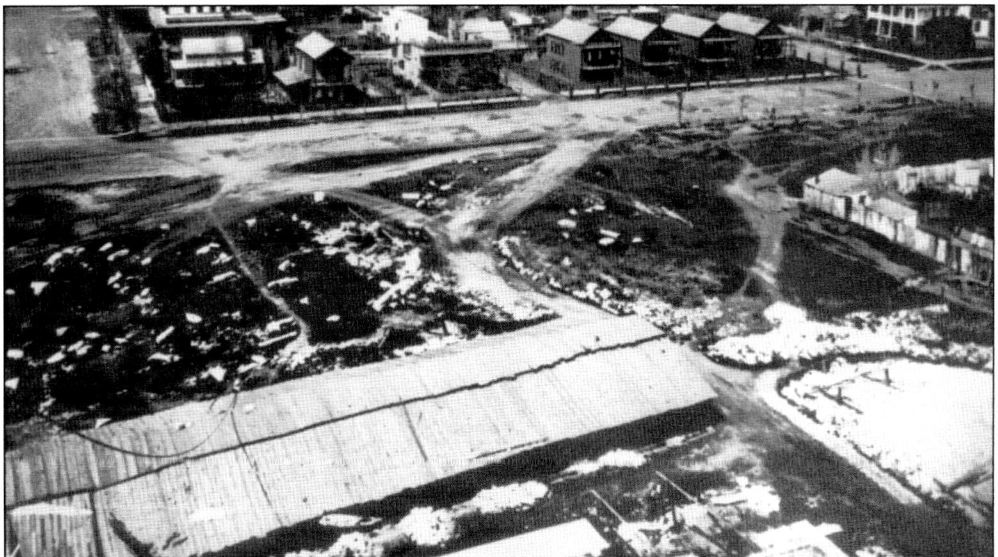

War loomed in the eastern states as construction began in the fall of 1860. The structures on the four-block site were removed or leveled, and the land was surveyed. The official "birthday" of the capitol could be said to be May 15, 1861, when the cornerstone was laid at the northwest corner of the foundation. This 1868 photograph was taken from the capitol and shows part of the construction site around the building. (CSL.)

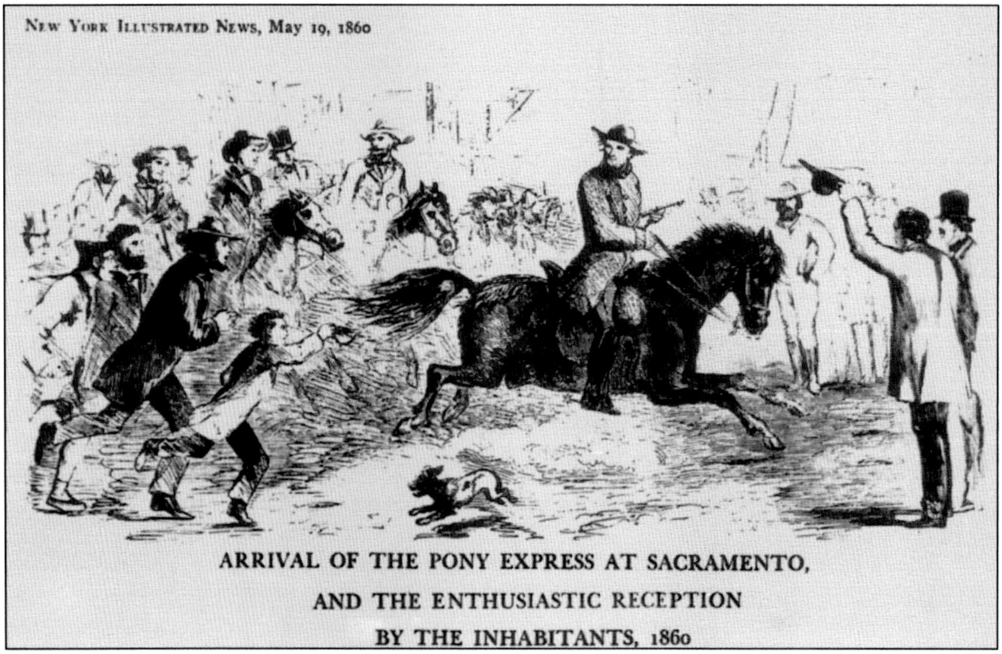

While work was just beginning on the capitol, another major undertaking was going on a few blocks away. Through the streets of Sacramento, the first Pony Express riders were completing the final stage of their 1,966-mile run. Between April 1860 and October 1861, relays of the riders connected the city and St. Joseph, Missouri, in 10 days. This is an engraving of Sacramentans greeting the arrival of the first Pony Express rider on April 13, 1860. (CSL.)

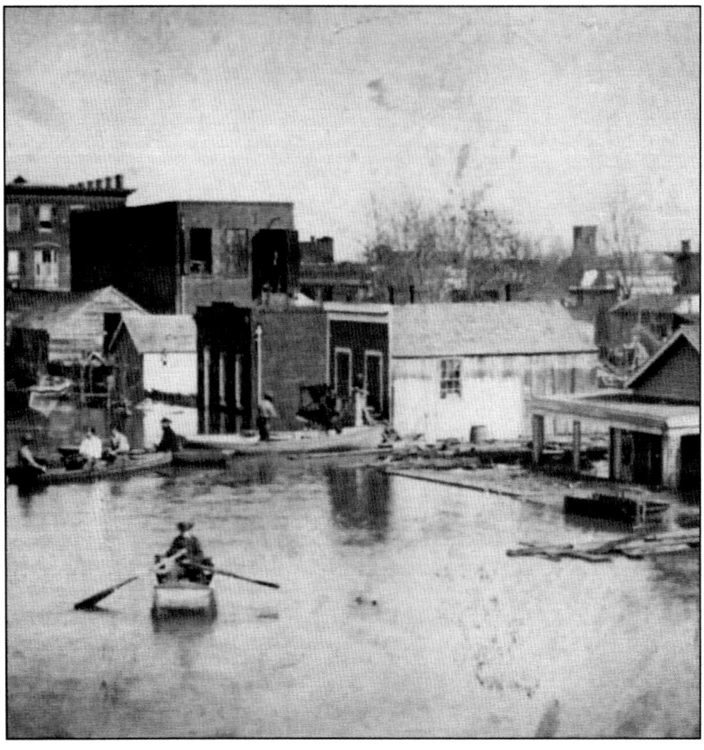

As construction on the foundations was under way in 1861, the worst flood in the state's recorded history inundated Sacramento and the Central Valley. Between December 1861 and the following spring, much of the city was underwater. This forced the recently elected governor, Leland Stanford, to have to be rowed in a boat to his inauguration ceremony at the courthouse. Soon afterwards, the legislature sought higher ground to complete its session. (JA.)

As the floodwaters continued to rise in January 1862, the legislators adjourned and headed for San Francisco to escape the deluge. They reconvened in the Merchants Exchange Building, pictured here, for the remainder of the session. (CSL.)

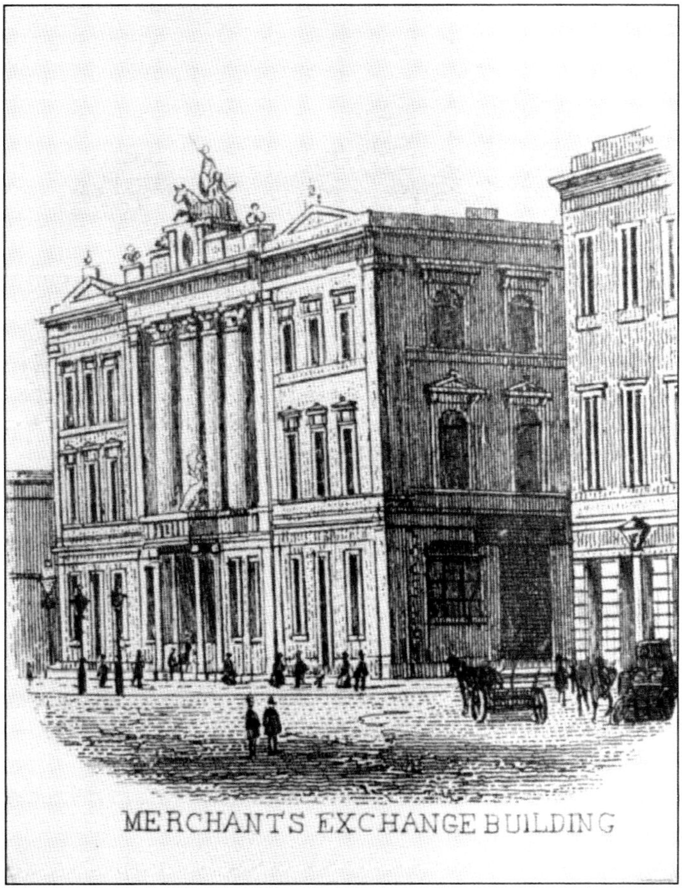

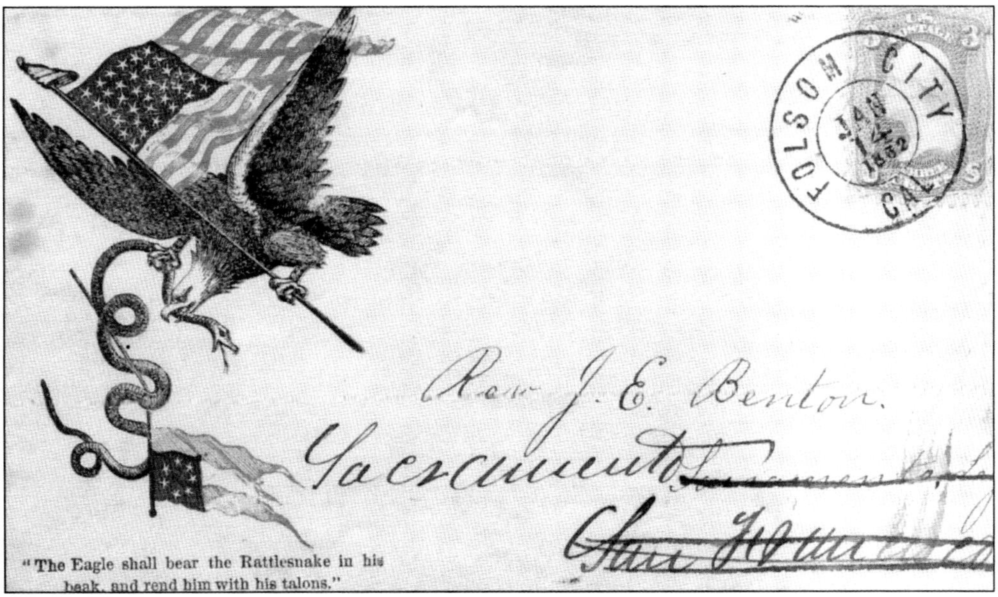

Here is a patriotic Civil War envelope addressed to a member of the assembly from nearby Folsom. The Sacramento postmaster has crossed out the address twice, unsure of where to even send it. (JA.)

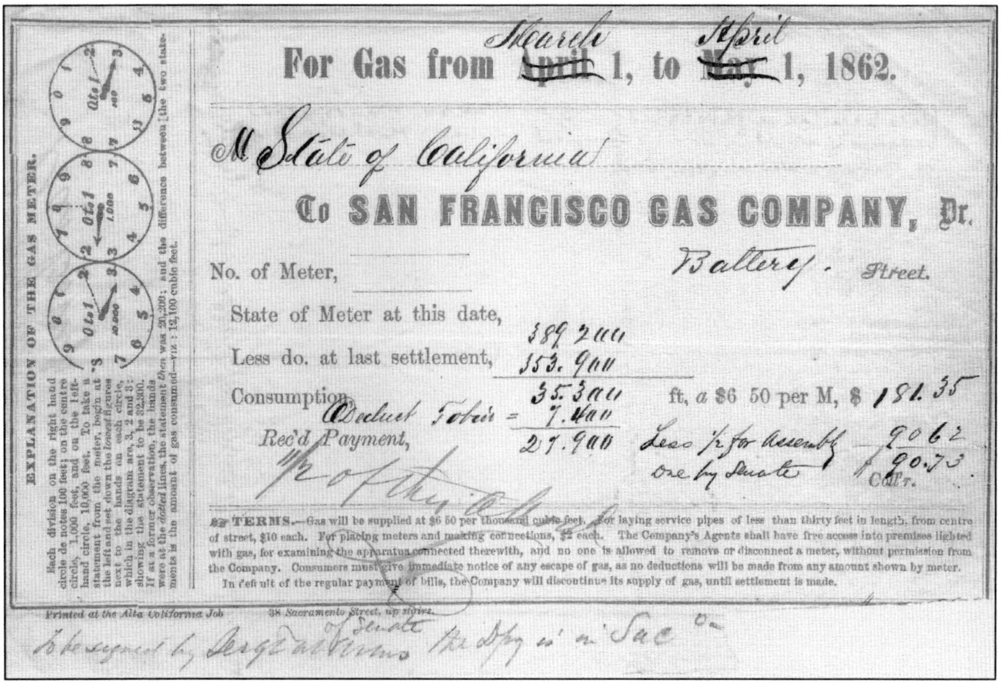

For Gas from ~~April~~ March 1, to ~~May~~ April 1, 1862.

State of California

To SAN FRANCISCO GAS COMPANY, Dr.

No. of Meter, Battery Street.

State of Meter at this date, 389.200

Less do. at last settlement, 353.900

Consumption 35.300 ft, a $6 50 per M, $ 181.35

Deduct Tobin = 7.400

Rec'd Payment, 27.900 Less ½ for Assembly 90.62

One by Senate 90.73

EXPLANATION OF THE GAS METER.

Each division on the right hand circle de notes 100 feet; on the centre circle, 1,000 feet, and on the left-hand circle, 10,000 feet. To take a statement from the meter, begin at the left and set down the *lowest* figures next to the hands on each circle, which in the diagram are, 3, 2 and 3: showing the statement to be 32,300. If at a former observation, the hands were at the *dotted* lines, the statement *then* was 20,200; and the difference between the two statements is the amount of gas consumed—viz: 12,100 cubic feet.

TERMS.—Gas will be supplied at $6 50 per thousand cubic feet. For laying service pipes of less than thirty feet in length, from centre of street, $10 each. For placing meters and making connections, $2 each. The Company's Agents shall have free access into premises lighted with gas, for examining the apparatus connected therewith, and no one is allowed to remove or disconnect a meter, without permission from the Company. Consumers must give immediate notice of any escape of gas, as no deductions will be made from any amount shown by meter.

In default of the regular payment of bills, the Company will discontinue its supply of gas, until settlement is made.

Printed at the Alta California Job 38 *Sacramento Street, up stairs.*

This is a receipt for a monthly gas bill for both the assembly and senate while they were in session in San Francisco. (JA.)

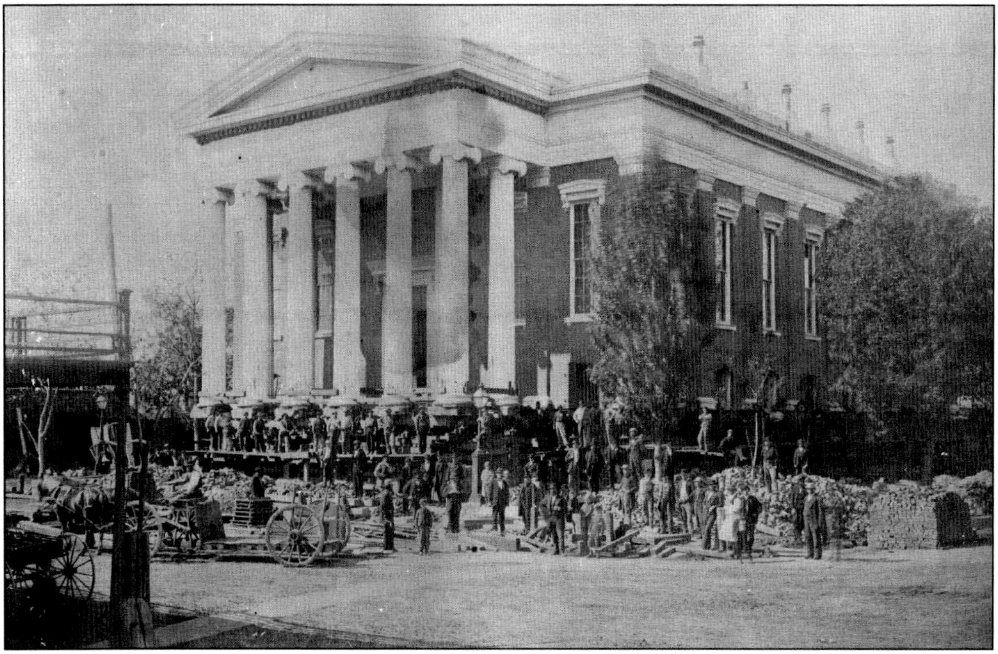

As part of the recovery of their flood-ravaged city, Sacramentans began to either raise their buildings or their streets. Construction resumed on the capitol in the spring of 1862 as the floodwaters eventually subsided. The original ground floor of the capitol was surrounded by landfill in an attempt to prevent future flooding. Here is a photograph of the Sacramento Courthouse being raised an extra story with screw jacks. (CSL.)

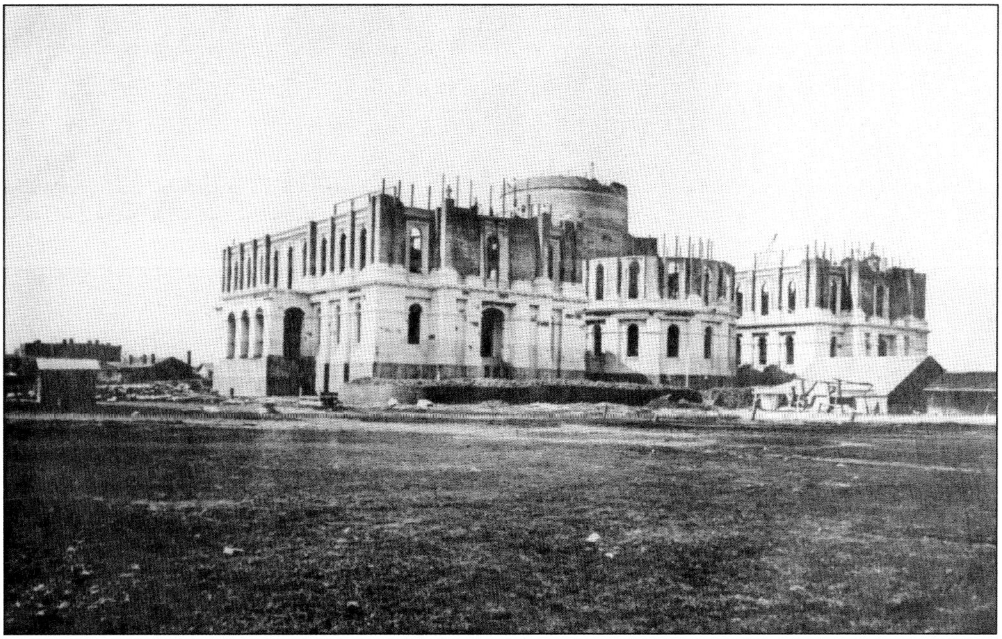

The flood forced major changes at the capitol construction site. The original first floor was turned into a basement. With this change to the foundation, the building was raised 13 feet higher. (CSL.)

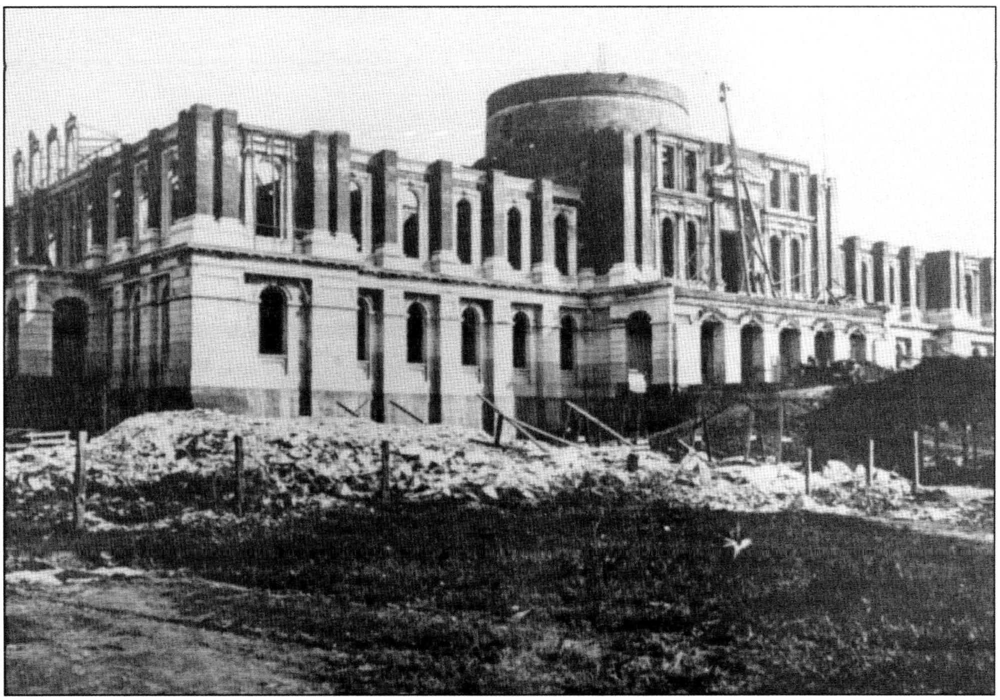

It had been the intention of the architects to encase the whole structure in granite, but as costs increased, this plan was abandoned. Instead, the Capitol Commission decided on completing the remaining two stories in less costly brick and a covering of mastic. A contractor would have to provide 29,000 bricks per day during this phase of construction. (CSL.)

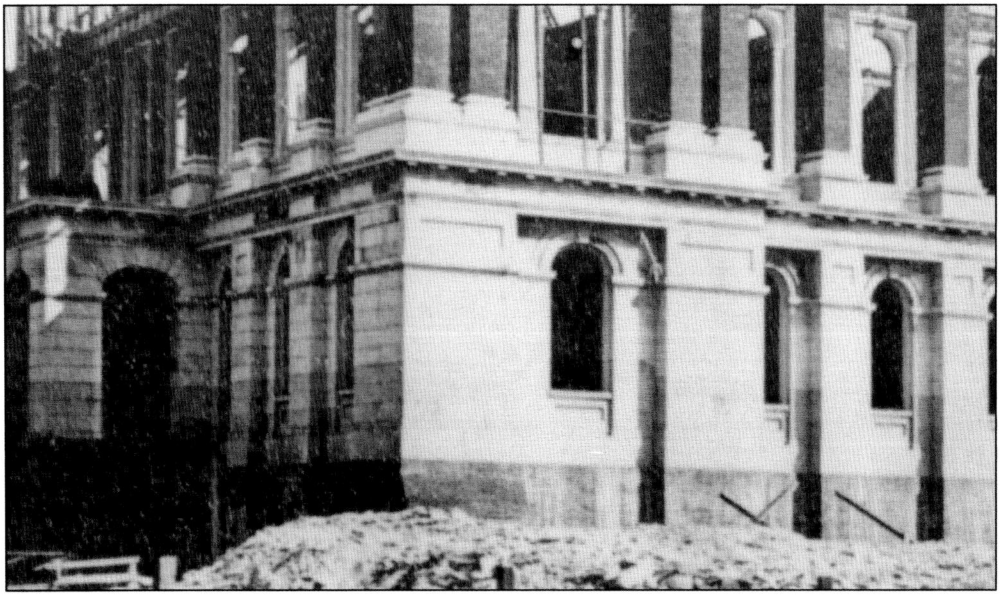

The stone used for the ground-floor podium was quarried locally. It came from two nearby sources: Folsom and Rocklin. The former supplied darker-colored granite, known as "Ambassador Black." The Rocklin granite, "Sierra White," was a much lighter and smoother stone and was preferred by many for its striking appearance. The contracts for quarrying and shipping the granite were subject to the competing railroad business interests to build a transcontinental railroad, as well as the political rivalries between the Democratic and Republican parties. (CSL.)

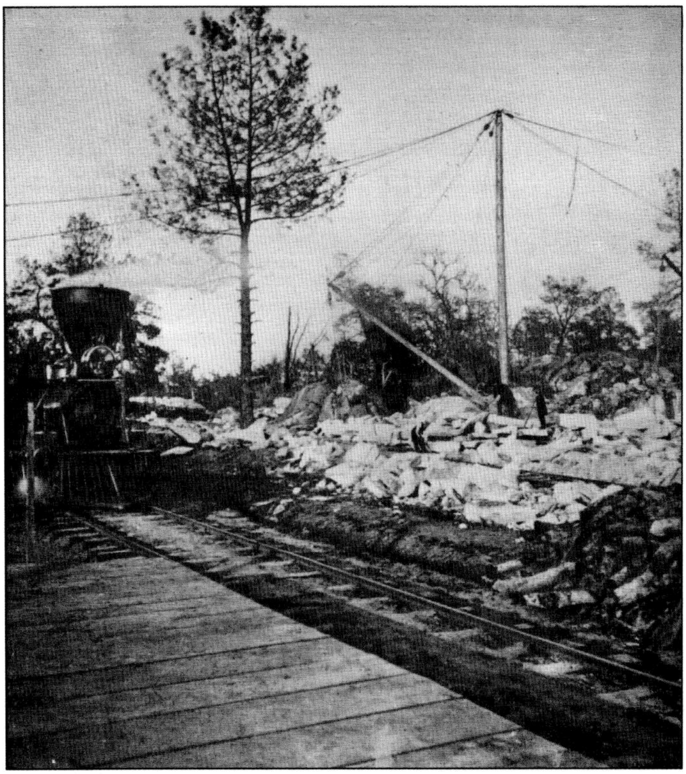

Leland Stanford was the new Republican governor and president of the Central Pacific Railroad. He was able to finally wrest the contract for supplying granite away from the competing Sacramento Valley Railroad and its Democratic supporters. Since the lighter-colored stone was quarried along the transcontinental railroad line in Placer County, hauling it became a lucrative source of revenue for the Central Pacific Railroad. A Central Pacific locomotive is pictured here in 1865, as it makes a stop at the side line of the Rocklin quarry. (CSL.)

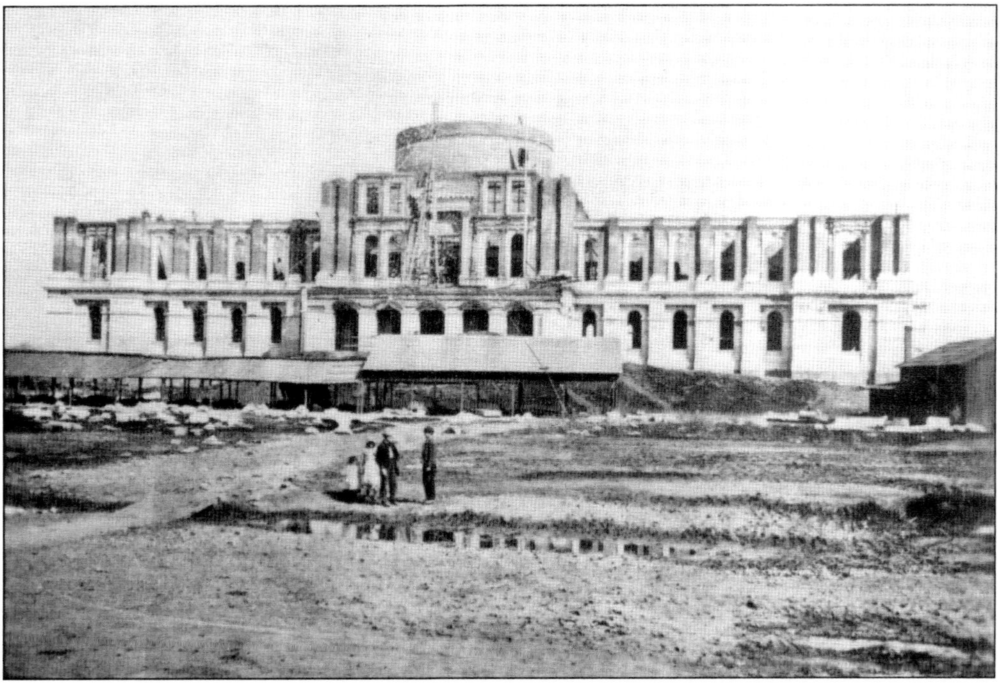

Tragically, the superintending architect, Rueben Clark, suffered a mental breakdown from the stress of the job and had to be removed in 1865. His assistant, Gordon Cummings, replaced him. Cummings would carry construction forward for the next five years. During this crucial stage, the exterior walls, roof, and dome, as well as much of the interior construction would be completed. (JA.)

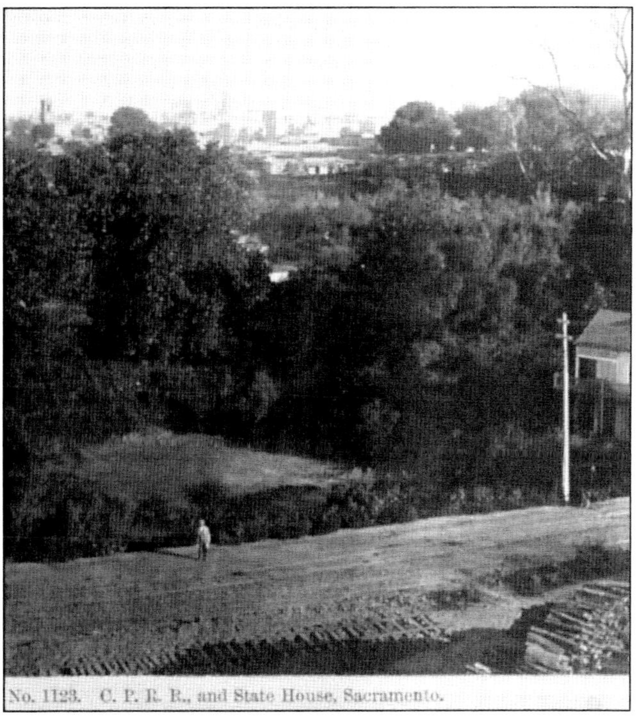

As work proceeded, the skyline of Sacramento began to change with the capitol rising above the city. The capitol can be seen here in the distant center behind the church belfry of St. Rose of Lima. Part of Sacramento's Chinatown is in the immediate foreground in this 1870 stereoview. (JA.)

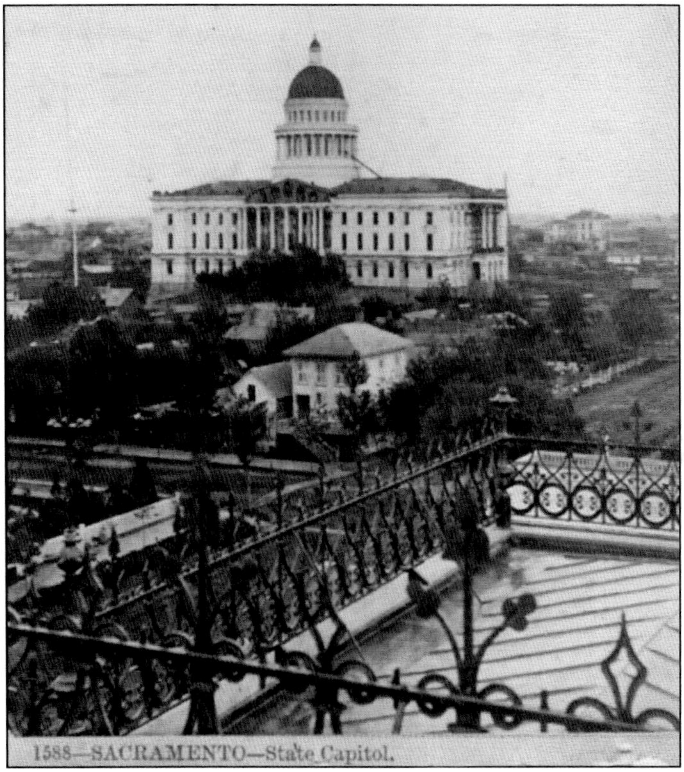

In another 1870s stereoview, the capitol is at last nearing completion. The massive iron columns are finally in place in both the outer dome and porticos. The columns that grace the three porticos of the new capitol are hollow, 30-foot-long cast-iron tubes. This photograph was taken from the roof of Gov. Leland Stanford's nearby mansion. (JA.)

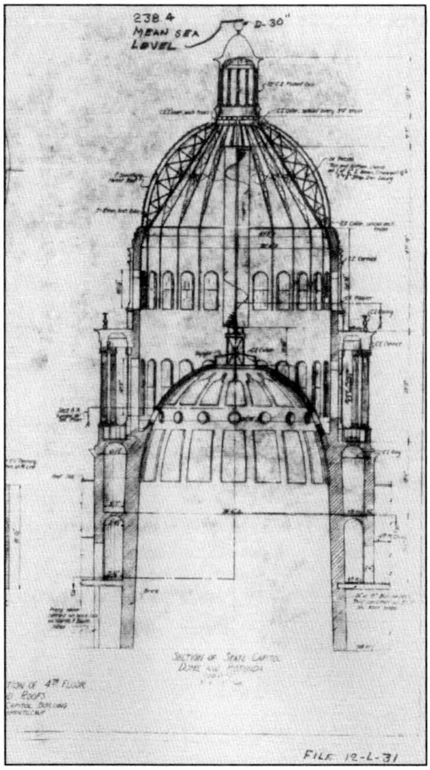

Here is a cutaway of the dome and rotunda. Many visitors assume that the dome they see on the exterior is the same as the one in the interior. In fact, there are actually two separate domes, both of which are plainly evident in this blueprint. The outer dome stands 210 feet high, and the inner one is 120 feet. A copper ball, gilded with $300 worth of gold, crowns the cupola. (SCM.)

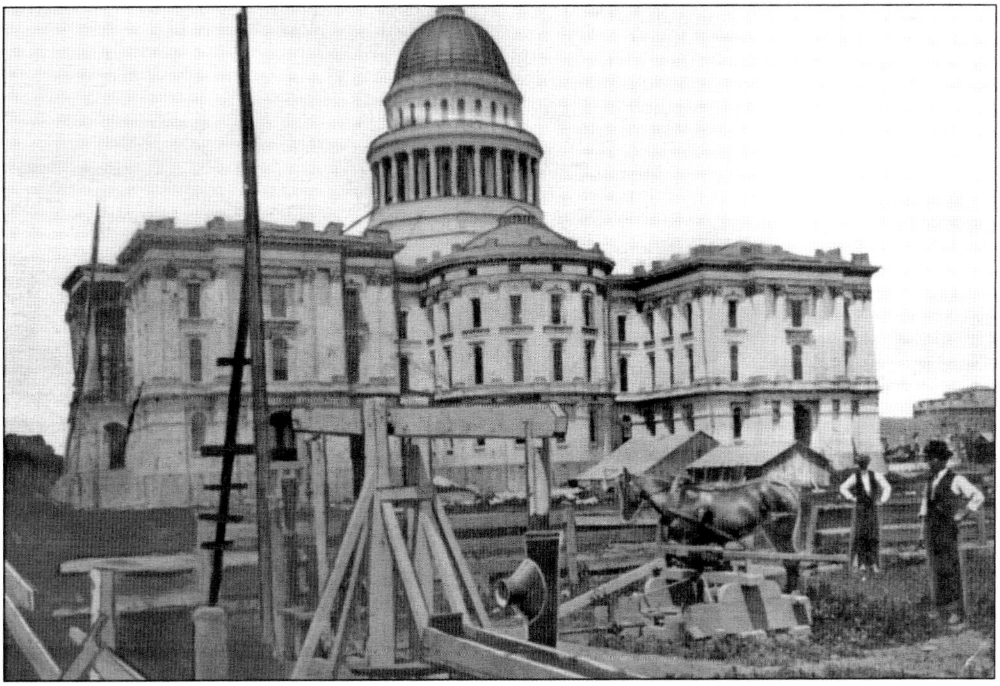

Another architect replaced Gordon Cummings in 1870. A.A. Bennet made numerous modifications to the building. He also omitted the "heavy, costly, and useless" staircase from the west portico that had been a part of the original plan. This is a view of one of the capitol's most distinctive features, the east side apse. (CSL.)

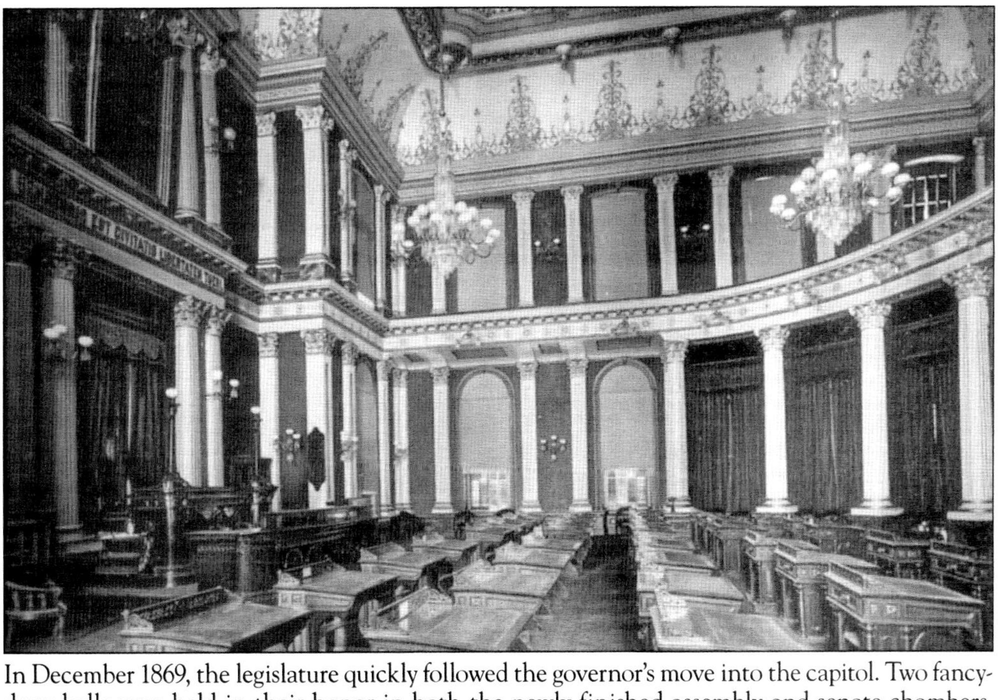

In December 1869, the legislature quickly followed the governor's move into the capitol. Two fancy-dress balls were held in their honor in both the newly finished assembly and senate chambers, pictured here in an 1897 photograph. (CSL.)

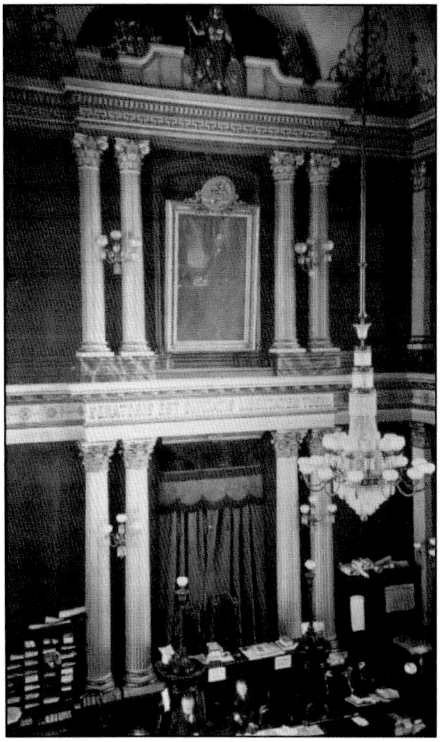

Here is the senate chamber backdrop topped by a gilded statue of Minerva. Engaged Corinthian columns and pilasters frame a portrait of George Washington. The senate was decorated with red carpets and accents, while the assembly was finished in green. The Latin motto at the left reads, "It is the duty of a Senator to protect the liberty of the people." The motto for the larger assembly chamber is "It is the duty of the Legislators to pass just laws." (CSL.)

Gordon Cummings would return to his former job in 1872. He would oversee the final work on the capitol's interior, such as tile and mosaic work, plastering, painting, woodwork, sculptural details, and so on. Pictured here is the original parquet flooring in the California State Library. The construction project finally came to an end on February 8, 1874, when the architect received his final payment. (CSL.)

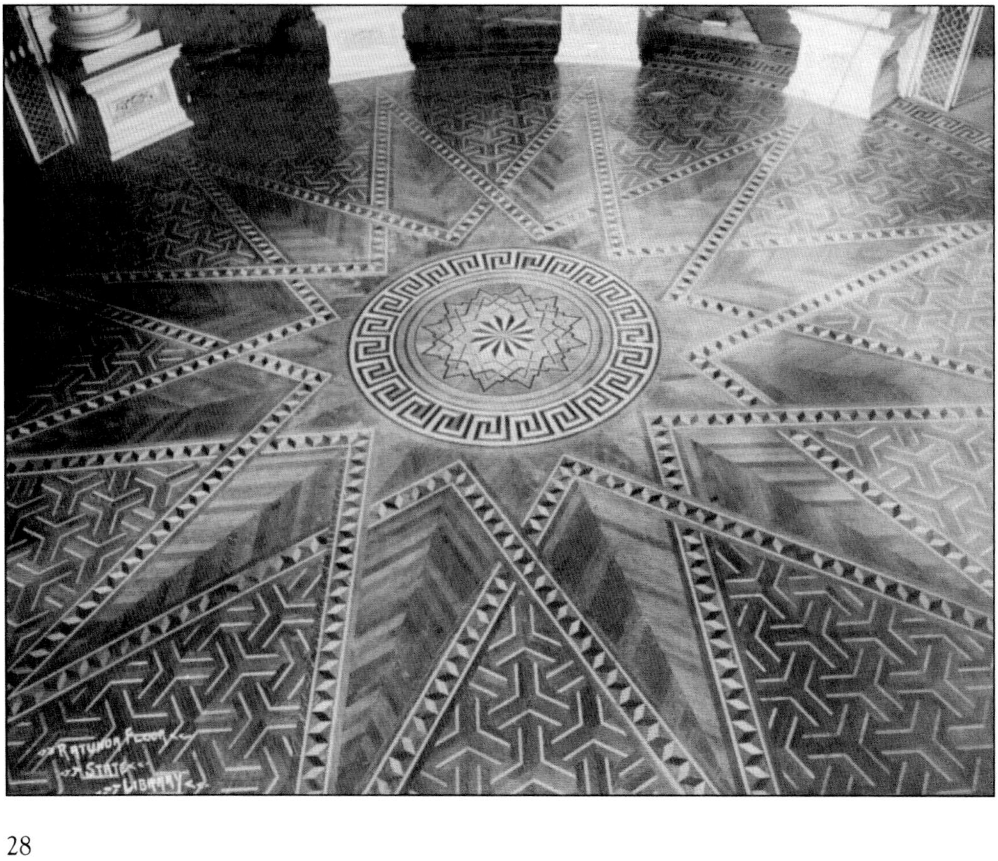

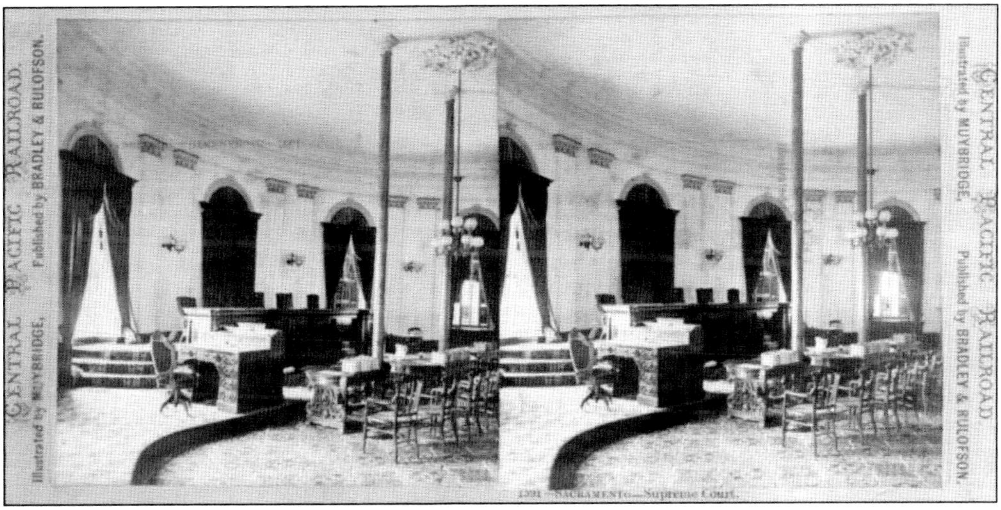

The State Supreme Court also moved into its new home in the capitol. This is an 1870s stereoview of the courtroom interior on the ground-floor level of the apse. For the first and only time in the state's history, all three branches of the government were all under the same roof. (JA.)

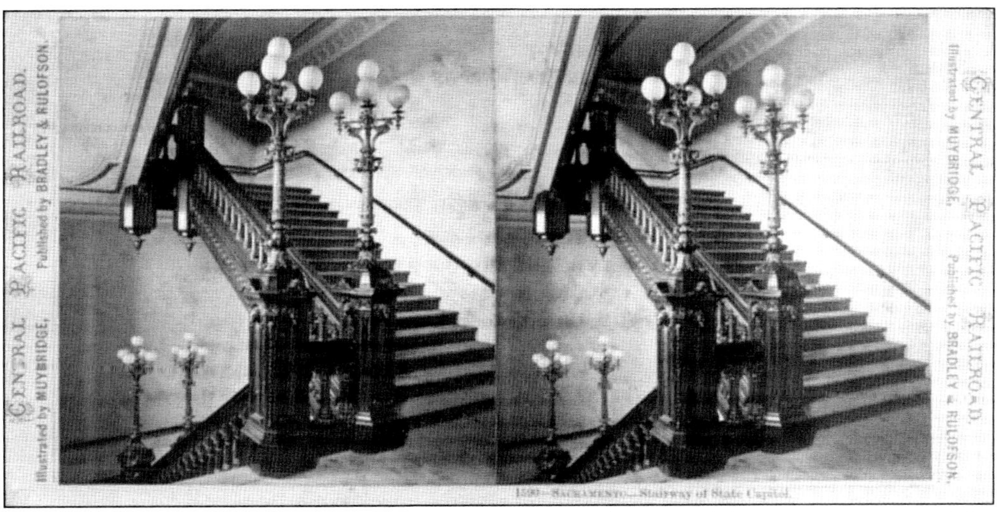

This is a photograph of one of the magnificent staircases that graced the original interior of the capitol. The Sacramento millwrights that made the original railing and newel posts were still in business a century later. The firm had the honor of replicating the long-lost originals for the 1976–1982 capitol restoration project. Today, Burnett & Sons continues to proudly carry on this family tradition. (JA.)

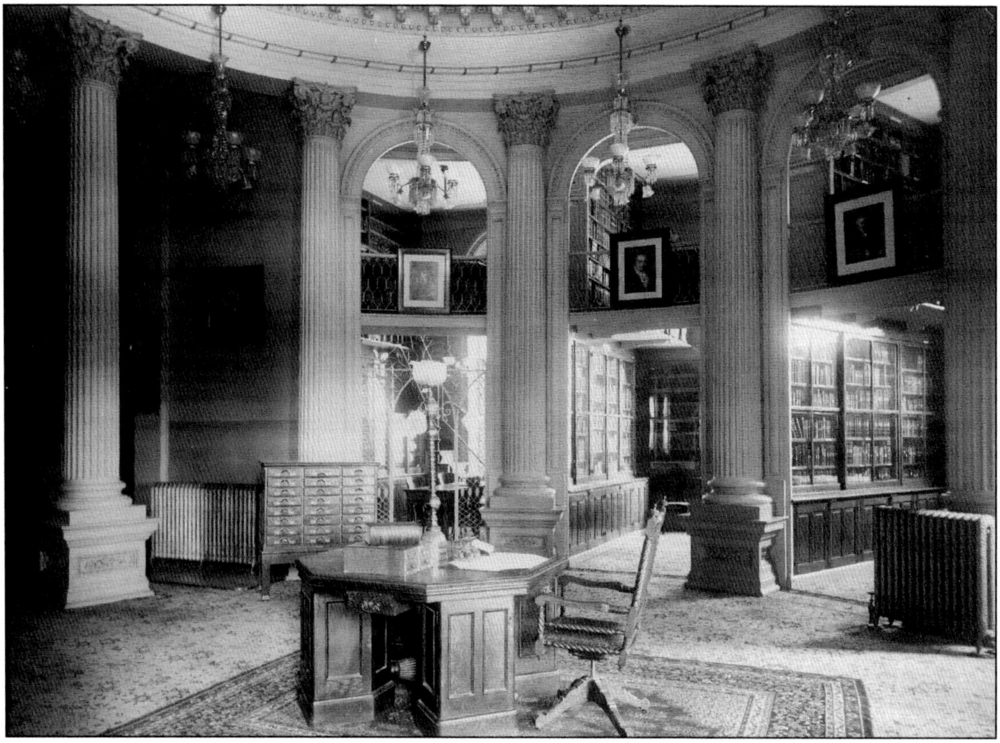

The California State Library, one of the oldest historical institutions in the West, occupied the upper floors of the apse. In this early-20th-century view, some of the splendor of the interior is visible. The multistory book stacks and radiating aisles were designed to accommodate the shape of the semicircular apse. (CSL.)

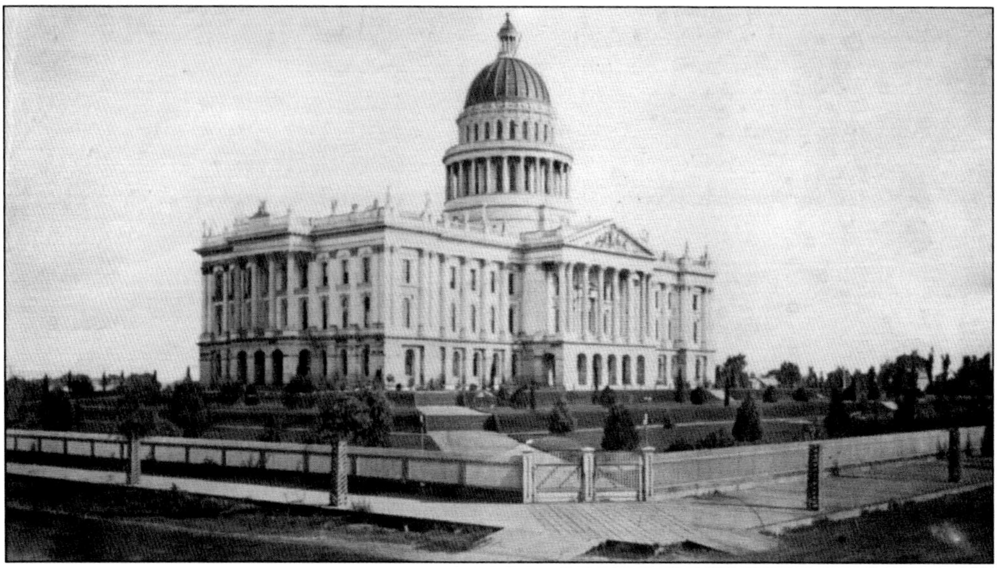

This is a photograph of the recently completed capitol with a new picket fence. Much of the original scaffolding used in the construction was recycled to make the first fence that surrounded the building. The 50,000-square-foot, three-story structure had a facade measuring 287 by 120 feet. (JA.)

Three

This Ole Capitol

The most perfect combination of stone, iron, brick and mortar I have ever seen and seems intended to last forever.

—Gordon Cummings

The newly completed capitol proudly signaled to Californians that a new era had begun. As a statement in brick, iron, and stone, it told the citizens of the state that California had finally come of age. After early years of chaotic development and the travails of the Civil War, Californians could now look on with pride at this magnificent structure. Like the many churches, courthouses, and schools that went up in California communities, the capitol helped to reassure its people that theirs was no longer an unstable, transient society. Stately structures, like the capitol, signaled that the chaos and impermanence of the state's early years was now a thing of the past.

The capitol has always been a "work in progress." It has never been fully completed. The structure has been subject to an endless process of maintenance, remodeling, and new additions over the last 150 years. The only thing "permanent" about the building has been change itself.

There would be four major construction phases during the 20th century. The first was to modernize the building with electricity, elevators, and a fourth floor around 1905. Then, in the 1920s, the West Annex was built across Tenth Street to help relieve the serious overcrowding in the capitol. World War II brought drastic changes to California. As the state's population exploded, government had to grow in order to keep pace. This meant yet another major expansion project, the East Annex.

Overtime, however, some observers began to have concerns over many of the changes that were being made to the building and the "thoughtless modernity" that they were ushering in. There were also calls for replacing the aging structure altogether. It was the proposal to replace the original capitol with two steel-and-glass towers in the 1970s that finally helped to galvanize support to save the historic building. The citizens of the state rallied to preserve and restore the stately but deteriorating structure to its former glory. Out of this struggle would come the 1976–1982 capitol restoration project, the largest such project at the time.

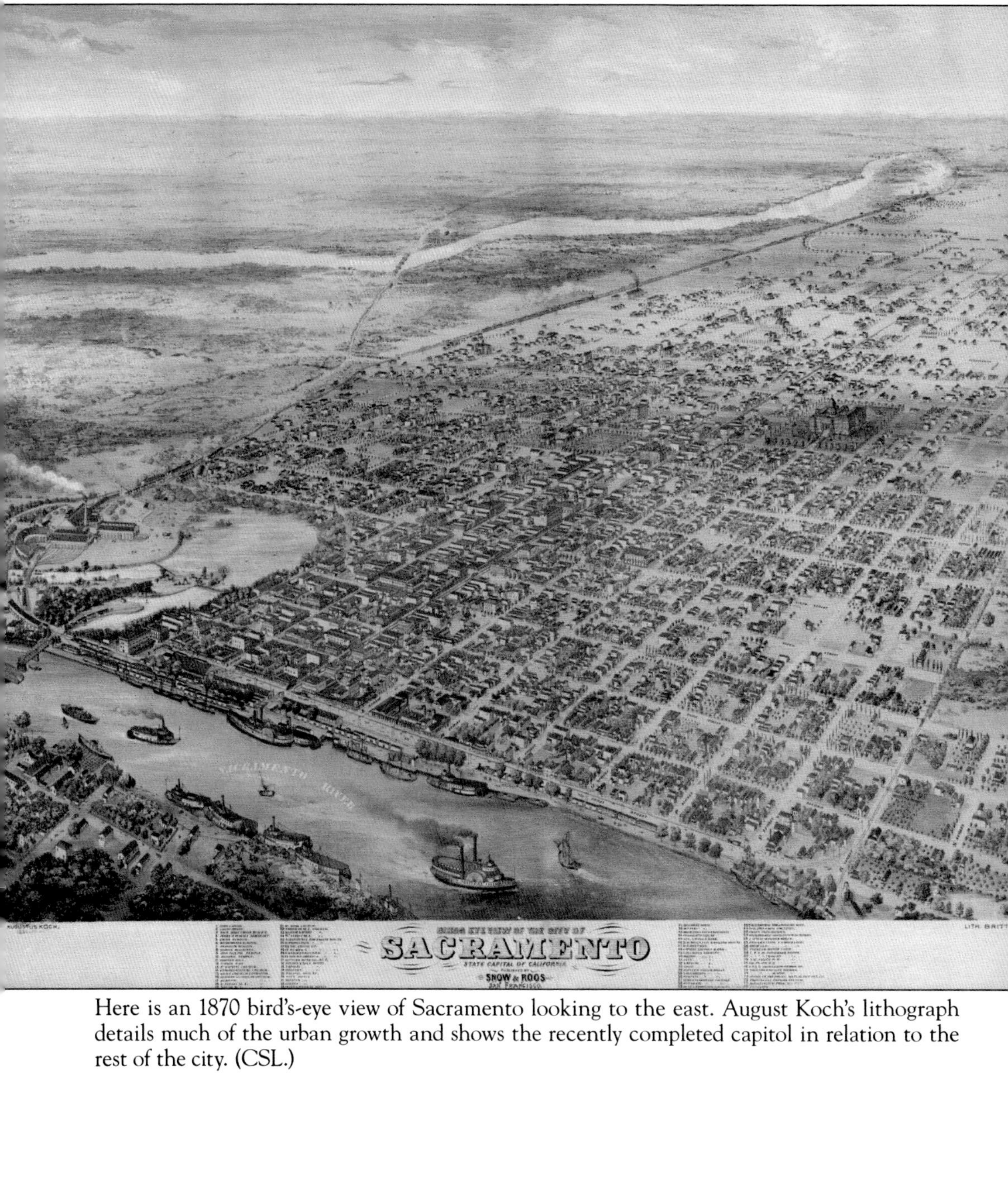

Here is an 1870 bird's-eye view of Sacramento looking to the east. August Koch's lithograph details much of the urban growth and shows the recently completed capitol in relation to the rest of the city. (CSL.)

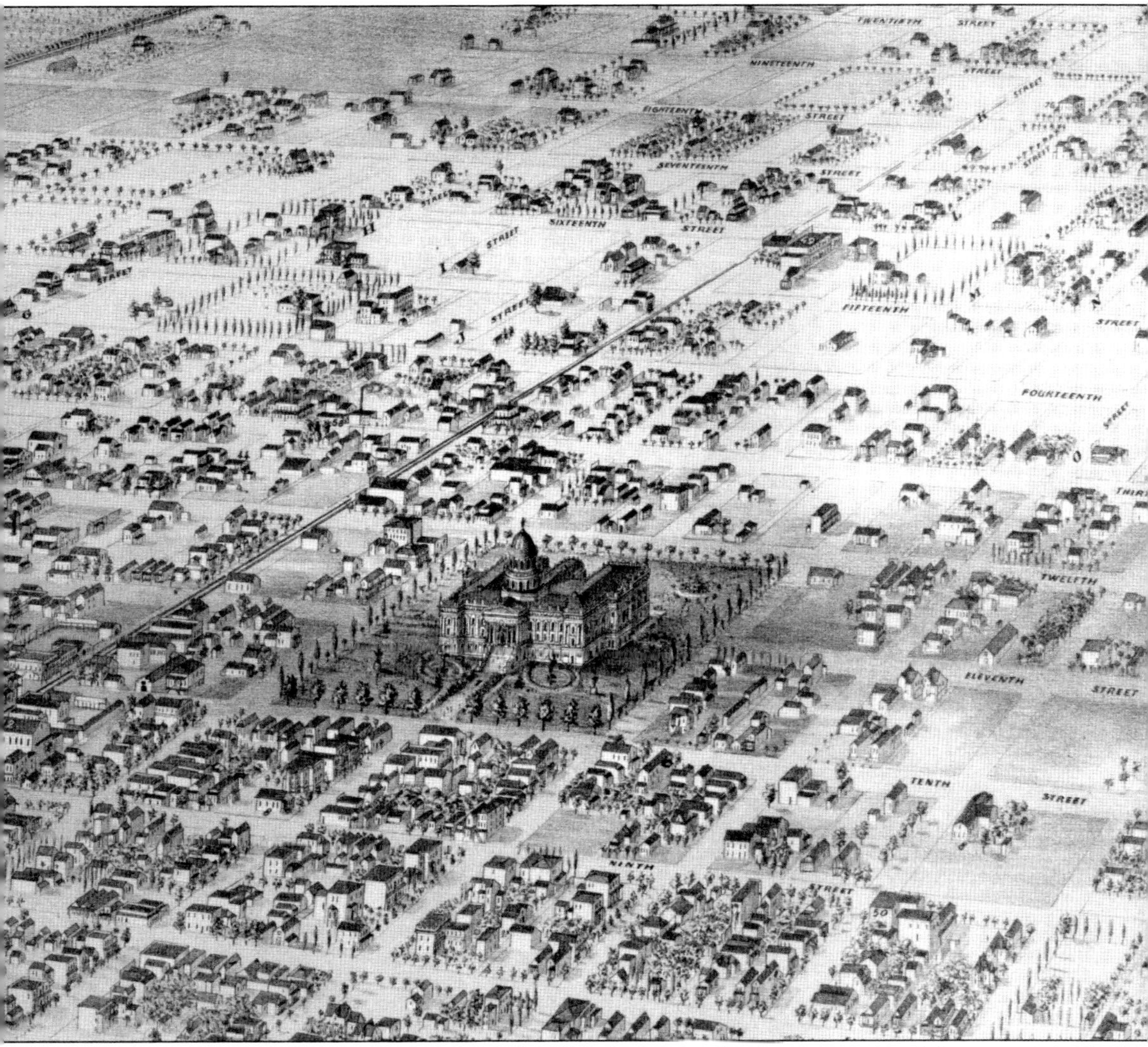

This close-up of the same print reveals that there has been new development around the capitol. As urban growth continued to increase over time, the city's center of gravity shifted to the area surrounding the capitol. (CSL.)

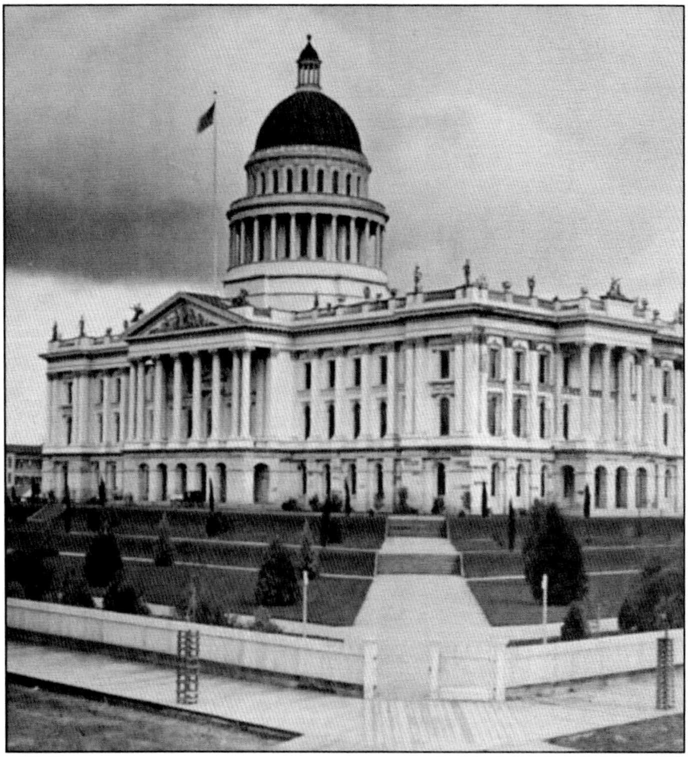

By 1877, the capitol was already in need of its first new coat of paint. In this contemporary photograph, a horse and carriage have stopped in front of the west entrance. (JA.)

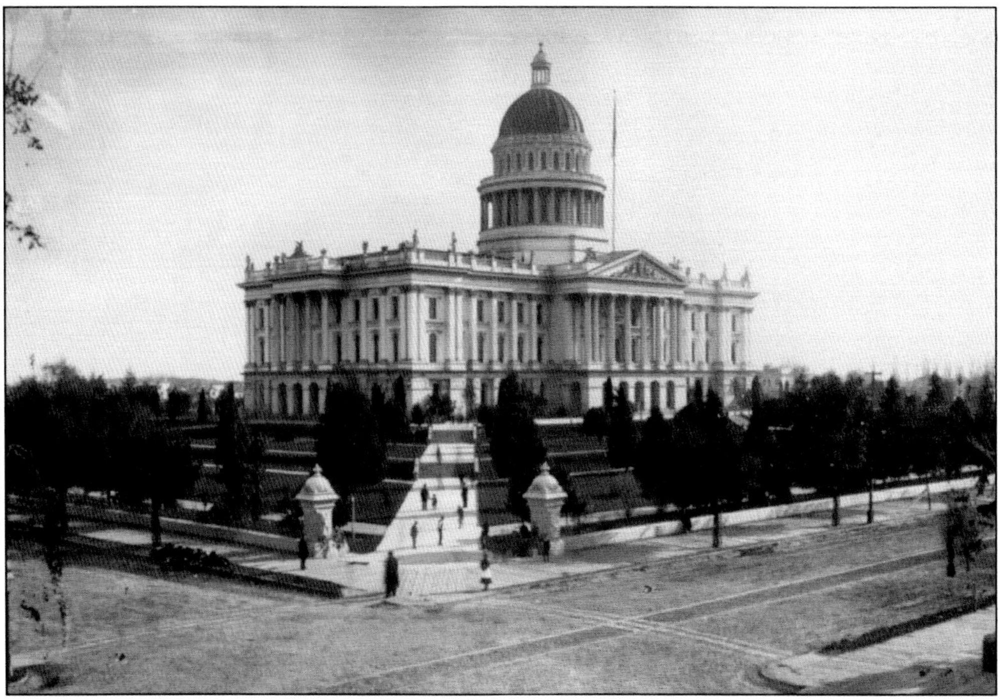

As seen in a later glass-plate photograph, the trees have grown higher. On April 21, 1892, an earthquake hit the Sacramento region. The capitol sustained serious damage to the assembly chamber. Some of the exterior statuary fell off the balustrade, as well. (JA.)

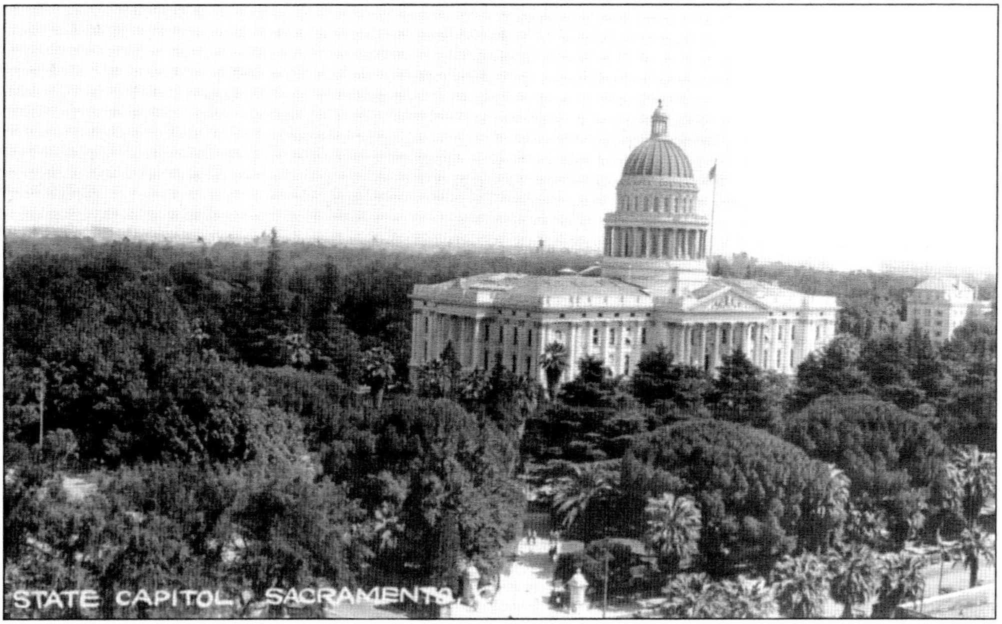

This view shows some of the changes made to the exterior at the beginning of the 20th century, including the addition of a fourth floor, a new venting system, and the removal of most of the exterior statuary. The windows for the newly constructed fourth-floor offices can be seen just below the balustrade. (JA.)

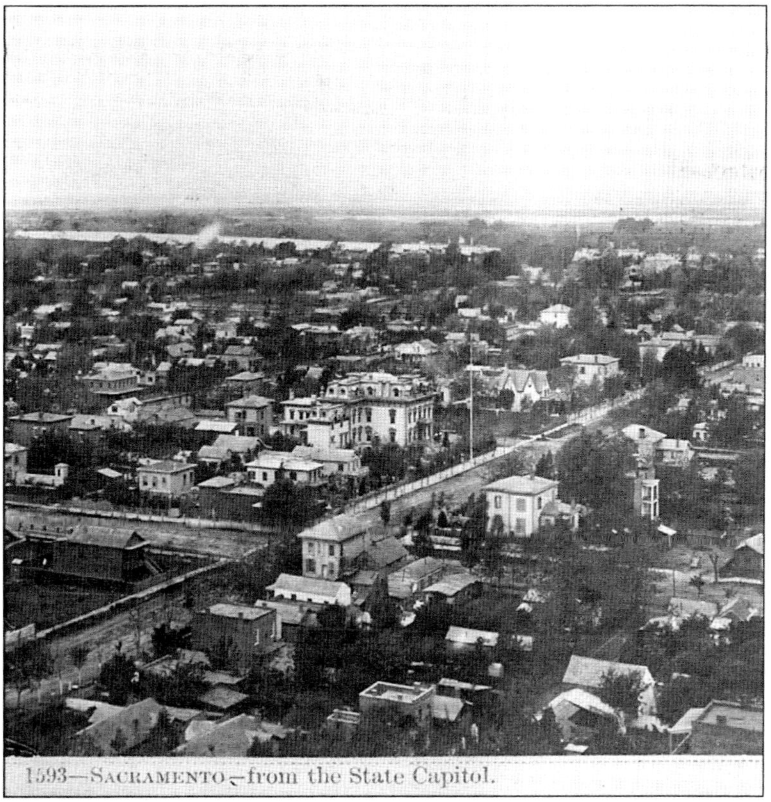

This is a view of Sacramento in an 1870s stereoview. This photograph was taken from atop the state capitol looking toward the southwest. In the middle distance, next to the flagpole, is the stately remodeled home of Gov. Leland Stanford. The mansion served as the home and office for three governors—Stanford, Frederick Low, and Henry Haight. (JA.)

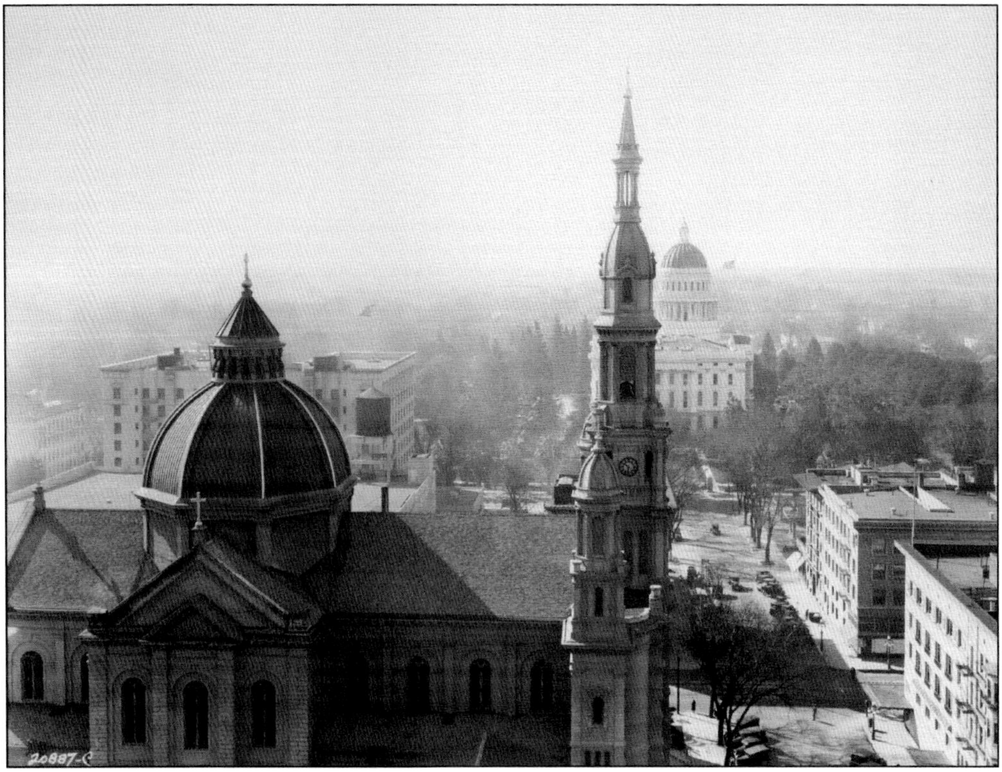

This view is looking south from the Elks Temple. In the foreground is the Cathedral of the Blessed Sacrament, completed in 1889. Its dome serves as an architectural counterpoint to the dome of the capitol. (CSL.)

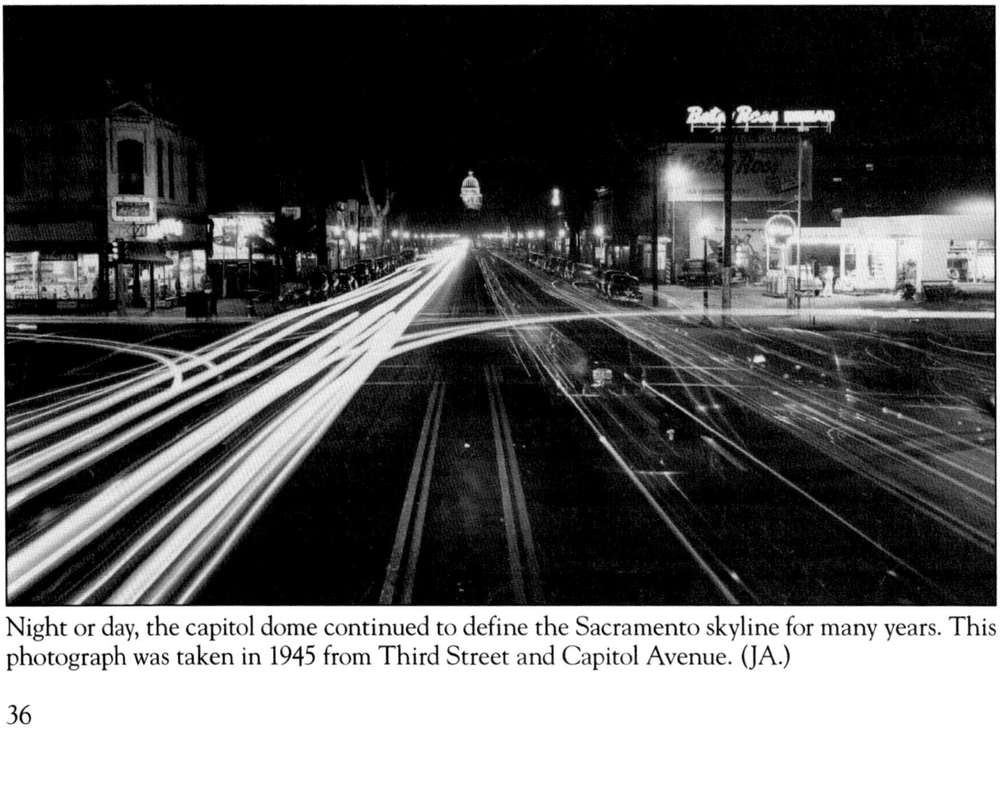

Night or day, the capitol dome continued to define the Sacramento skyline for many years. This photograph was taken in 1945 from Third Street and Capitol Avenue. (JA.)

This current view is of the magnificent inner dome over the rotunda. The glass oculus at the center was designed to let in exterior light from the outer dome. Above the coffered dome is the outer dome. The two are separated by an intervening space of 90 feet. (SCM.)

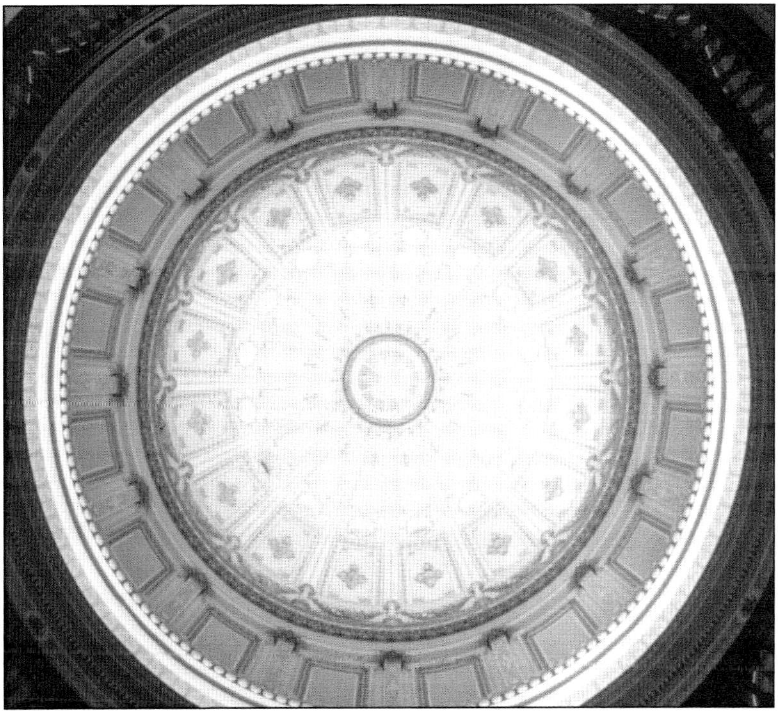

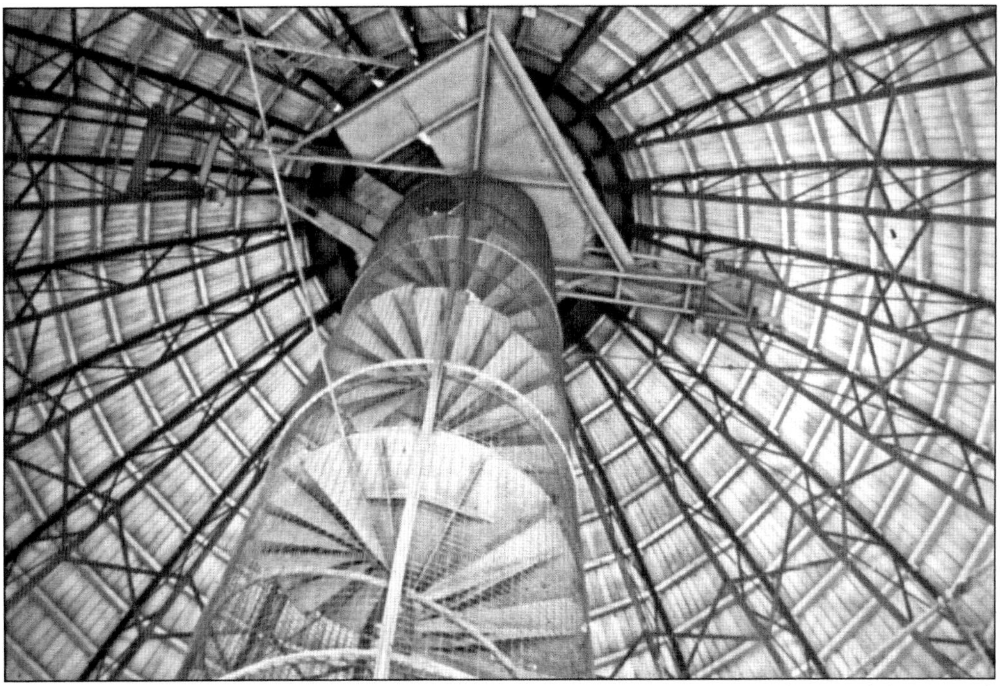

This photograph is of the spiral staircase connecting the inner and outer domes of the capitol. The use of inner and outer domes was an architectural convention that went back to the Italian Renaissance. The outer iron-and-wooden dome was designed to reflect the grand scale of the exterior structure, while on the other hand, the lower brick one was more in keeping with the building's interior proportions. (CSM.)

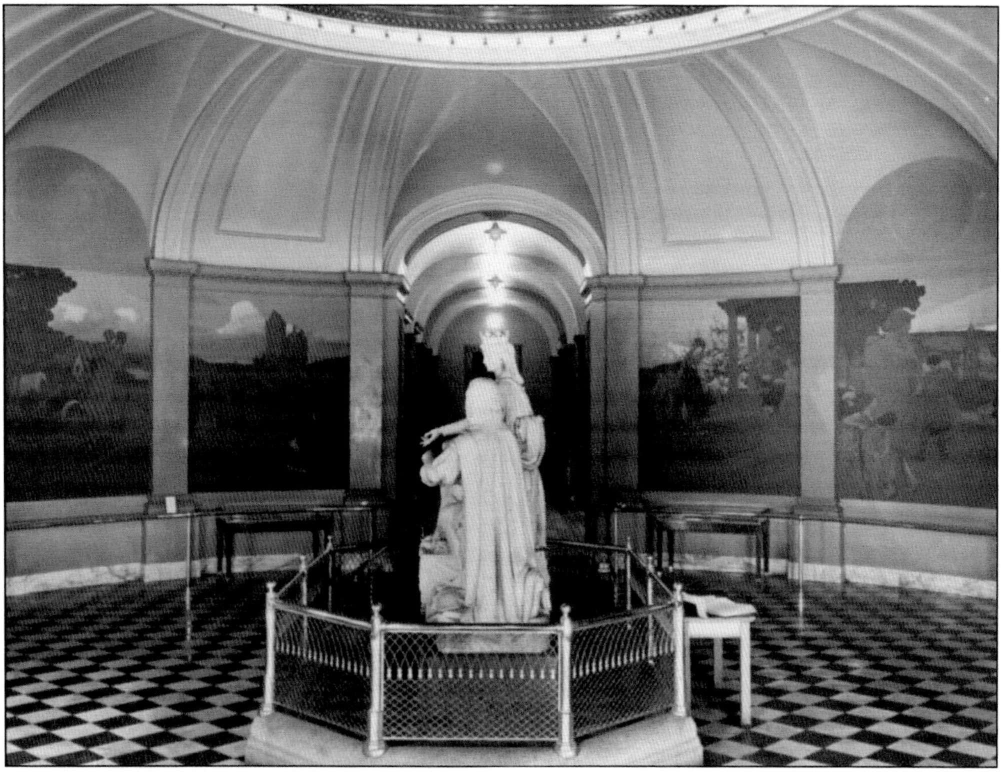

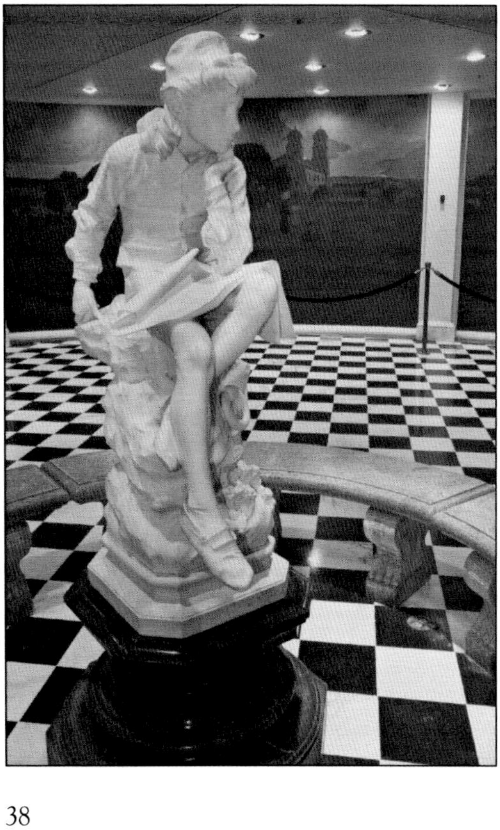

Here is an early-20th-century view of the ground floor of the rotunda with the statue *Columbus' Last Appeal to Queen Isabella* in the center. A series of wall murals painted by Arthur Mathews can be seen in the background. This cycle of 12 panels, *The Story of California*, was originally painted for the 1915 Panama Pacific International Exposition. First exhibited in San Francisco, they were later removed and installed in the rotunda. (CSL.)

Mathews's murals were later placed in the basement rotunda after the 1970s restoration. Today, they are still located there. This is the staging area for the daily tours of the State Capitol Museum. (SCM.)

This is an early photograph of the marble statue of Queen Isabella and Christopher Columbus. American artist Larkin Meade sculpted it. The nine-ton statue was purchased by Sacramento banker Darius Ogden Mills for $30,000 and installed in the rotunda in 1883. (JA)

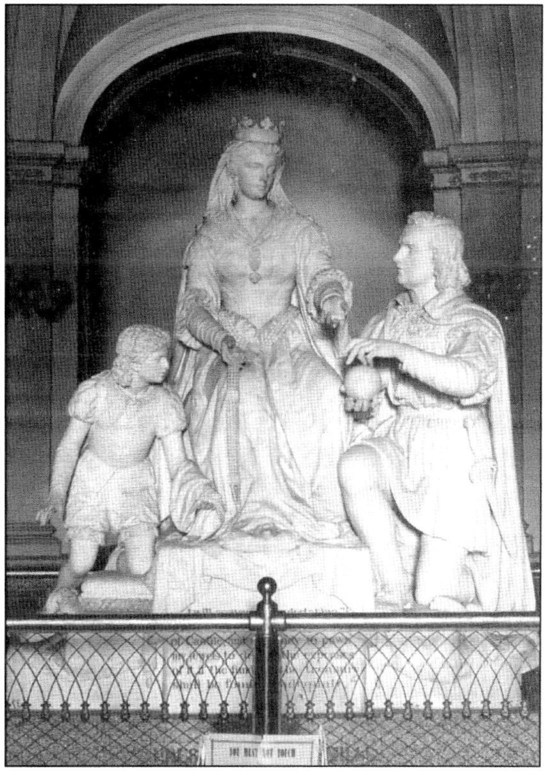

This early-20th-century view is of the senate chamber and visitors' gallery. Many of its original details can still be seen here. The original ornate ceiling was lost when it was lowered to accommodate a fourth floor above it. The senate, which has only half the number of members as the assembly, still uses the traditional voting system of verbal roll calls. (CSL.)

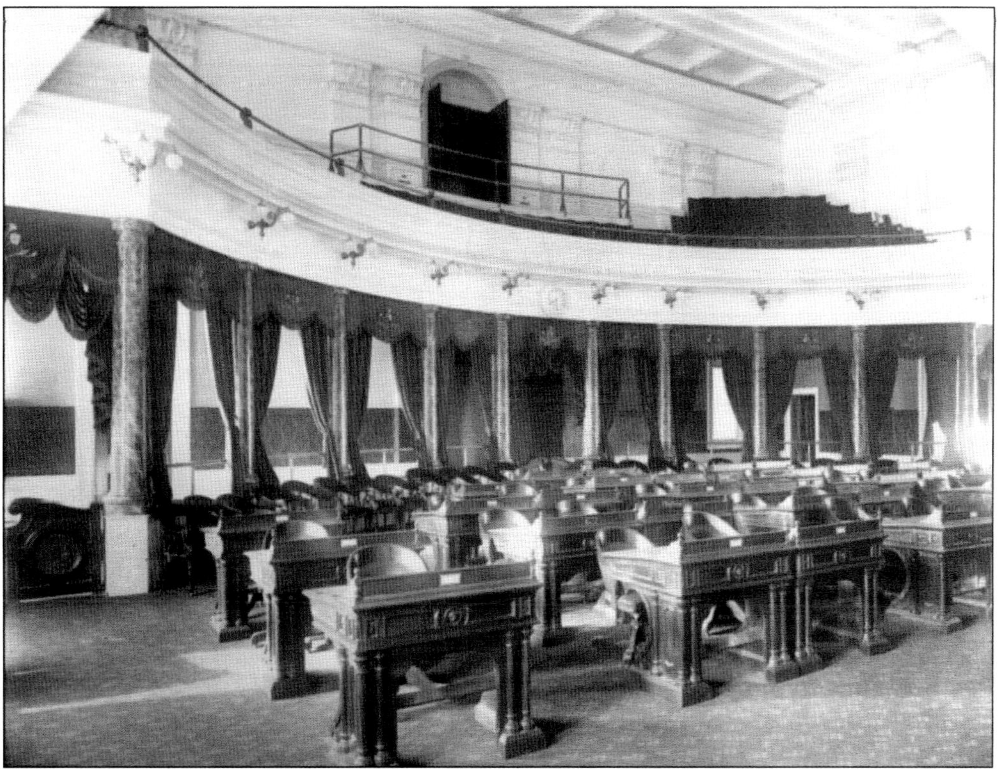

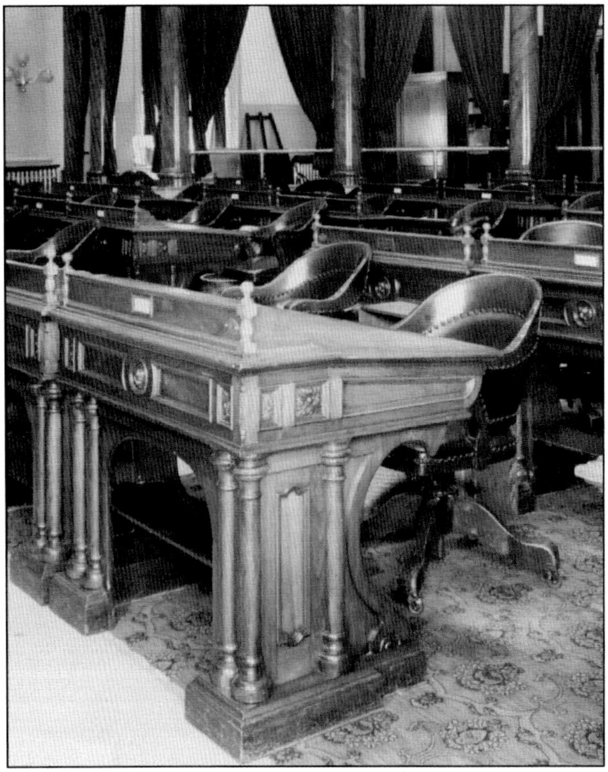

One of the original senate chamber desks made by furniture maker John Breuner is seen here. He was commissioned to make 120 walnut desks for the legislature and other furniture for the building in 1869. The desks were patterned after school desks in his native Germany. The Breuners became a prominent business family in Sacramento and ran Breuner's Department Store for over 100 years. (CSL.)

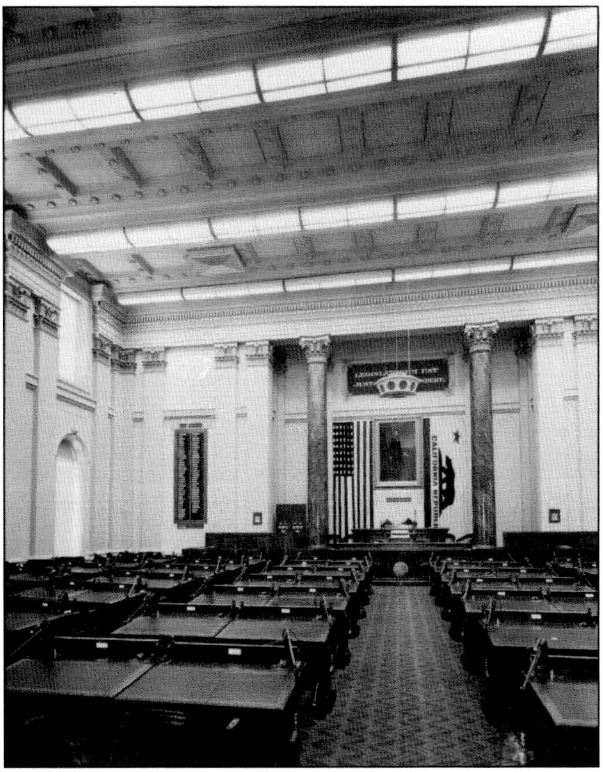

This 1948 photograph shows the assembly chamber. Gone now are almost all of the chamber's original architectural details and light fixtures from numerous remodels. In 1935, an electronic voting system was installed with buttons on each member's desk and large boards that registered their votes with colored lights. (CSL.)

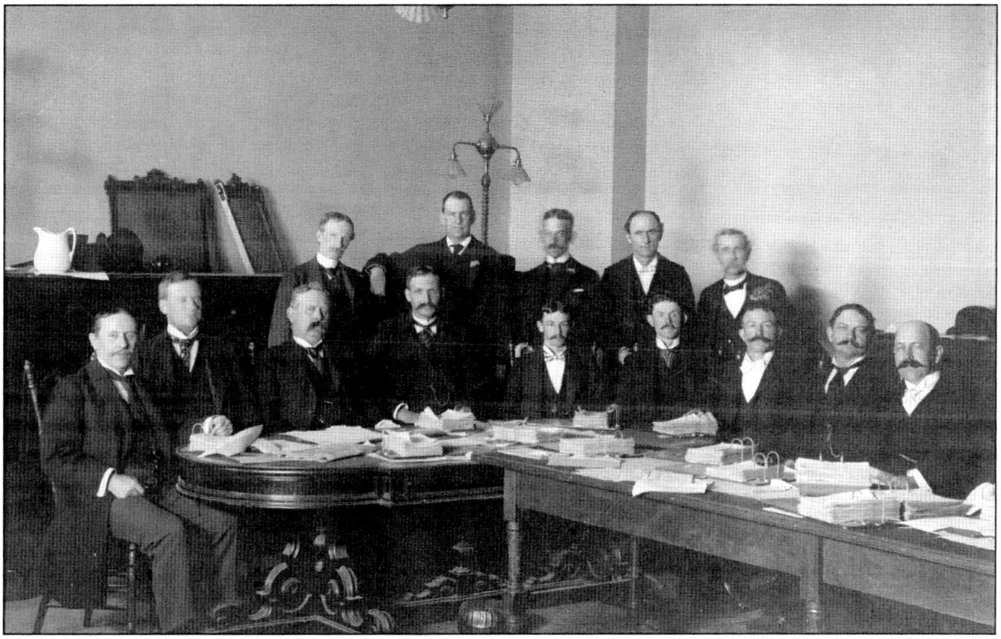

The capitol also had many legislative hearing rooms. The red-and-green color schemes were carried over to these rooms, as well. It was in rooms like this one that much of the legislature's work was conducted. (CSL.)

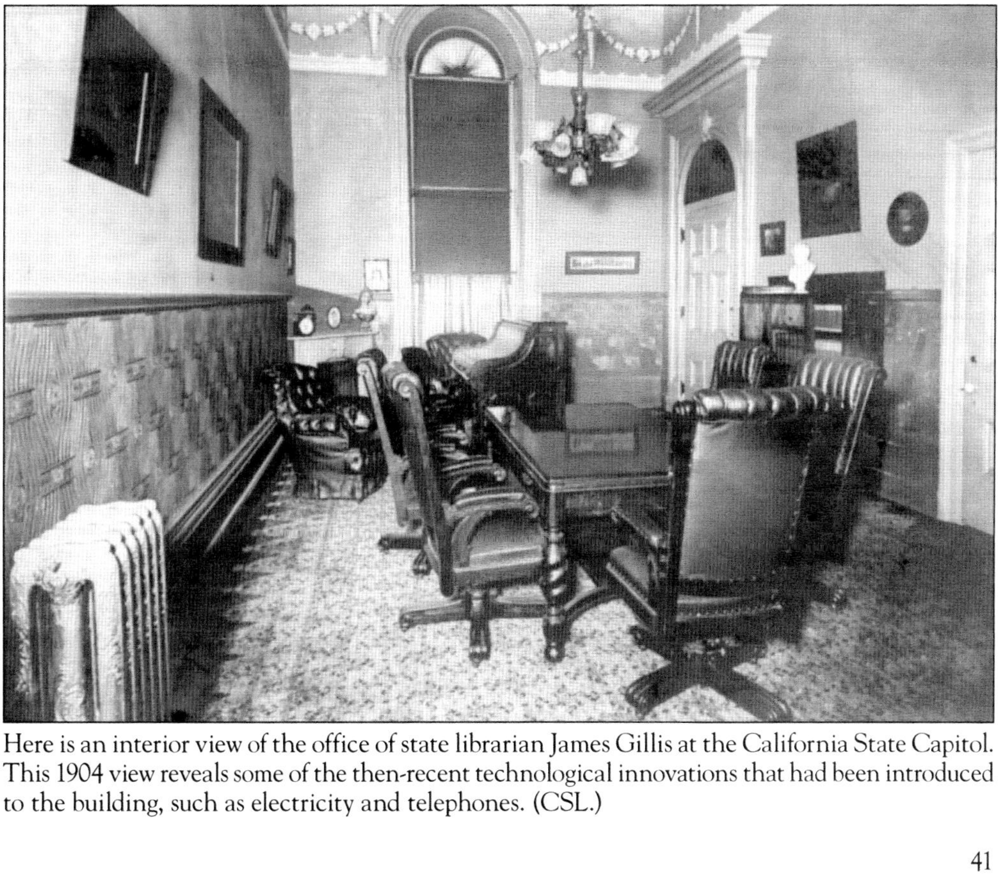

Here is an interior view of the office of state librarian James Gillis at the California State Capitol. This 1904 view reveals some of the then-recent technological innovations that had been introduced to the building, such as electricity and telephones. (CSL.)

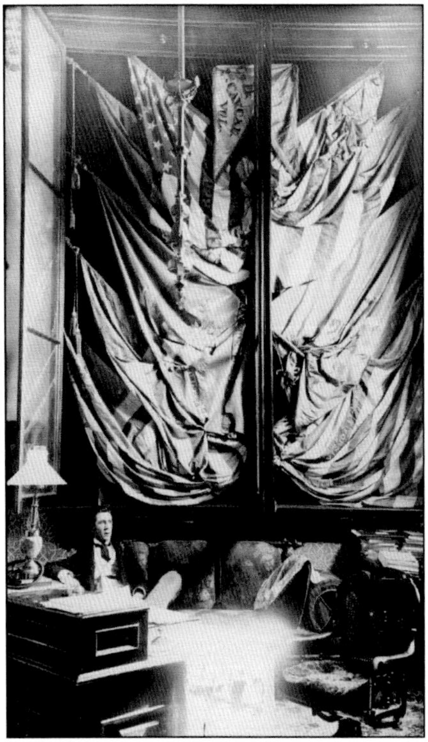

Here is an interior view of the State Adjutant General's Office around 1900. Many of the original Civil War flags in the capitol's collection can be seen in the case. (CSL.)

For over half a century, the State Treasury Office was housed in the capitol. Here is a later view of the interior in the 1920s. Gone are the original ornate features and furniture from an earlier era. Instead, the walls are painted in an institutional green. Eventually, the State Treasurer's Office was relocated across the street to Office Building No. 1, where it still resides. (CSL.)

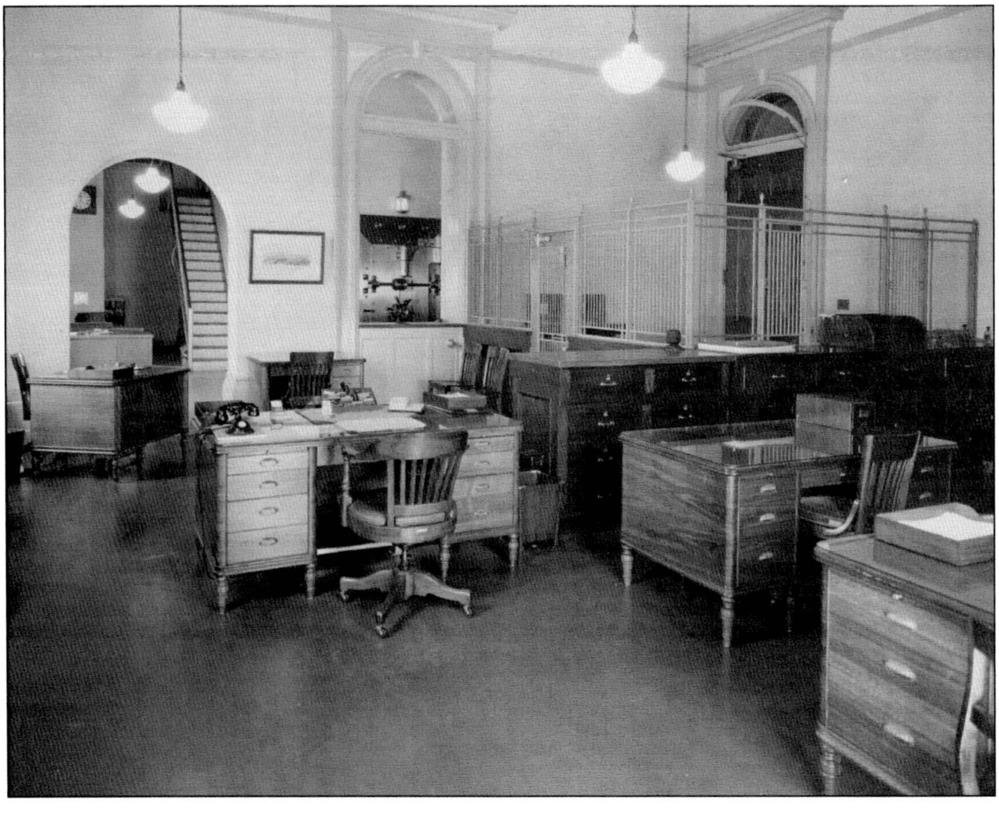

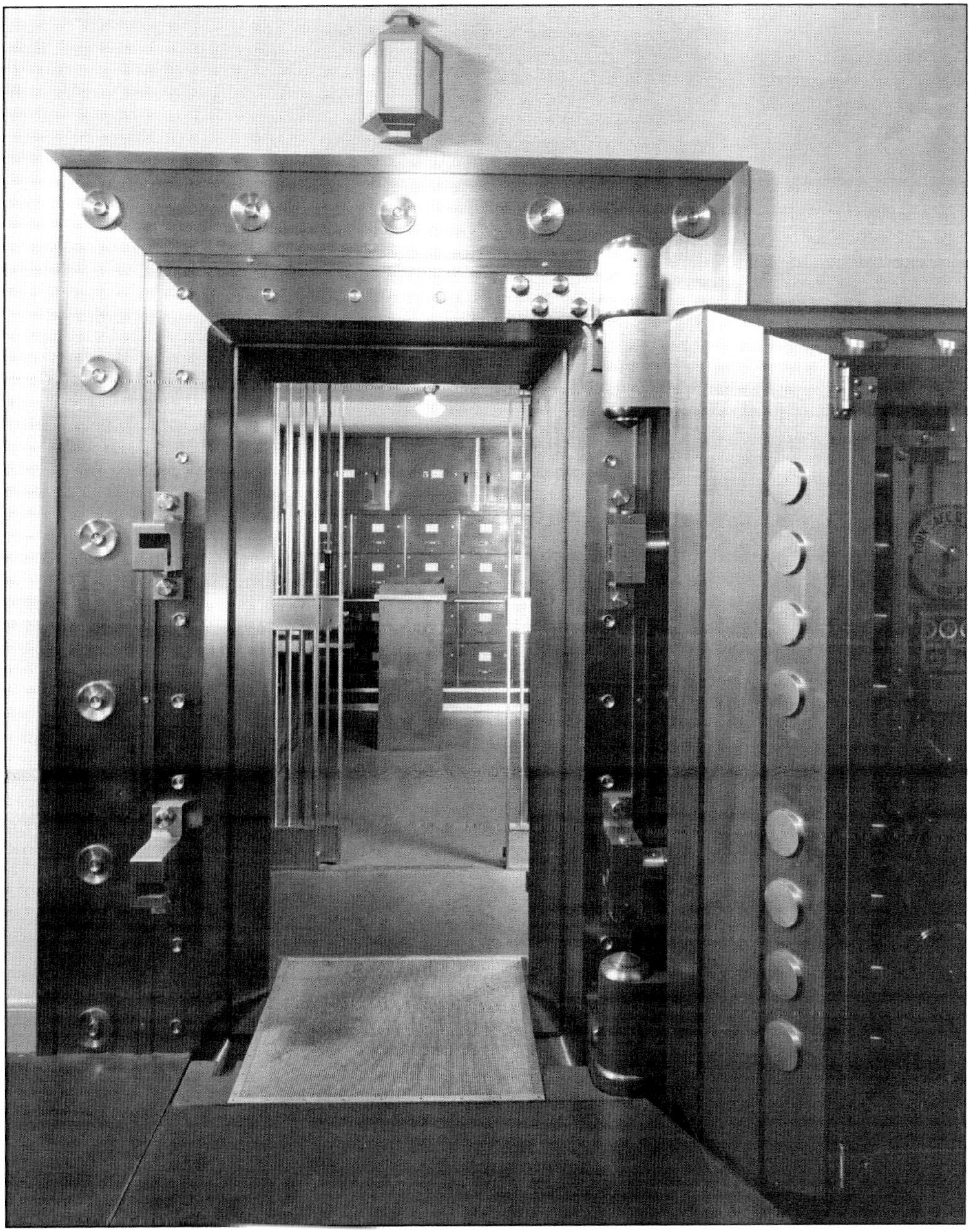

The State Treasury Office served as the state's official bank. All state monies were kept in its vaults until the early 20th century, when major banking reforms were made. These then allowed the state to deposit state revenues in private banks and finally receive interest. This massive vault on the first floor had an elevator that went down to a separate vault in the basement. (CSL no. 3279.)

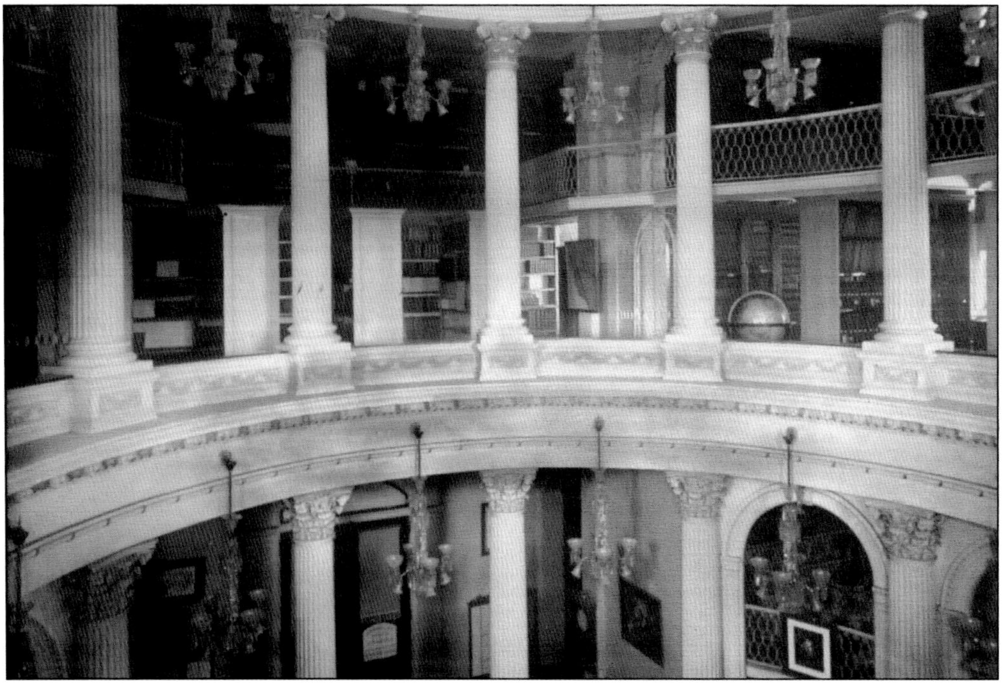

By 1900, the capitol, especially the California State Library, was literally running out of room. With space at a premium, plans were made for a capitol expansion. California state librarian James Gillis was able to secure funding for construction of the first two new state buildings in Sacramento since the 1860s. (CSL.)

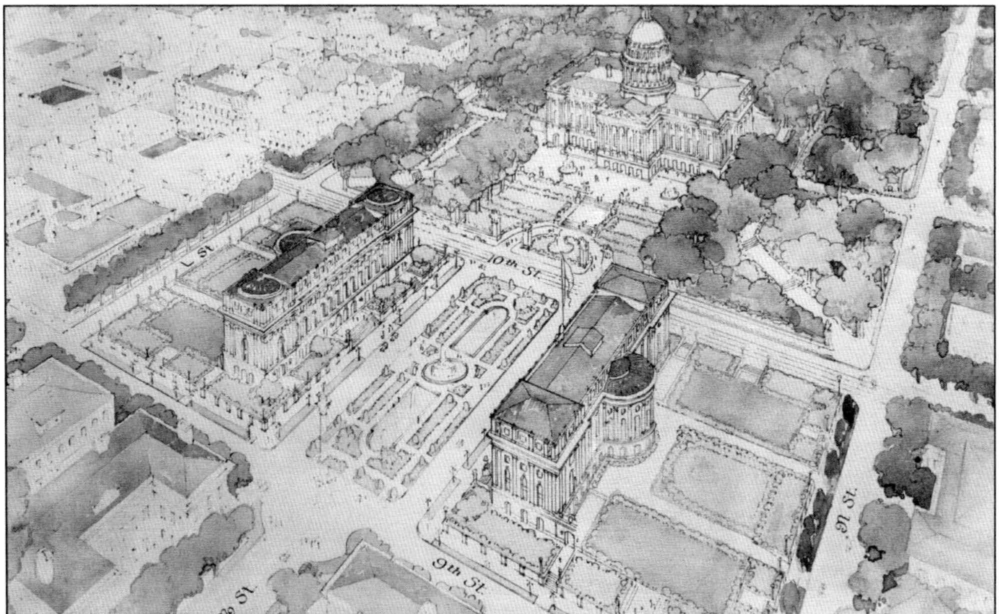

Here is one of the unsuccessful proposals for the capitol expansion. This architect's drawing was only one of 64 entries submitted but not used. The winning contract went to San Francisco architectural firm Weeks and Day. (CSL.)

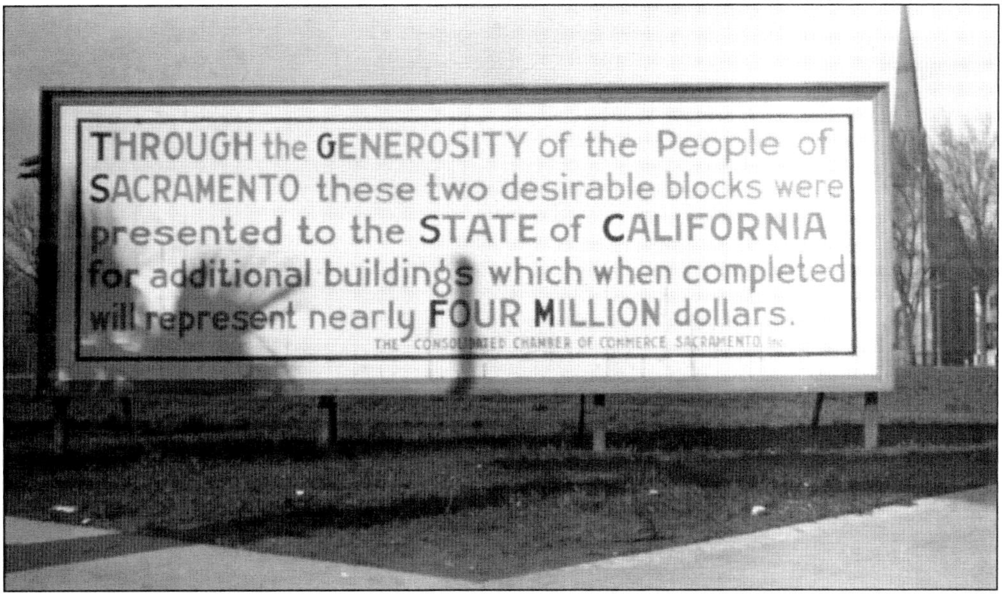

Shown is a construction sign on the vacant lot where the future capitol expansion, or West Annex, was to be built. Construction was held up because of shortages caused by World War I. (CSL.)

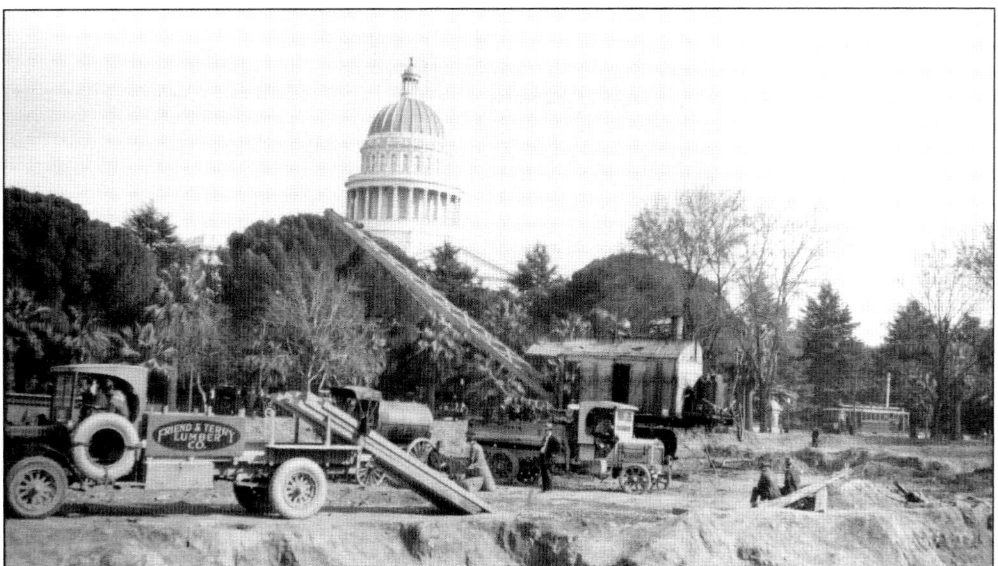

Construction finally began in 1924 and would not be fully completed until five years later. (CSL.)

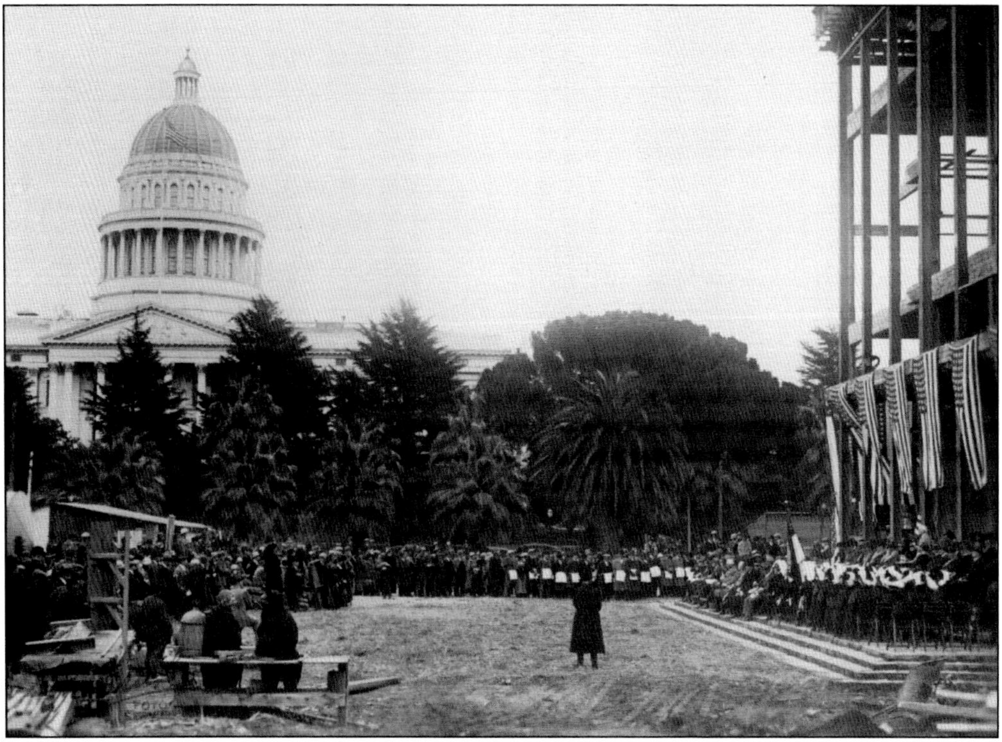

A cornerstone ceremony was held in March 1924 for the California State Library and Courts Building (now known as the Stanley Mosk Building). Construction continued over the next five years. (CSL.)

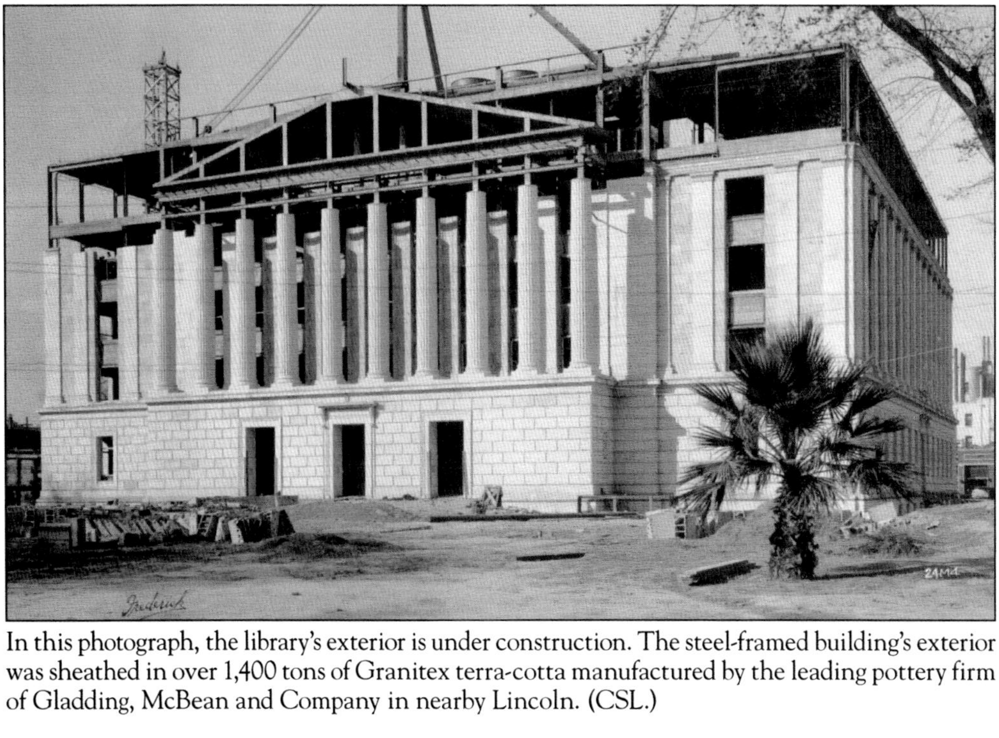

In this photograph, the library's exterior is under construction. The steel-framed building's exterior was sheathed in over 1,400 tons of Granitex terra-cotta manufactured by the leading pottery firm of Gladding, McBean and Company in nearby Lincoln. (CSL.)

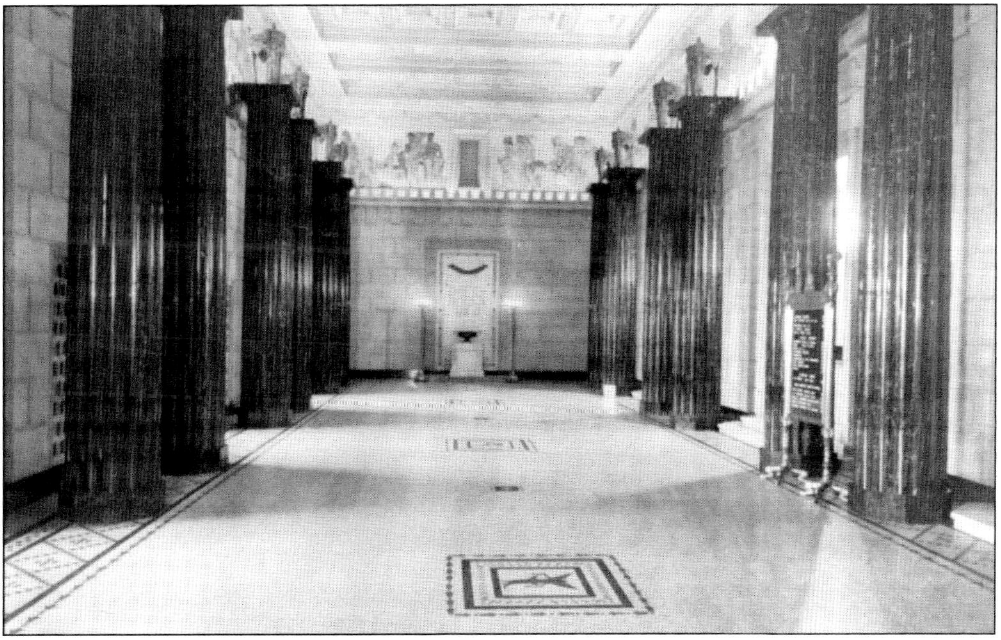

Here is an interior shot of the California State Library's Memorial Vestibule, which was dedicated to the war dead of the First World War. A continuous frieze runs around the whole of the room between its 16 massive columns and the hall's coffered ceiling. Titled *A History of War*, this mural was completed by Frank Van Sloun in 1928. (CSL.)

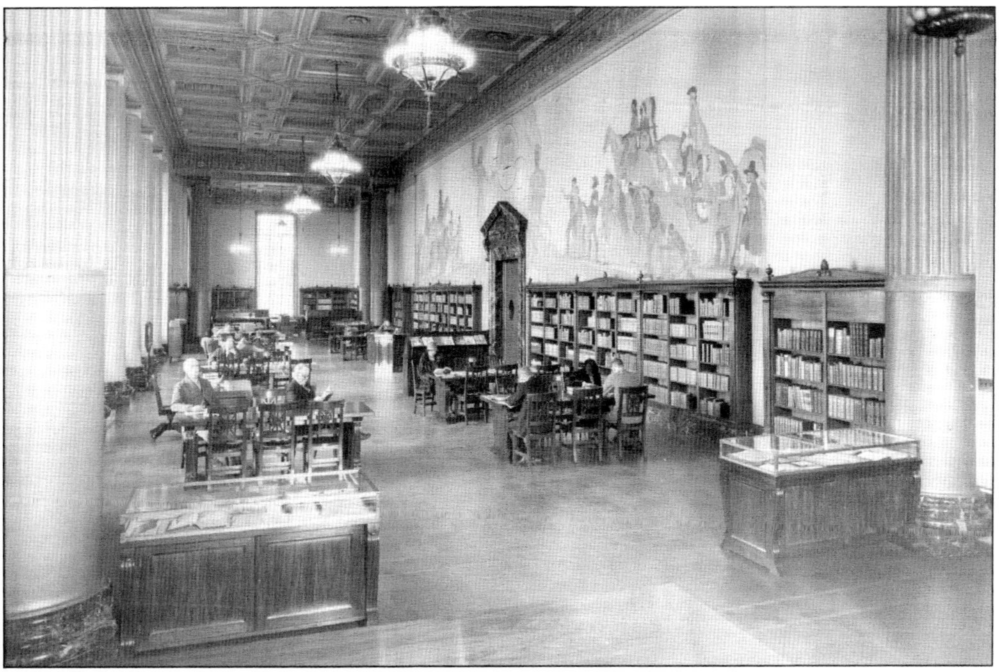

This 1929 view is of the library's stunning Gillis Hall. It has a magnificent 1928 mural by the great Western artist Maynard Dixon. Called *A Pageant of Tradition*, it runs nearly the whole width of the library building. It has been fully conserved as part of a major building restoration project that began in 2011. Other Dixon murals also grace the building. (CSL.)

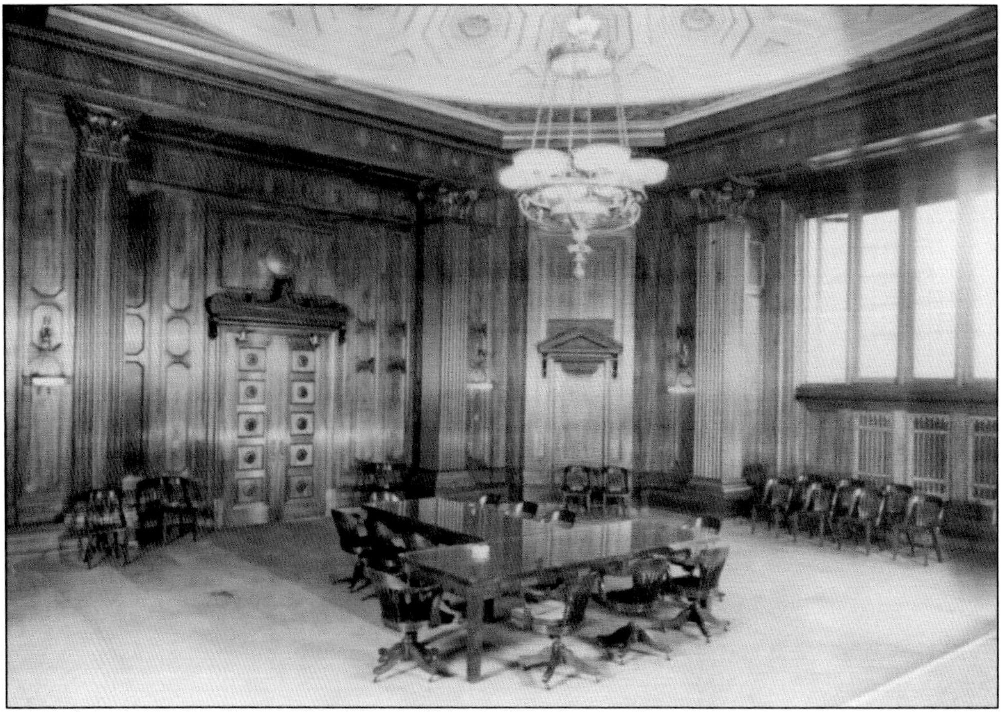

The original octagonal courtroom on the fifth floor was intended for the use of both the California State Supreme Court and appellate courts. It was never used as intended because the justices did not wish to occupy the room during the hot summer months—and they were not alone. Stories still persist of library staff lying down at times on the marble floors to try to keep cool. (CSL.)

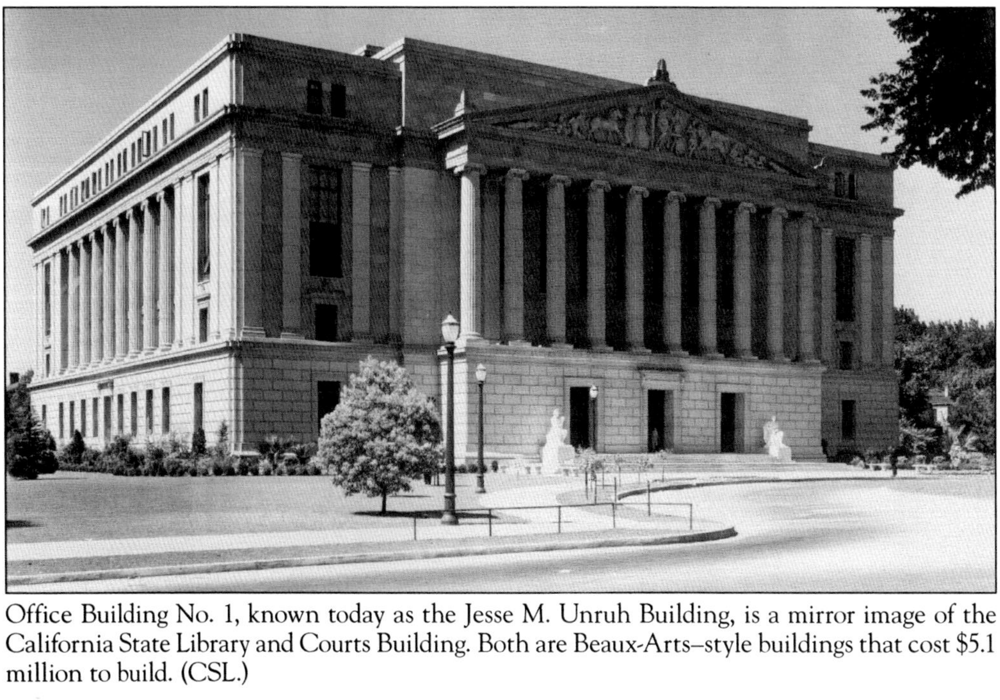

Office Building No. 1, known today as the Jesse M. Unruh Building, is a mirror image of the California State Library and Courts Building. Both are Beaux-Arts–style buildings that cost $5.1 million to build. (CSL.)

Here, sculptor Edward Field Sanford Jr. is examining his own work on the library pediment. He sculpted the pediments for both the library building and Building No. 1, along with four marble statues and ten plaques. (CSL.)

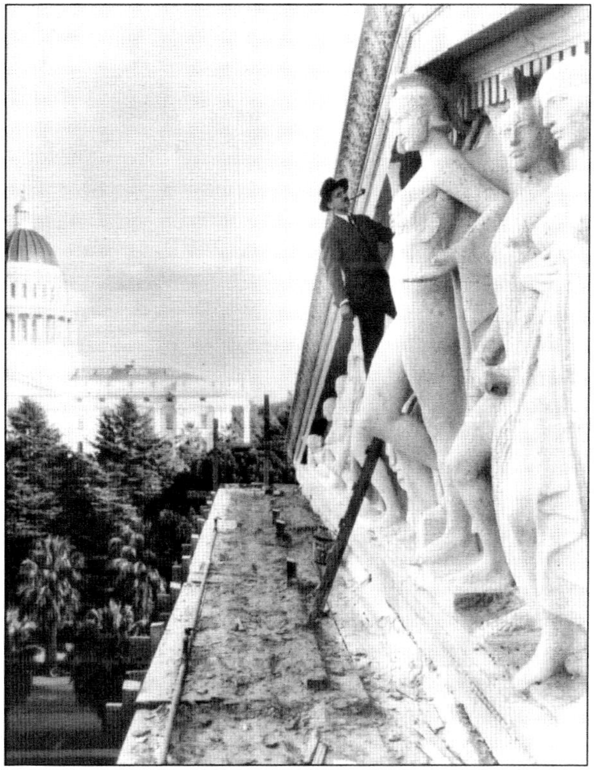

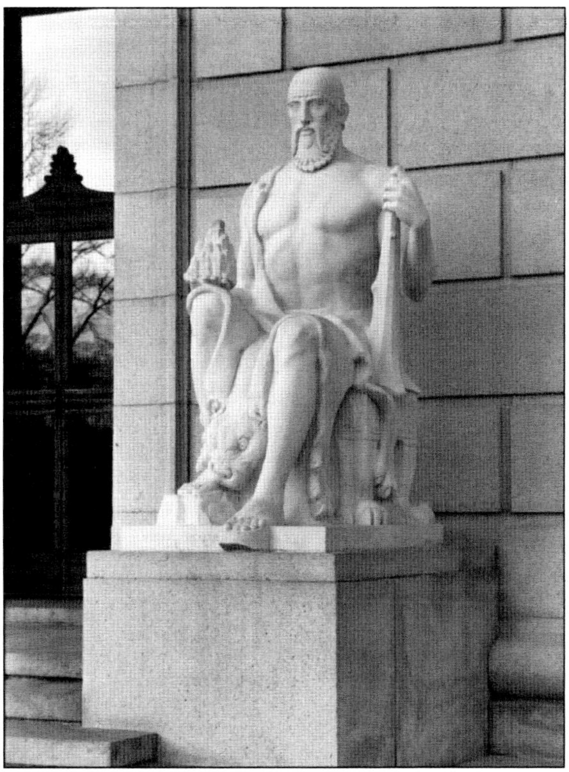

The statue of the allegorical figure of mineral wealth is in front of the library building. It is one of Sanford's four granite statues at the entrances of both buildings. (CSL.)

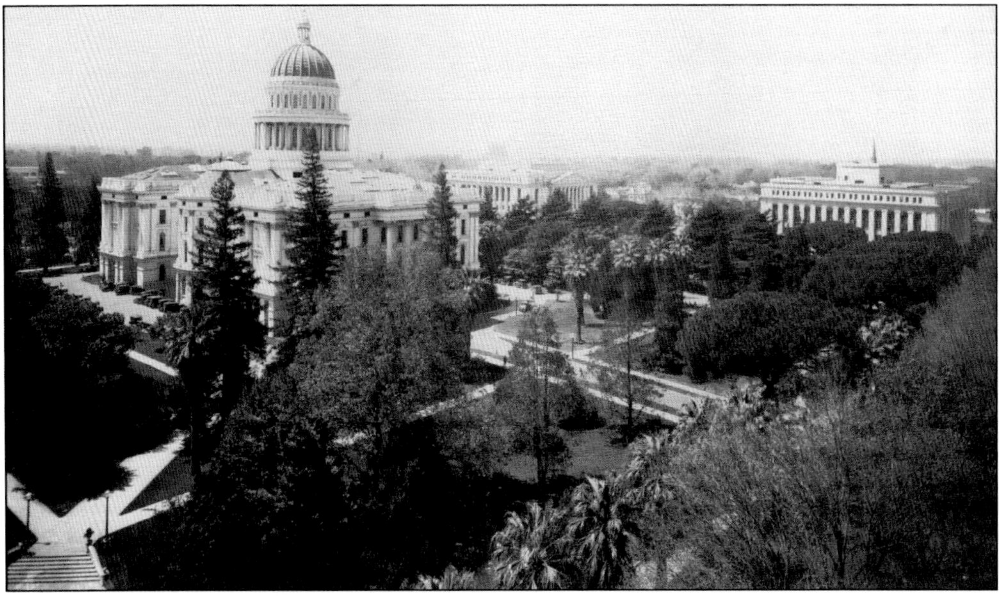

Looking southeast from the Senator Hotel, the newly completed West Annex can be seen across from the capitol. (CSL.)

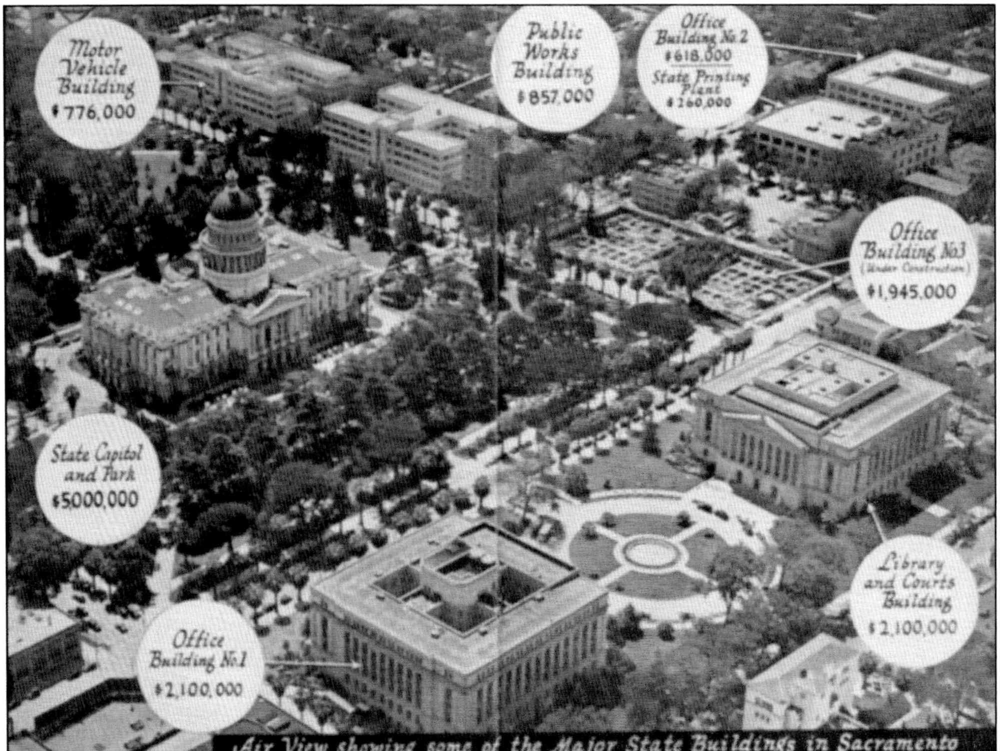

This aerial view from a 1930s promotional brochure shows not only the recently completed capitol expansion project but also other state buildings, either completed or under construction, and their costs. With the exception of State Building No. 2 that housed the printing plant, all other structures are still in existence. (JA.)

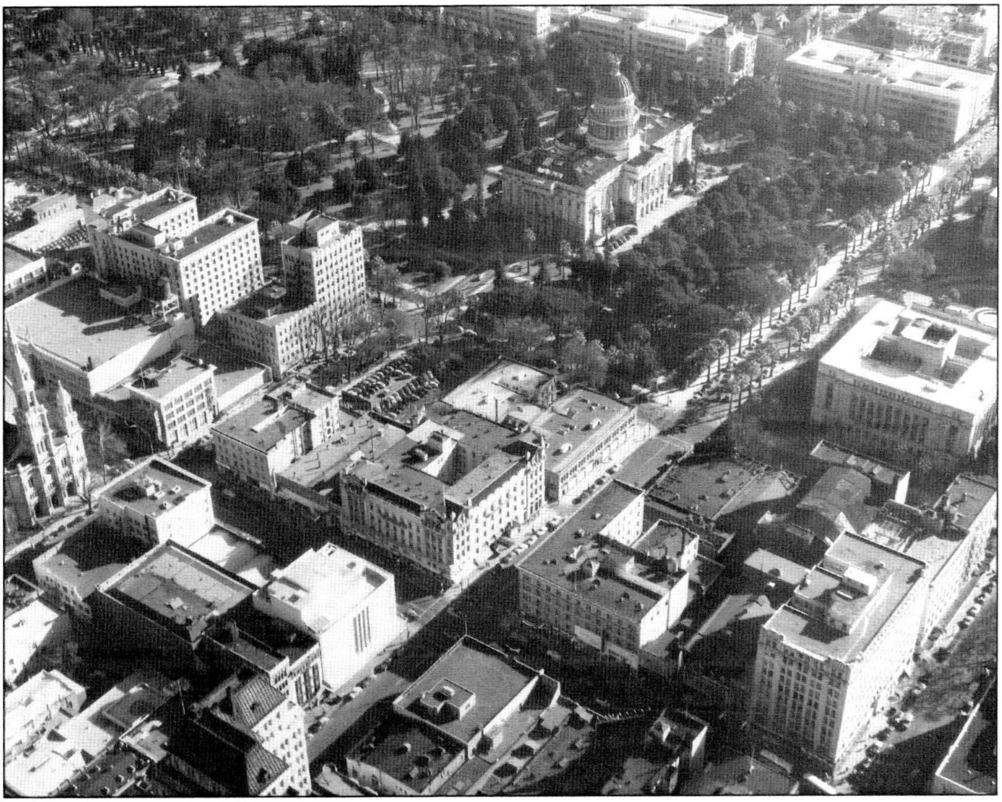

Here is an aerial view of the capitol at the time of World War II. As California's population continued to grow, the old building was experiencing its own growing pains. (CSL.)

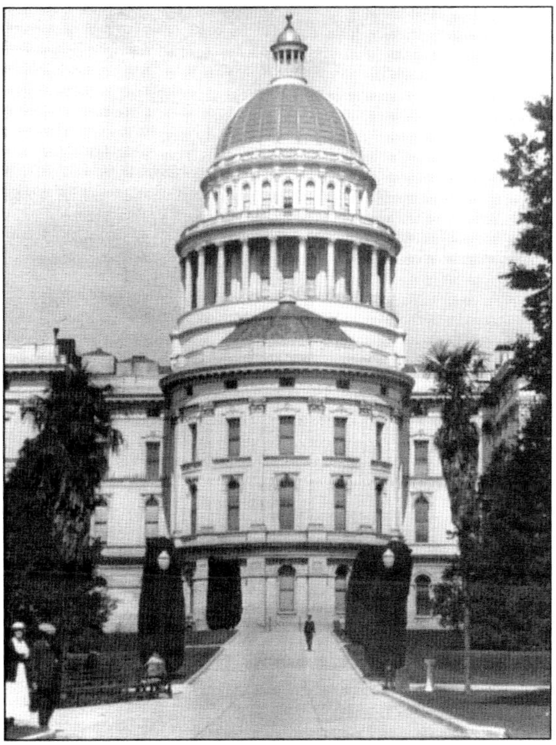

The stately old apse had always been one of the most distinctive architectural features of the capitol. Sadly, it would eventually fall victim to the plans for the expansion of the capitol. (CSL.)

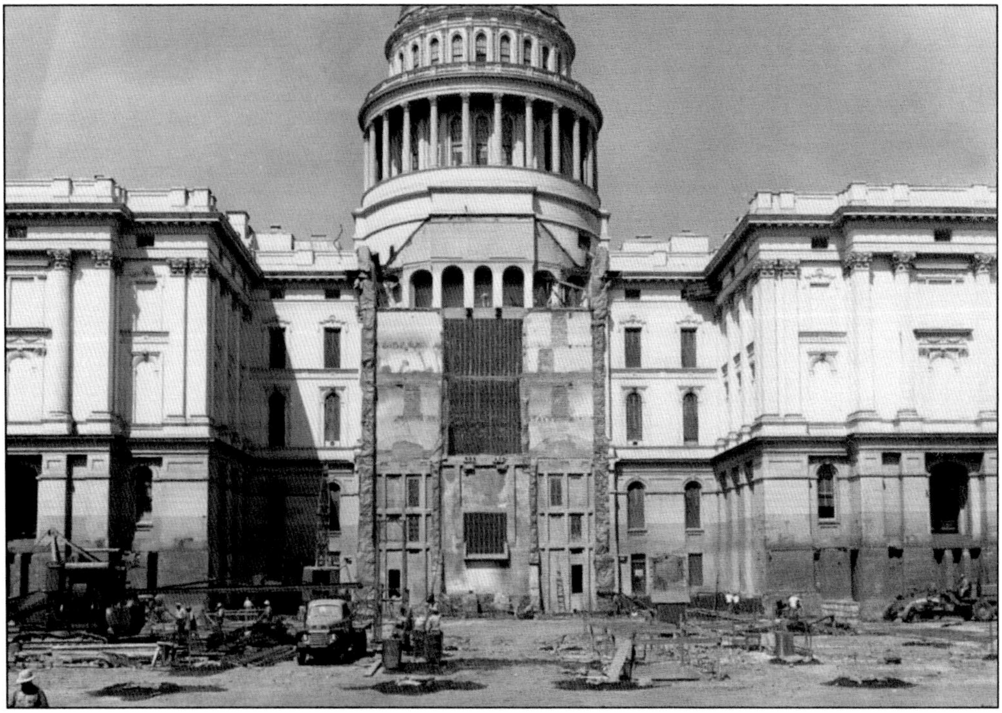

Construction on the East Annex began in June 1949 and would be completed in December 1950. This view shows the final stages of the demolition of the apse. Over time, many Sacramentans came to regret this loss of one of city's greatest architectural treasures. (CSL.)

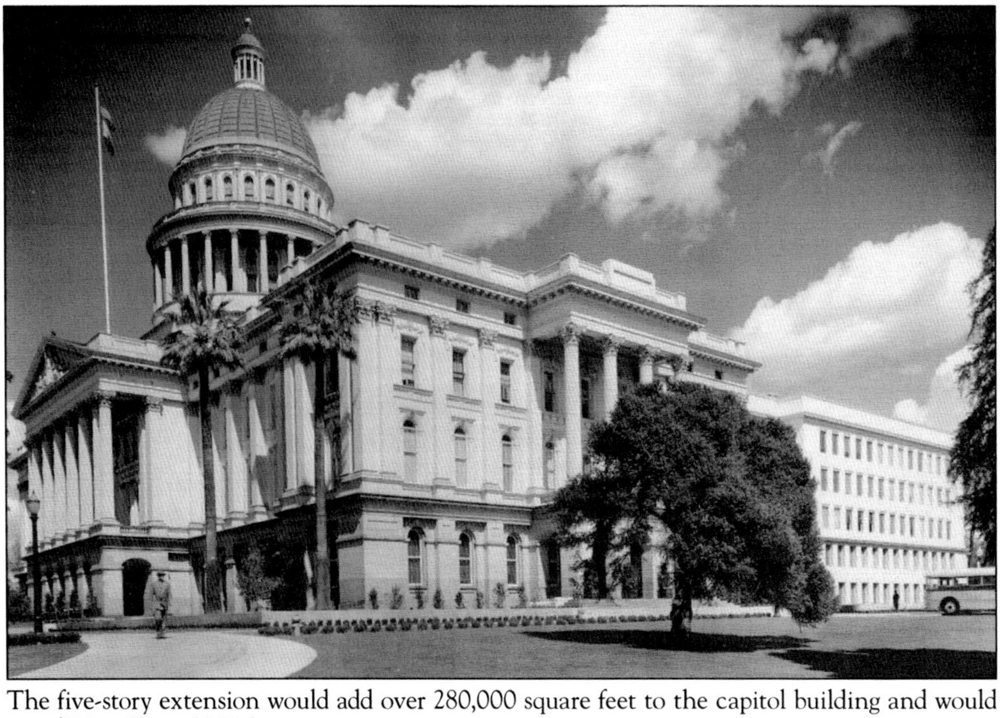

The five-story extension would add over 280,000 square feet to the capitol building and would cost $7.2 million. (CSL.)

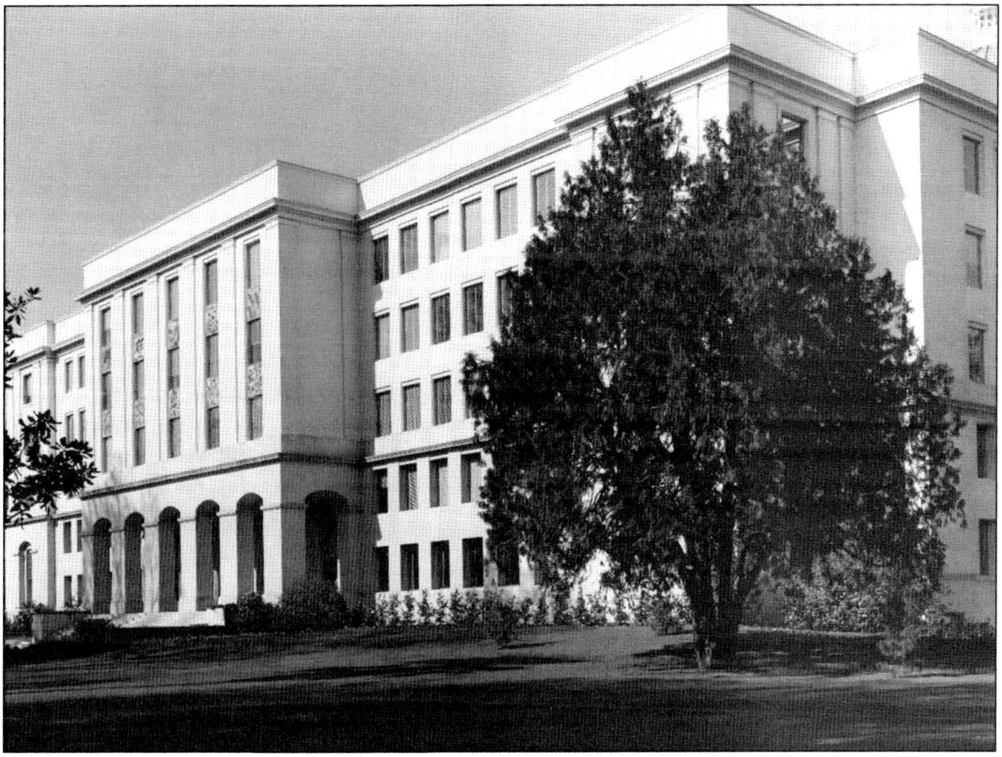

The newly completed East Annex portico was built in a modified Classical Revival style. The new addition had its detractors and critics. State senator James Mills called it an example of "early-prison architecture." (CSL.)

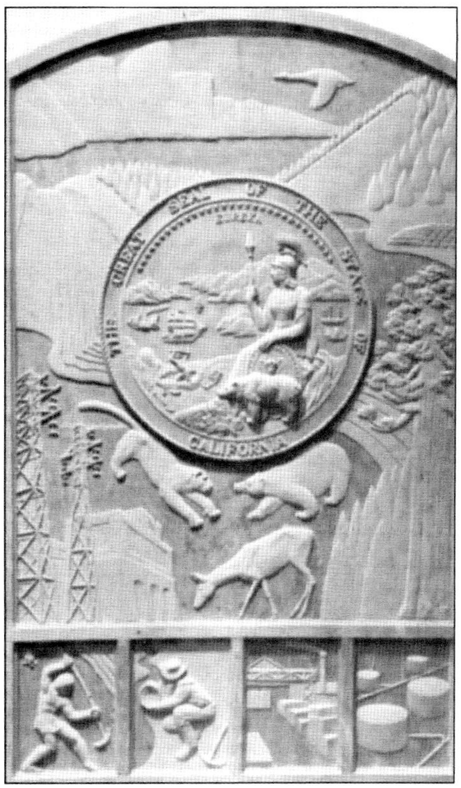

Noted American sculptor Olof C. Malmquist was commissioned to produce five major panels and nine plaques for the entrance to the East Annex. These beautiful Art Deco–style sculptures were based on California historical themes and flora and fauna. (SR.)

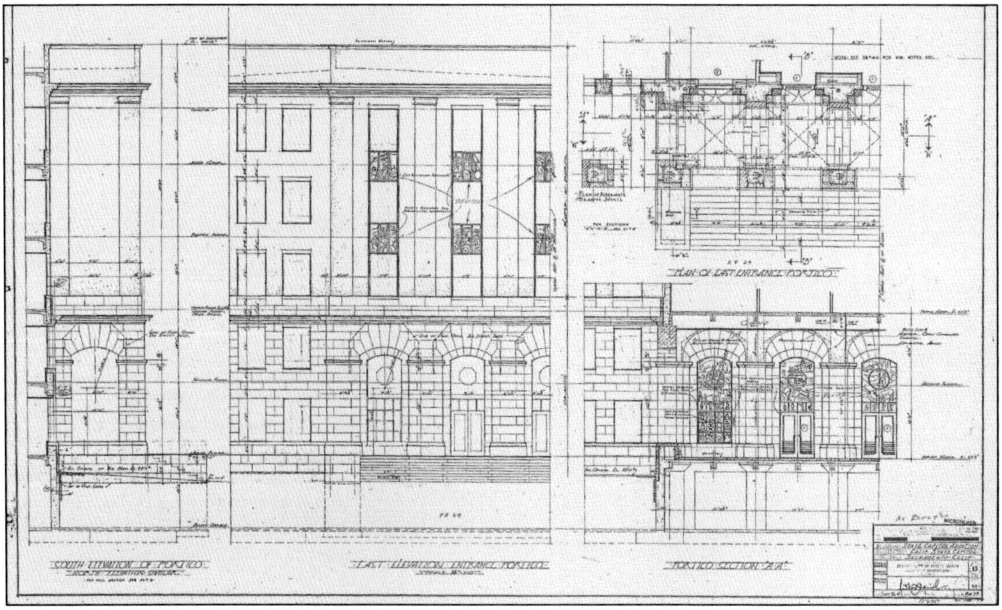

A blueprint of the east entrance shows the placement of Malmquist's series of aluminum sculptural panels. (SRC.)

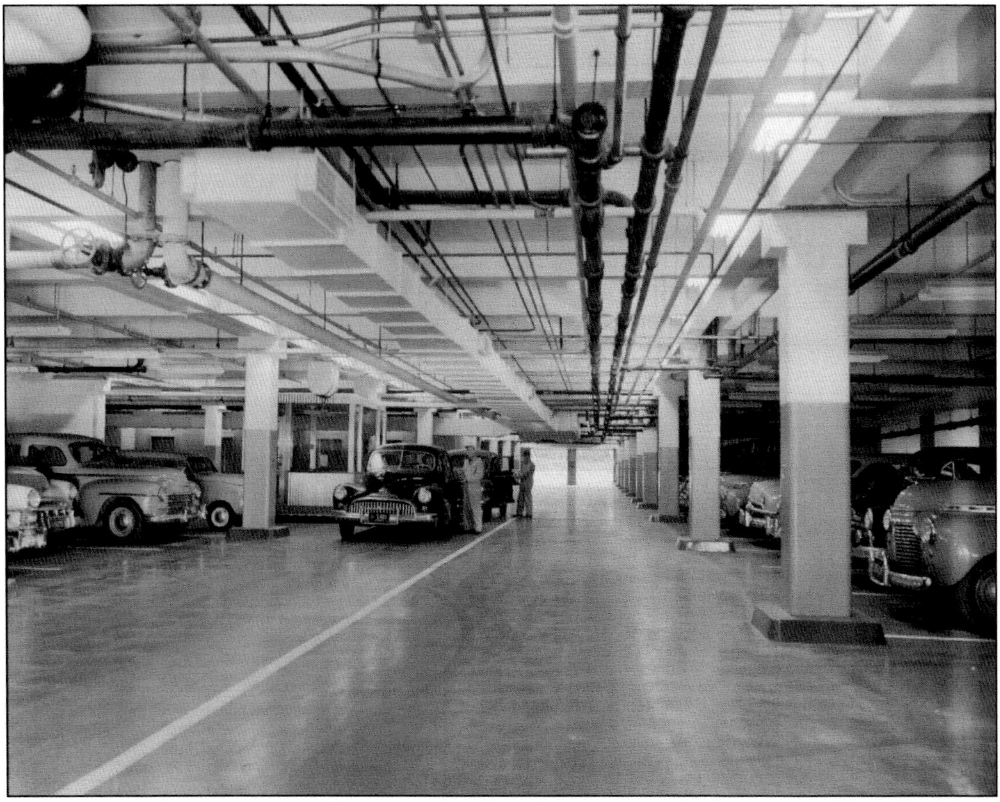

The new East Annex came with its own garage. Shown is a 1955 photograph of the basement garage underneath the new wing of the capitol. (SCM.)

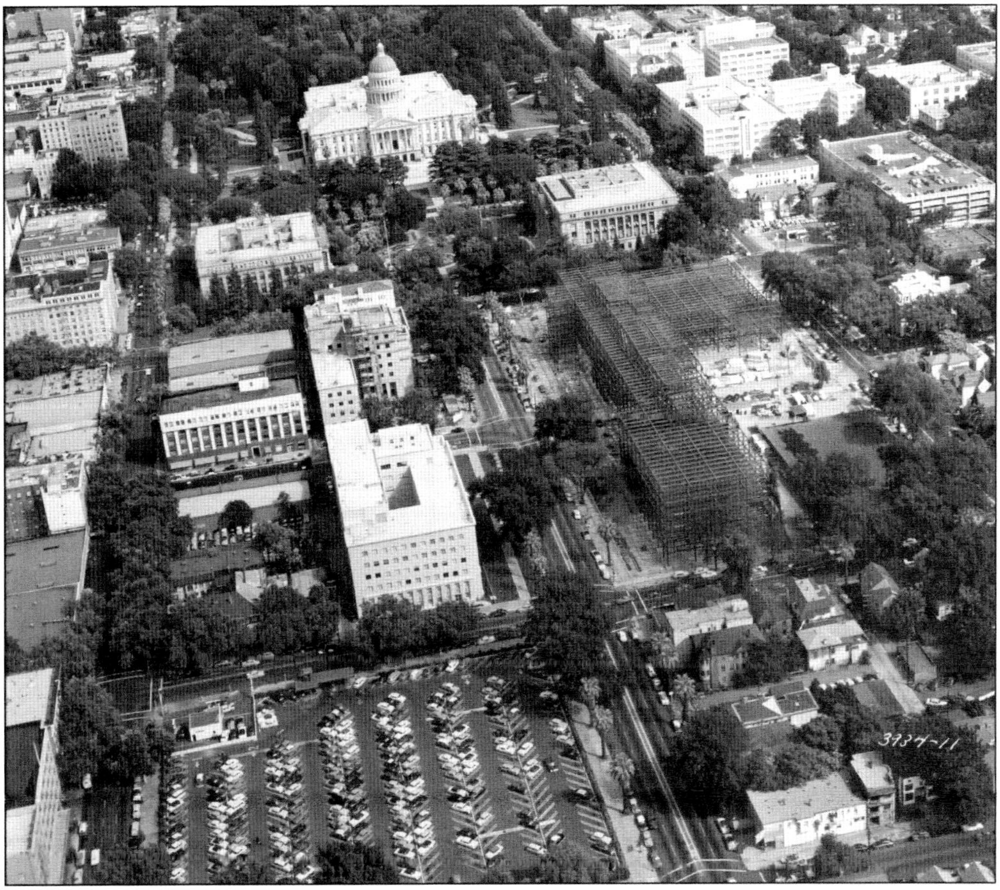

The postwar era unleashed a wave of new construction along Capitol Mall. Above is a 1954 aerial view of the capitol and surrounding area. Construction on the Employment Development Department Building can be seen in the foreground. By the late 1960s and early 1970s, the century-old capitol was showing the advanced signs of its age. Structurally, it had been deemed unsafe in the event of a major earthquake. Some legislators began calling for the building's demolition. In its place were to be two modern skyscrapers, as seen in this architectural drawing below. (Above, CSL; below, SCM.)

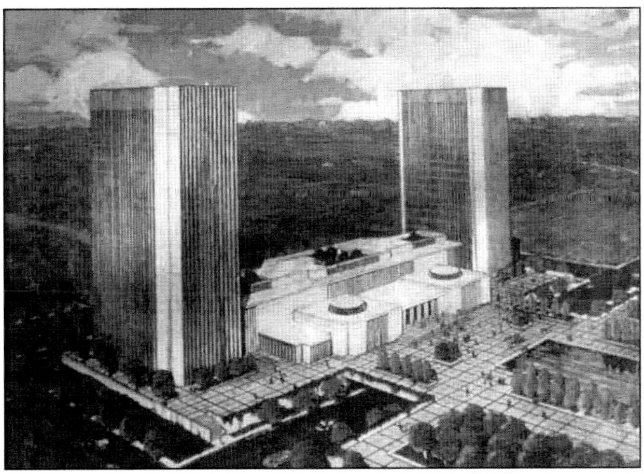

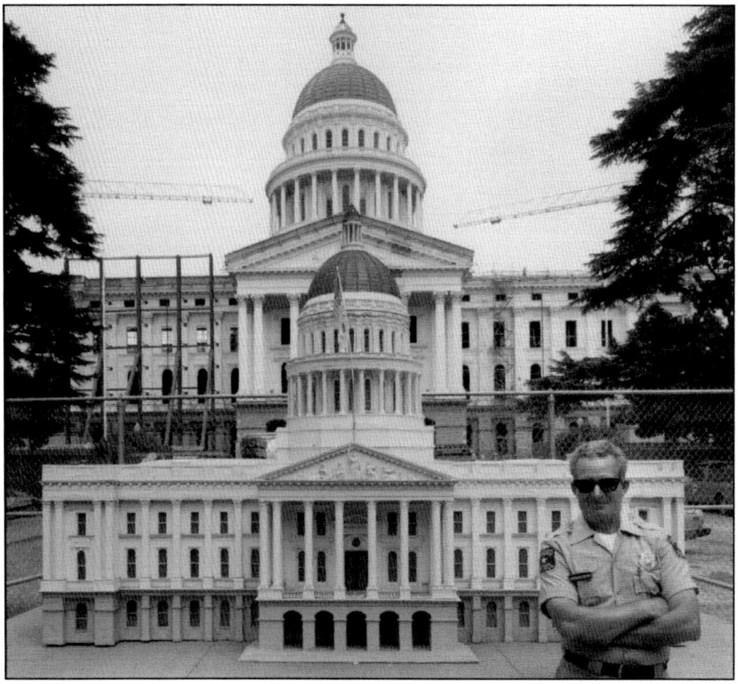

A scale model was in front of the capitol while it was undergoing restorations. Some states have chosen to build a separate modern capitol and then turn their original structure into a museum. Instead, the six-year-long capitol restoration project turned the capitol into both a modern working building and a museum. (CSL.)

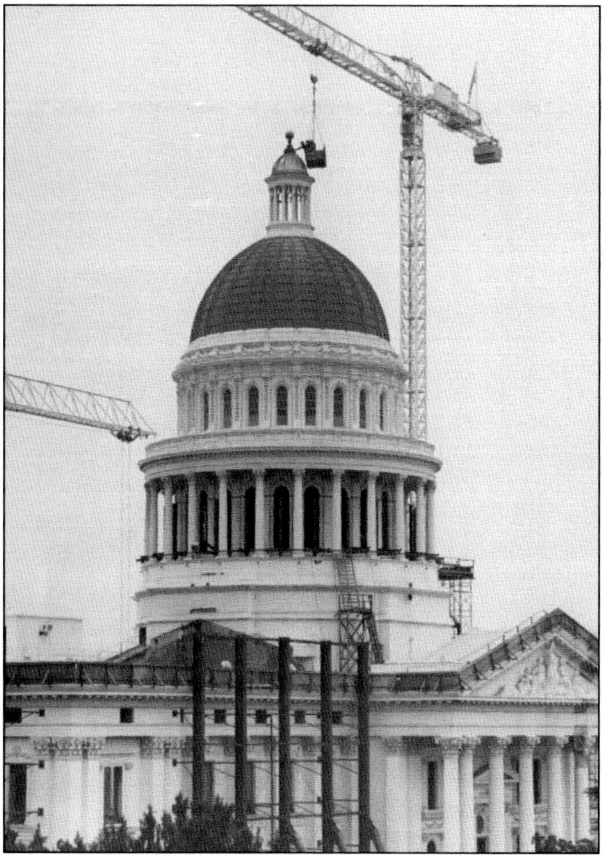

The capitol restoration began in 1976 and would take six years to complete. It was the largest project at the time, costing over \$67 million. Here, massive cranes dwarf the 210-foot-high dome. Both the upper and lower domes needed full restoration. (CSL.)

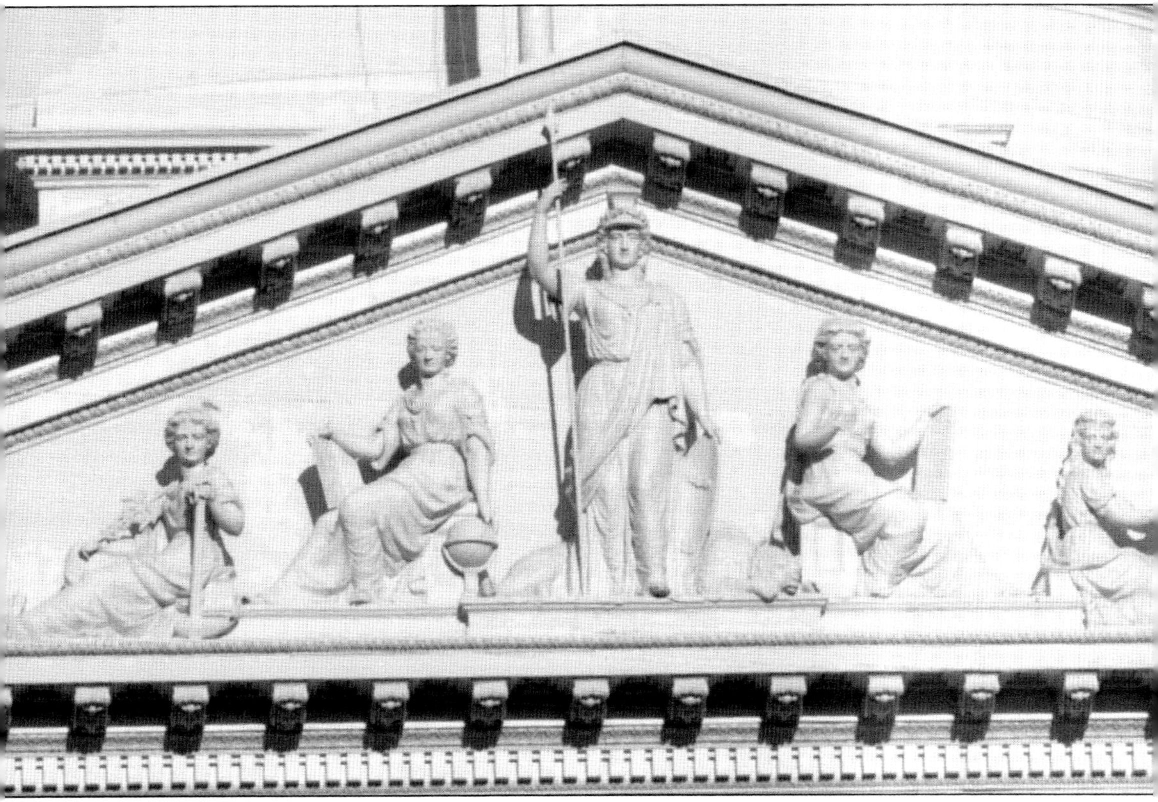

Here is an exterior view of the restored pediment over the west entrance. The seated figure in the center, *Minerva*, represents the Roman goddess of wisdom. Flanking her to the left are *Mining* and *Industry*; and to her right are *Education* and *Justice*. They are the only original sculptures of Pietro Mazzara to have survived. All others were removed in the early 20th century. (SCM.)

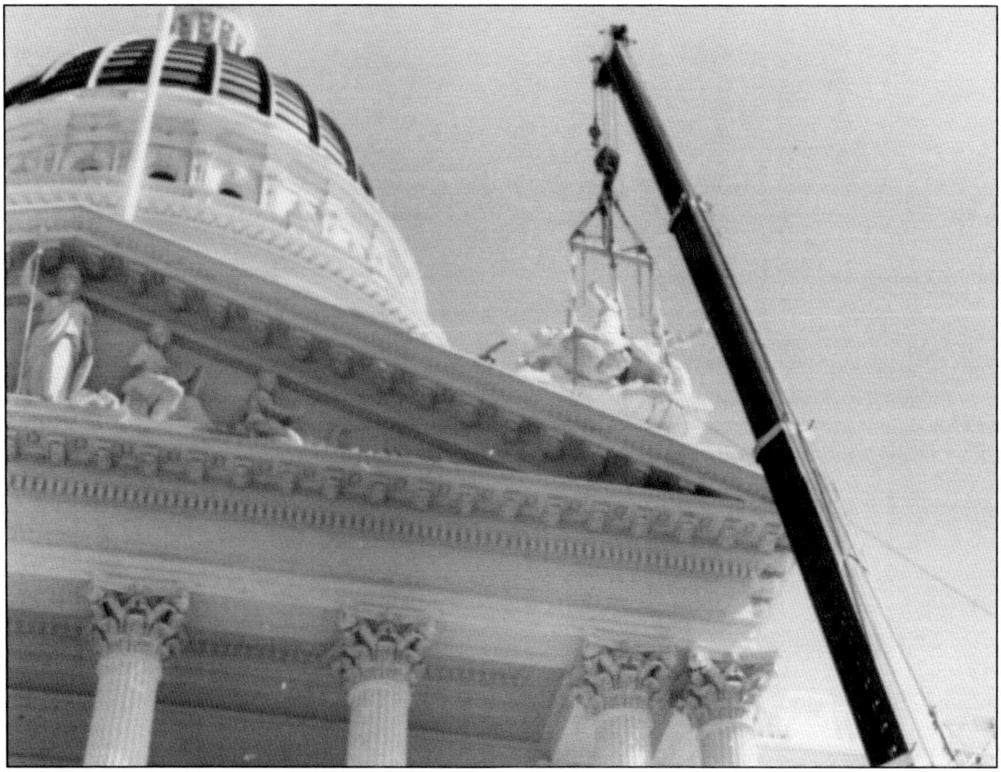

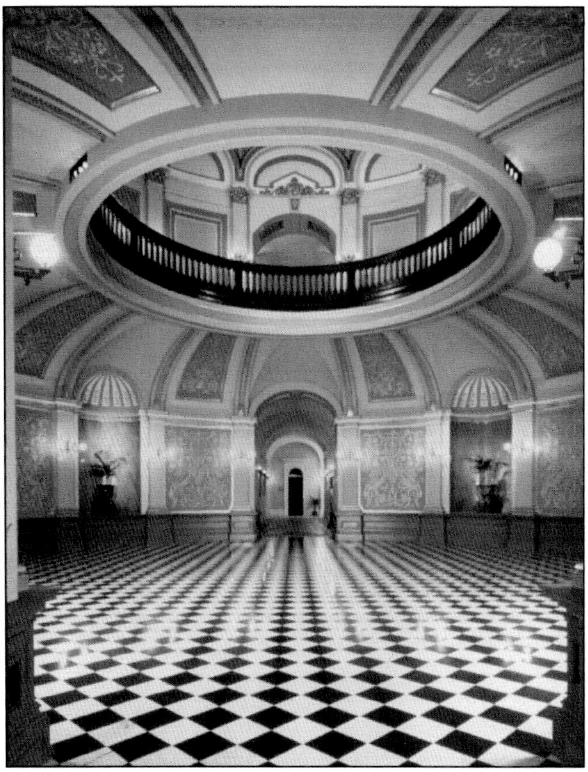

The original statuary that once graced the exterior balustrades was removed during remodeling work done at the turn of the 20th century. Here, one of the copies of the original pieces is being lifted into place on the western portico. (CSL.)

Here is an interior photograph of the newly renovated rotunda before the Columbus and Isabella statue was returned to the center. Some critics felt that space should have been left open in order to give a different spatial feel to the interior. (CSL.)

This is a view of the restored rotunda and interior dome with *Columbus' Last Appeal to Queen Isabella* in its original position. (SCM.)

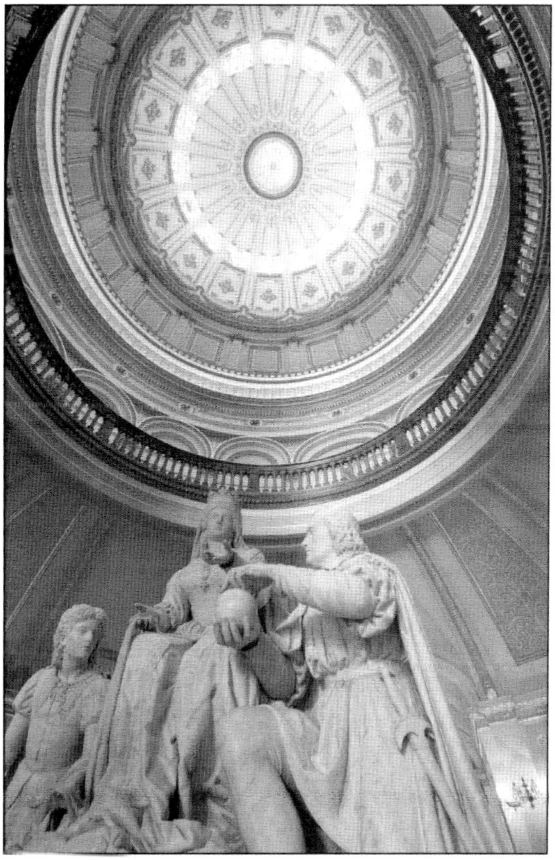

Here is a view looking into the rotunda from the west steps on the second floor. Some of the original surviving Maw & Co. tiles, manufactured in England, can be seen in the foreground. The remainder of the tile had to be replicated for the restoration. (SCM.)

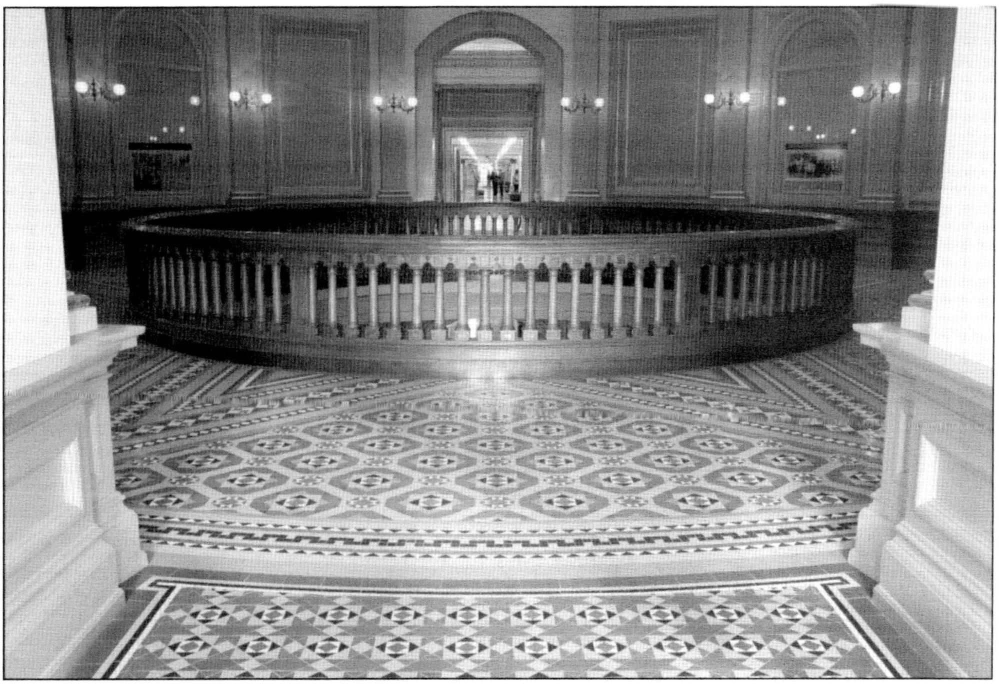

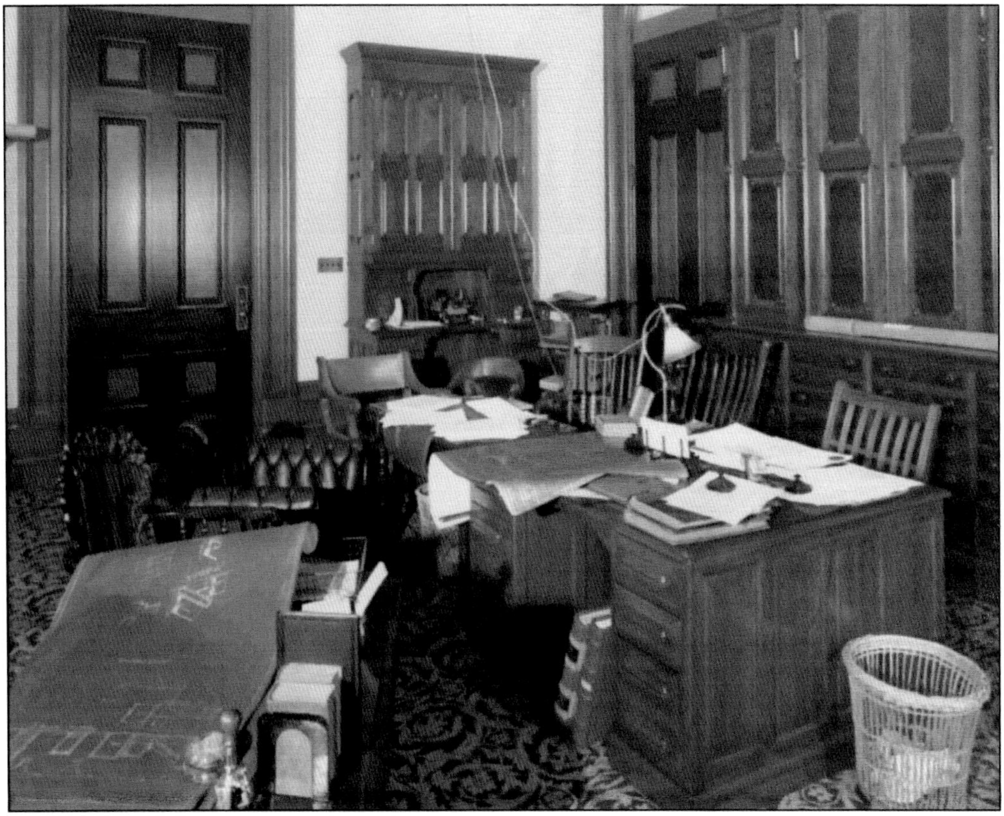

Here is the interior of one of the rooms in the Governor's Office, which had been restored to around 1906. It was at that time that modern conveniences, such as elevators, electricity, and telephones, were installed in the building. Note the wires hanging down from the ceiling for both the light and telephone on the desk. This anteroom is one of the five fully restored historic rooms in the capitol. (SCM.)

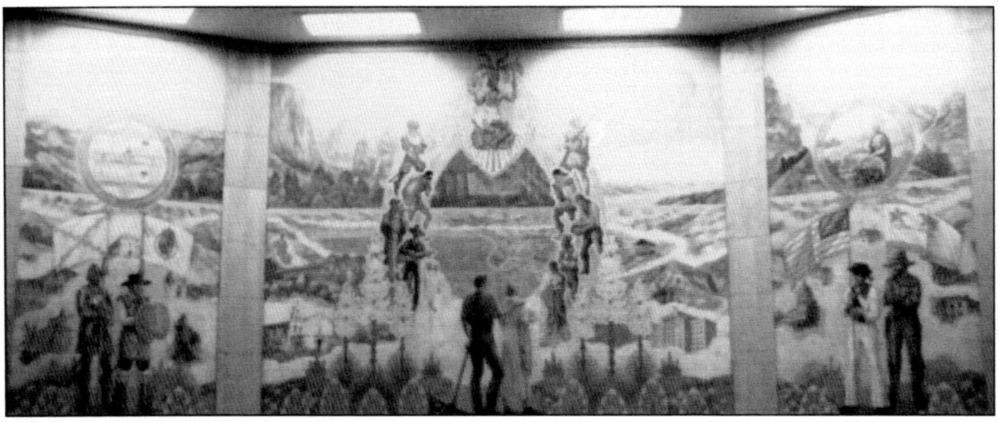

Following the restoration, a new addition was made to the artwork in the capitol. A magnificent mural that had originally been in the Los Angeles State Building was removed and placed in the legislative hearing room in 1991. Titled *The Origin and Development of the Name of the State of California*, this series of three murals was painted by WPA artist Lucile Lloyd in 1937. (SCM.)

Four

CALIFORNIA'S BACKYARD

This fine Capitol and its grounds should be kept up, not extravagantly, but economically, in a manner worthy of the state, they represent.

—Gov. George Waterman, Governor's First Biennial Message, 1885

A 40-acre park encompassing 10 city blocks surrounds the state capitol. Bounded by N and L Streets and Tenth and Twelfth Streets, the original park grew to include six more city blocks by the 1880s. For a time, the park would provide land for both the California State Fairgrounds as well as an unoccupied governor's mansion. The original four-block area immediately around the capitol was laid out in a "French system," a formal geometric pattern. Over time, as the park continued to expand to the east, the newer sections were laid out to have a more natural, parklike feel.

In an address to the California legislature, Waterman called Capitol Park "the greatest collection of diversified flora within any similar area of the globe." From its humble start, the first original plantings were made in 1870–1871. A Civil War Memorial Grove was added two decades later. Then, in 1914, schoolchildren throughout the state were asked to send plant specimens to be used in the California section of the park. Over more than a century, the park has also received the attentions of professional botanists, biologists, entomologists, arborists, and a staff of dedicated groundskeepers.

The park is also the home to numerous monuments and memorials. They range from war memorials and monuments dedicated to the memories of firefighters and peace officers lost in the line of duty and important individuals from California's past to a World Peace Rose Garden, to mention but a few.

Today, a rising wall of skyscrapers that now even dwarfs the capitol itself fences in this urban forest. Still, the magnificent Capitol Park, one of the largest in the nation, provides a wonderful natural setting in an otherwise major urban landscape. Each day, thousands visit the park.

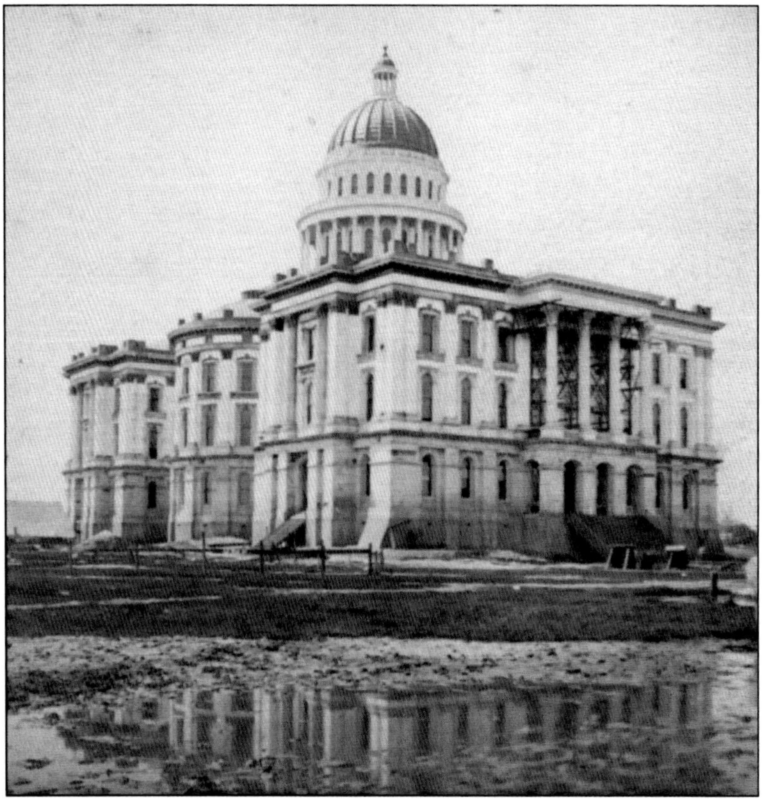

This early photograph of the northeast corner of the capitol shows the exposed basement and foundations before the earthen terraces were filled in at the base of the building. (SCM.)

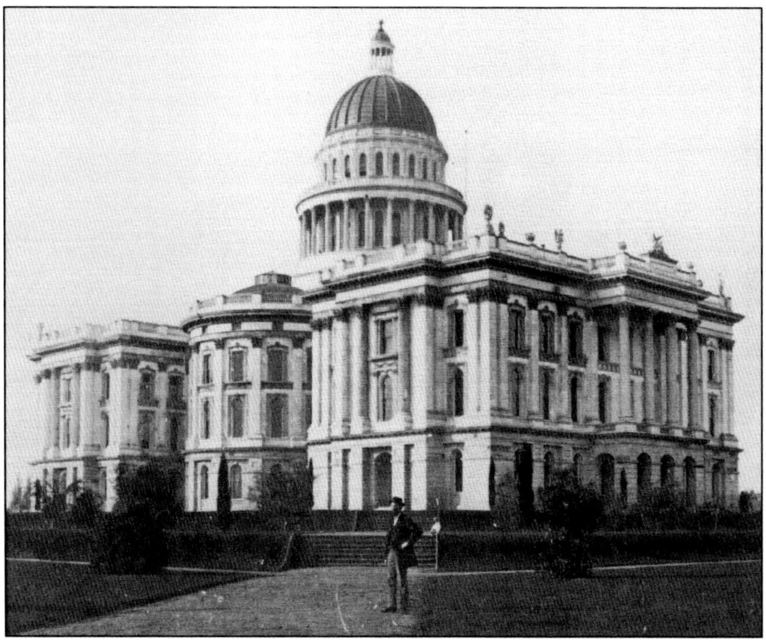

This image was taken from the same direction as the one above and shows the completed terracing and plantings around the capitol. (SCM.)

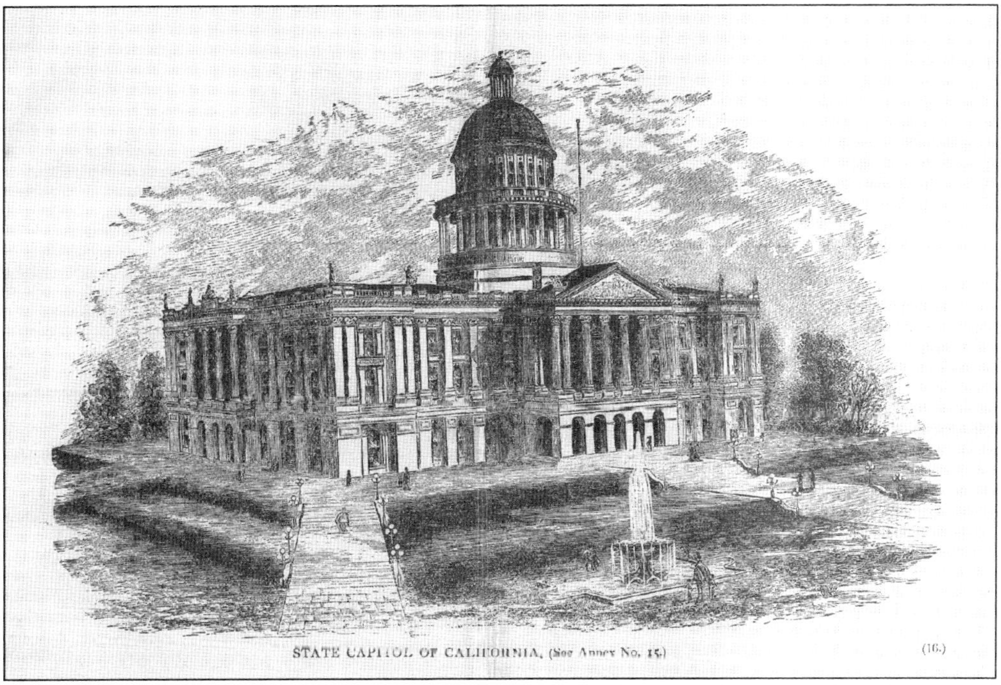

This wood engraving from the 1870s shows the plans for the grounds surrounding the capitol. The fountains pictured here were never in fact added to the park's grounds. (JA.)

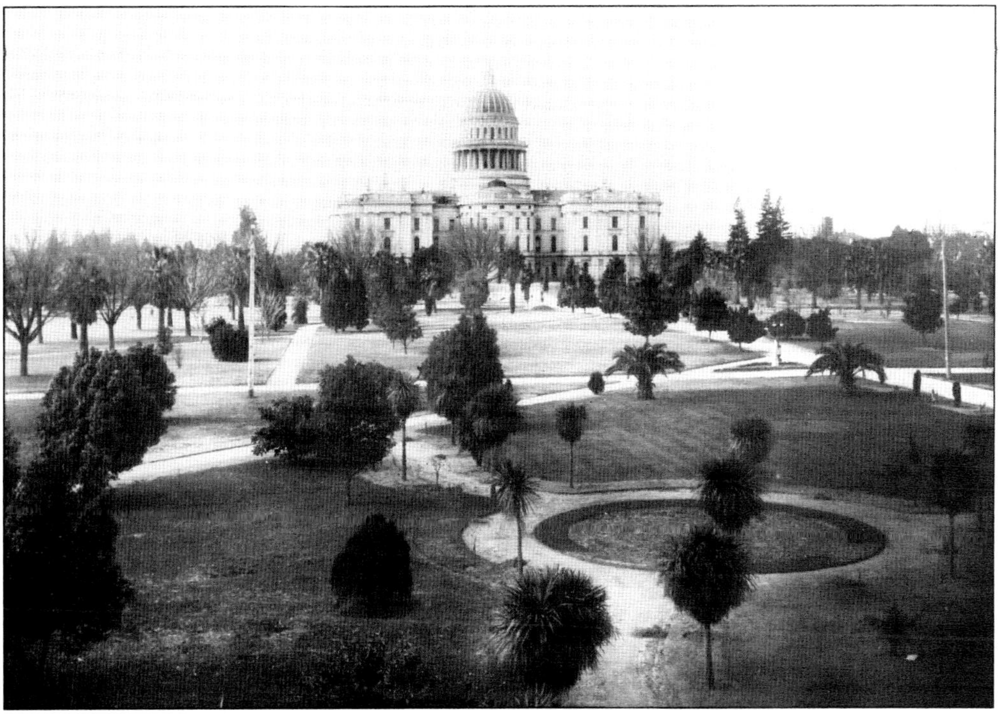

This view of park expansion is looking to the west. Gone now is the geometric design, as the park addition is opened up in a more parklike design. More flowing carriage lanes and walkways help to give newer sections of the park a less formal feel. (CSL.)

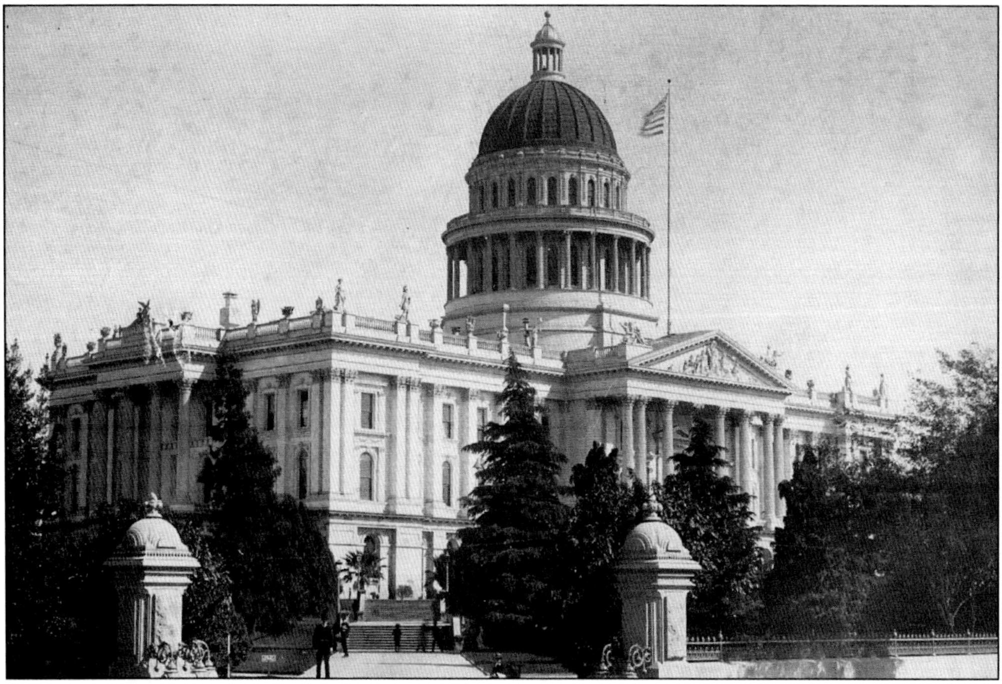

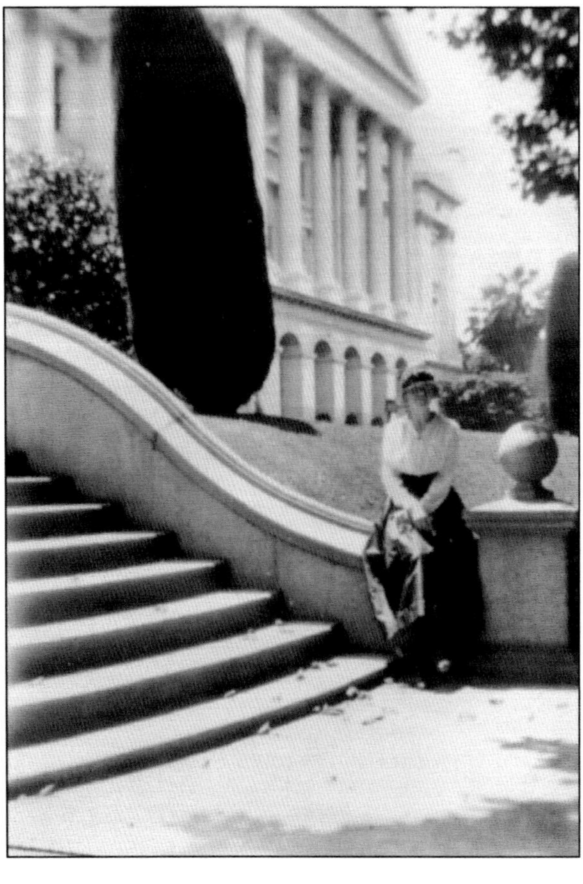

Monumental granite gateposts and a cast-iron fence replaced the earlier picket fence. They were all removed after World War II. Two of them went back to the place where they were originally quarried. Today, they can be found in the town of Folsom. This view is of the Tenth and L Streets entrance. (CSL.)

New granite staircases were added to each level of terracing. Here, a park visitor is seated on one of them in 1919. (JA.)

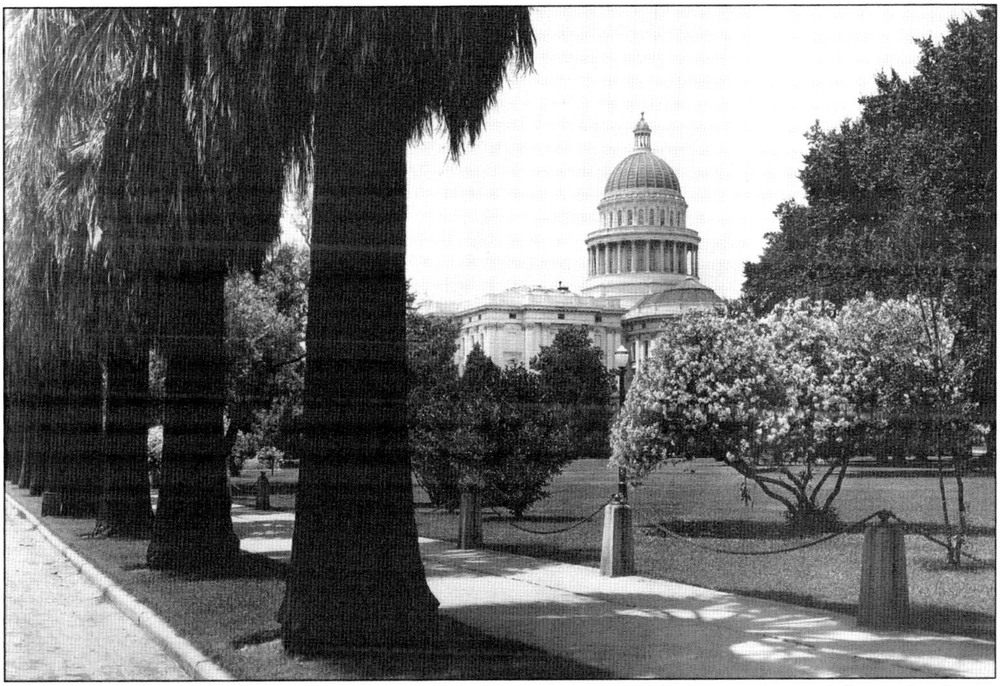

The park is home to hundreds of varieties of trees from all over the world, and flower beds are bursting with thousands of colorful blooms throughout the year. Since the beginning, the park has required constant maintenance and care. (JA.)

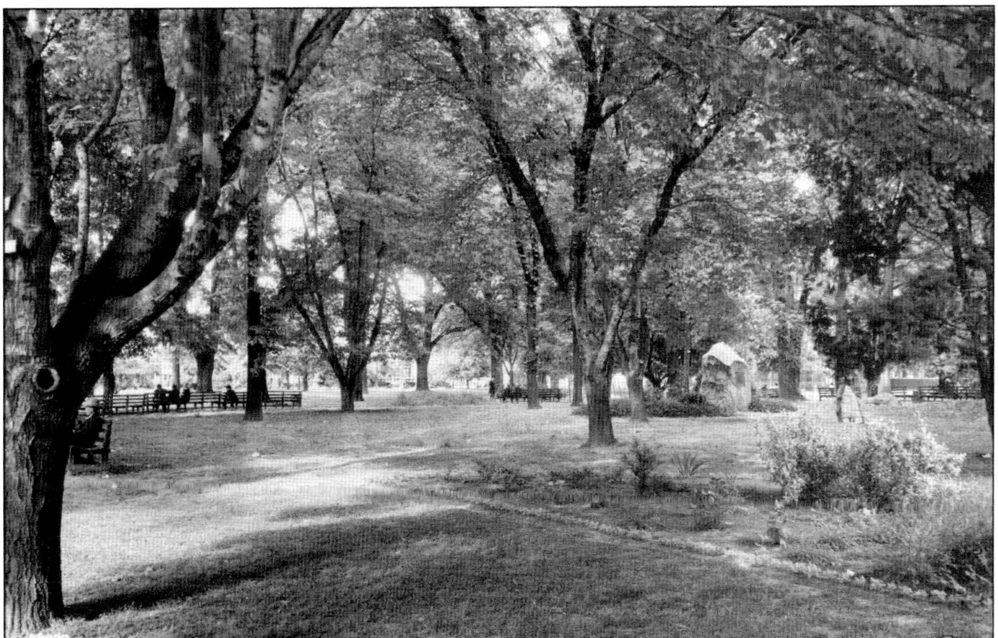

The Ladies of the Grand Army of the Republic dedicated Memorial Grove in 1897 in memory of California's Civil War veterans. It was the first memorial to be set up in the park. It was made up of plantings of trees from famous Civil War battlefields. Over the years, these trees have had to be replaced with new saplings. (CSL.)

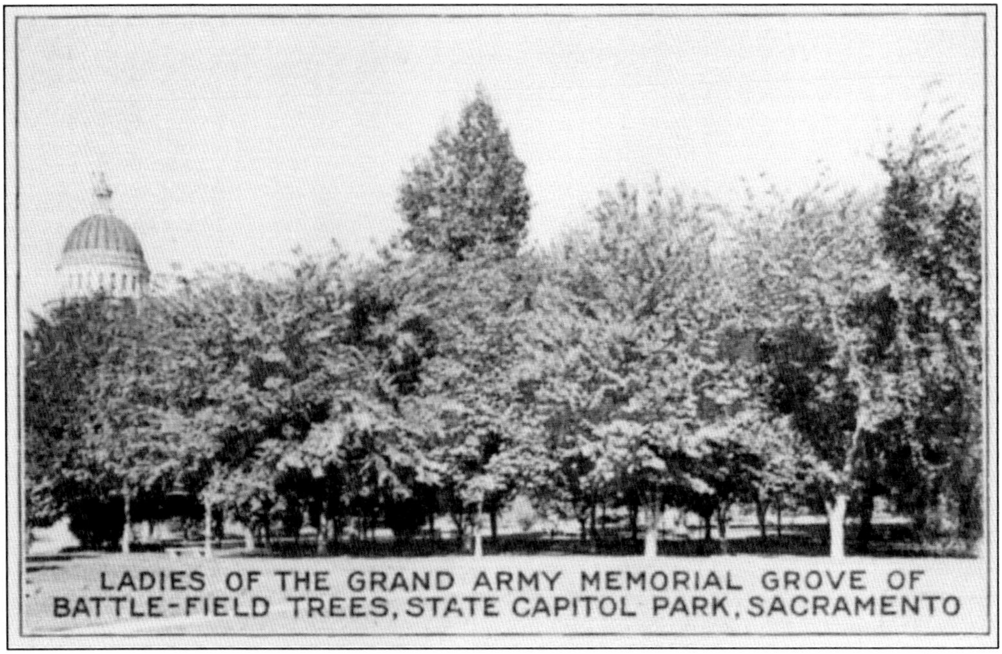

Here is an early-20th-century postcard view of the Memorial Grove, with the capitol dome in the distance. (JA.)

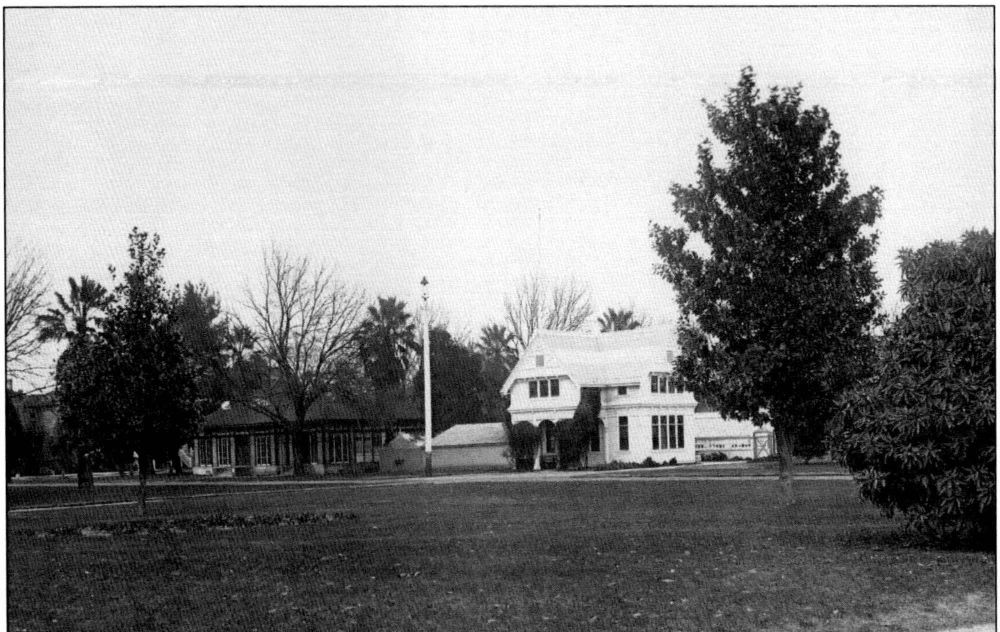

Early in the 20th century, the California Department of Agriculture became interested in finding alternatives to using pesticides. In order to better advance these studies, an insectary (to the left) was built in the park as a research station for developing better pest-control techniques. Experiments were carried out in the use of different types of insects to eradicate other harmful pests. The park was also home to a gardener's cottage (seen here on the right). (CSL.)

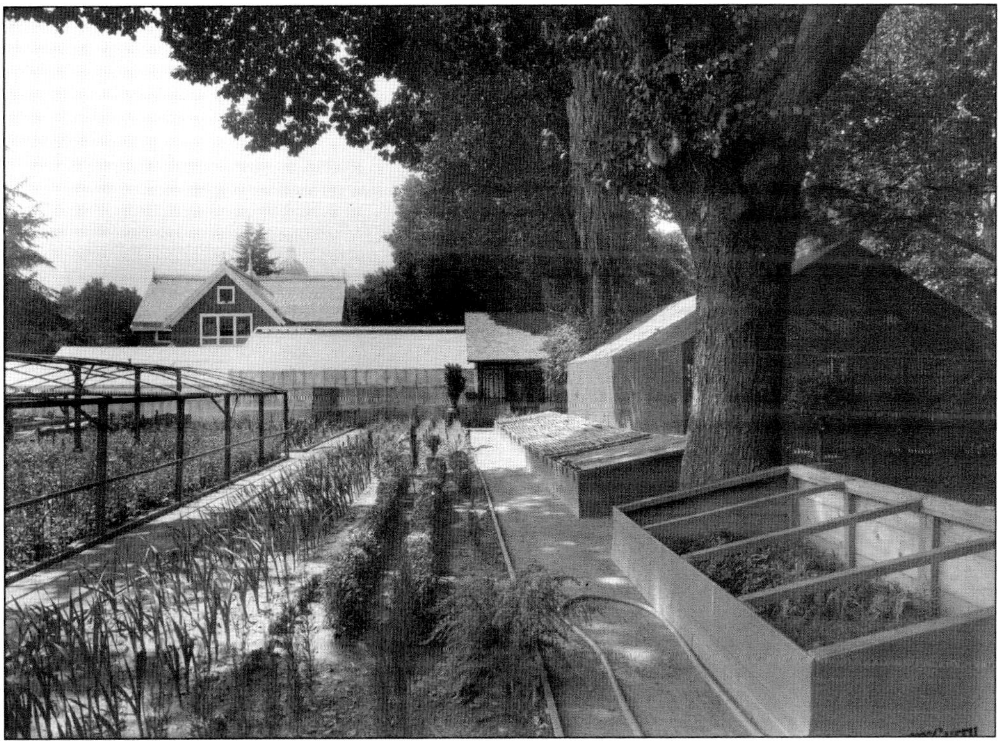

This shows some of the flower beds next to the gardener's cottage, which supplied many of the Capitol Park's flower beds. With 40 acres of park grounds, Capitol Park was in constant need of numerous new plantings throughout the year. The gardener was the only person to ever officially reside on the capitol grounds. (CSL.)

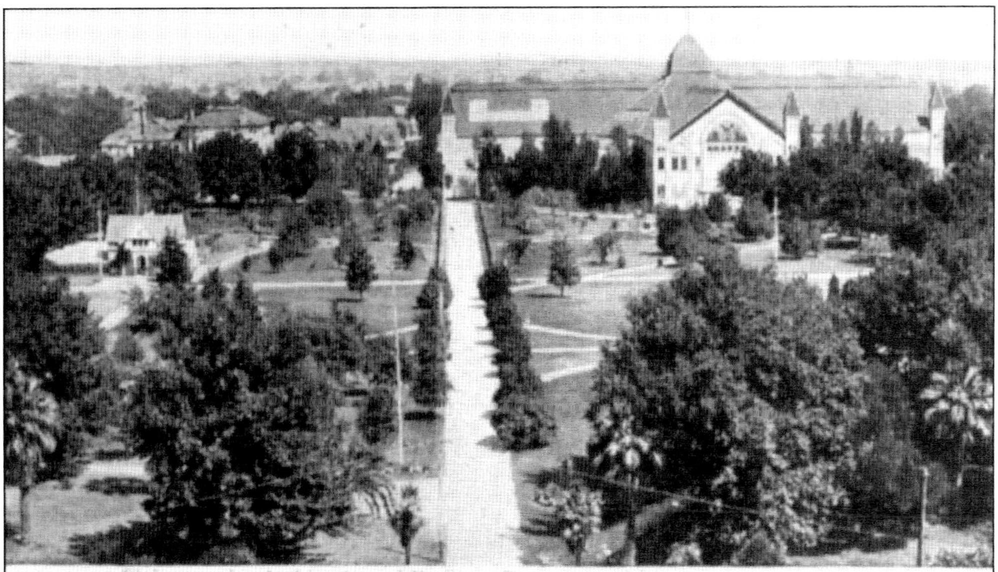

The first official California State Fair was held in 1854. Until 1861, when the state fair was permanently located in Sacramento, it called many places home. Pictured here is part of the fairgrounds at the southeastern end of the park. (JA.)

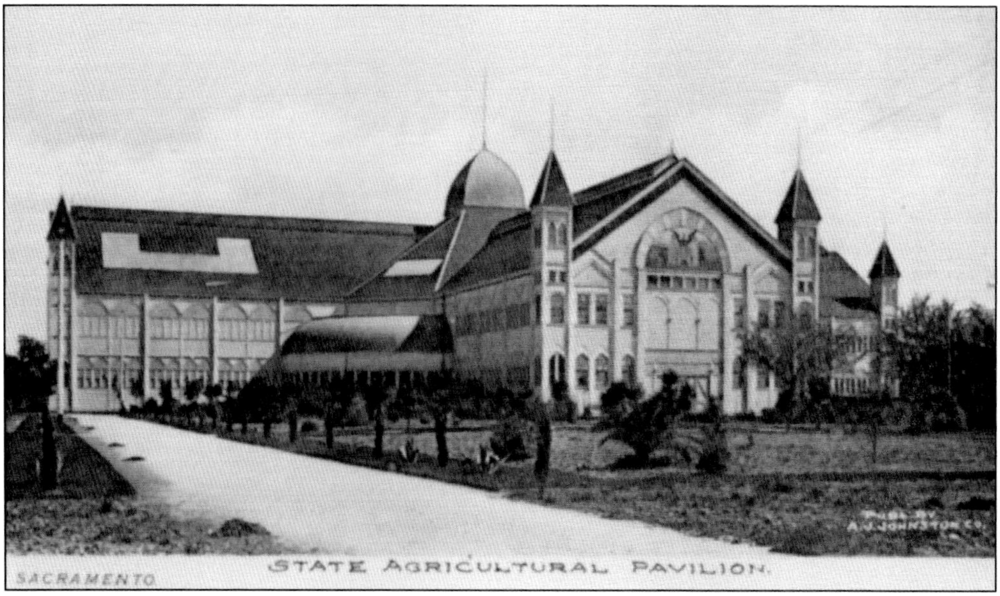

Completed in 1884, the Agricultural Hall, or State Fair Pavilion, served as the centerpiece of the California State Fair. Constructed of wood and glass, it was the largest structure of its type in America at the time. It remained in use until the fairgrounds was moved in 1909. At one point after the 1906 San Francisco earthquake, many refugees from that city found shelter in the pavilion. (CSL.)

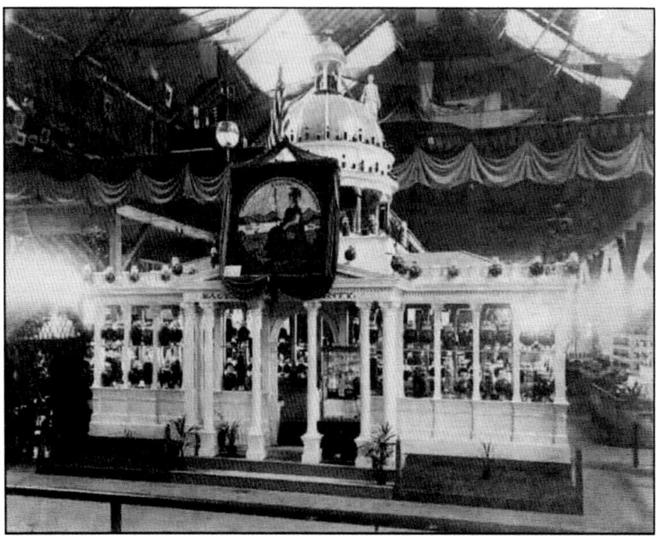

And what would a fair be without exhibits? Here is a display at the California State Fair made to resemble the capitol. (CSL.)

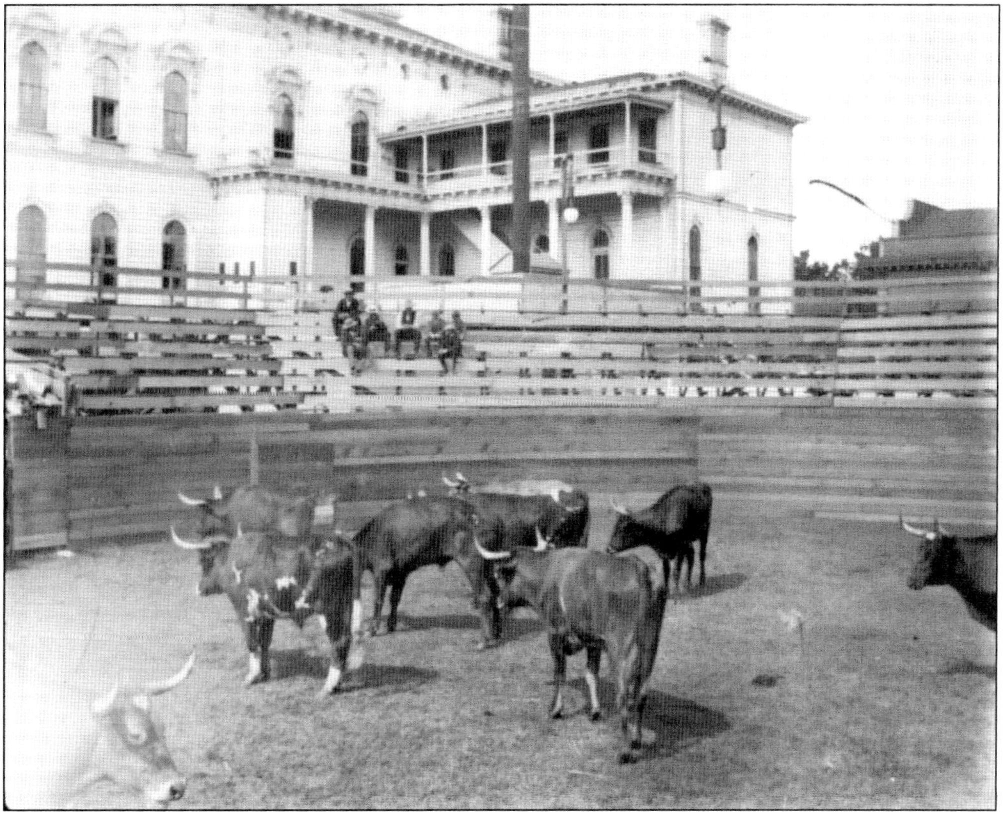

Here is a livestock arena on the park fairgrounds. The State Printing Office is in the background. A separate racetrack was located a few blocks to the north. (JA.)

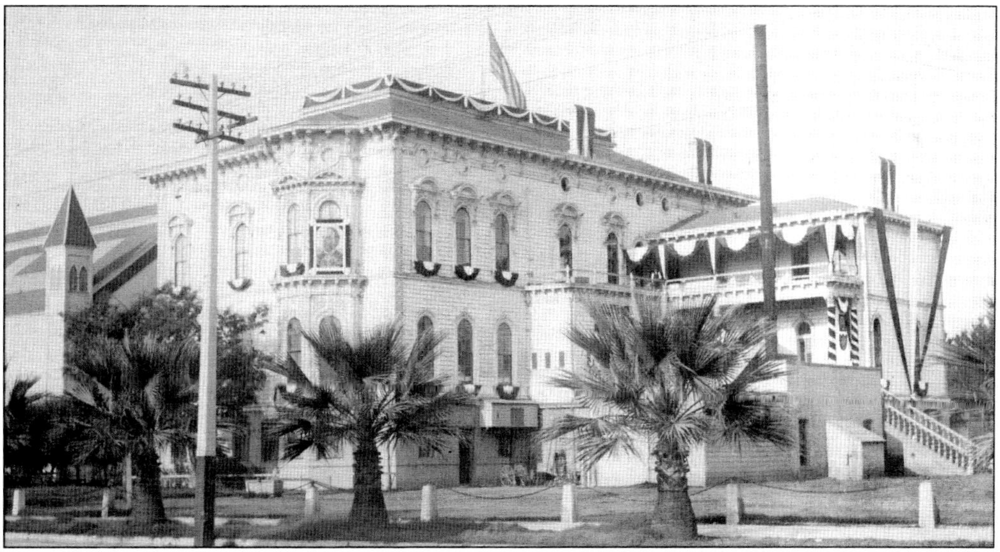

Shown in this 1901 photograph, the State Printing Office occupied the Capitol Park grounds at the corner of Fifteenth and L Streets. After failing to become the official governor's residence, the building was made into the State Printing Office. Here, it is draped with black bunting as a sign of mourning for Pres. William McKinley. (CSL.)

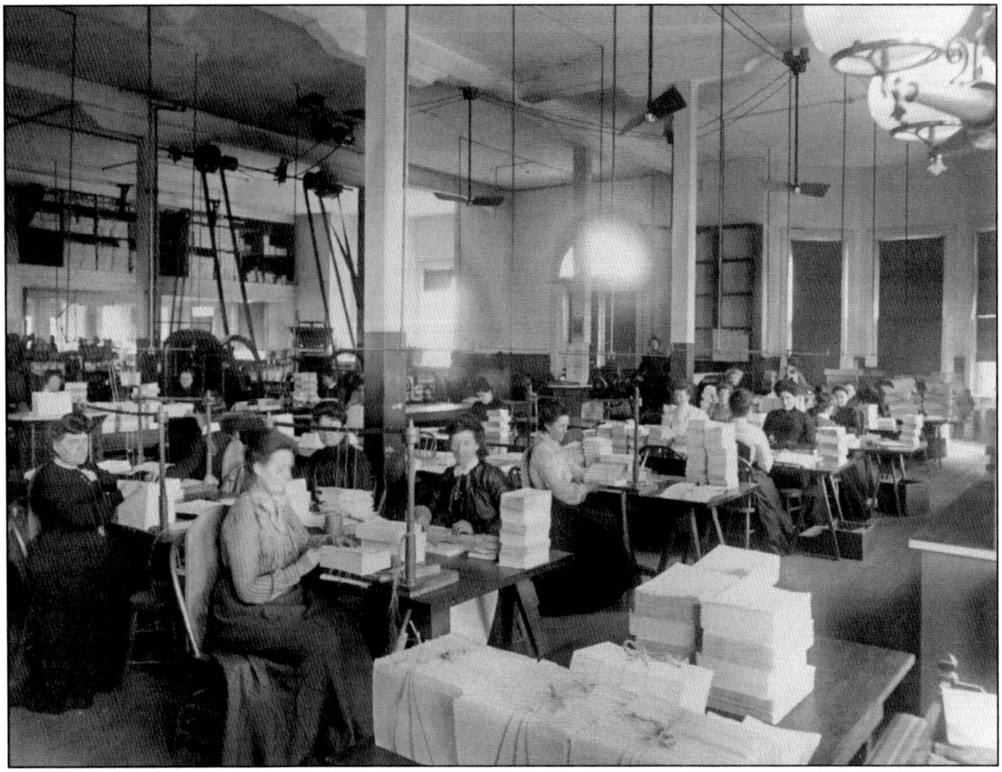

This interior view of the State Printing Office shows women binders at work. As the largest publisher west of the Mississippi River, the State Printing Office was responsible for producing bills, legislative statutes and journals, government reports, and the state's textbooks. (CSL.)

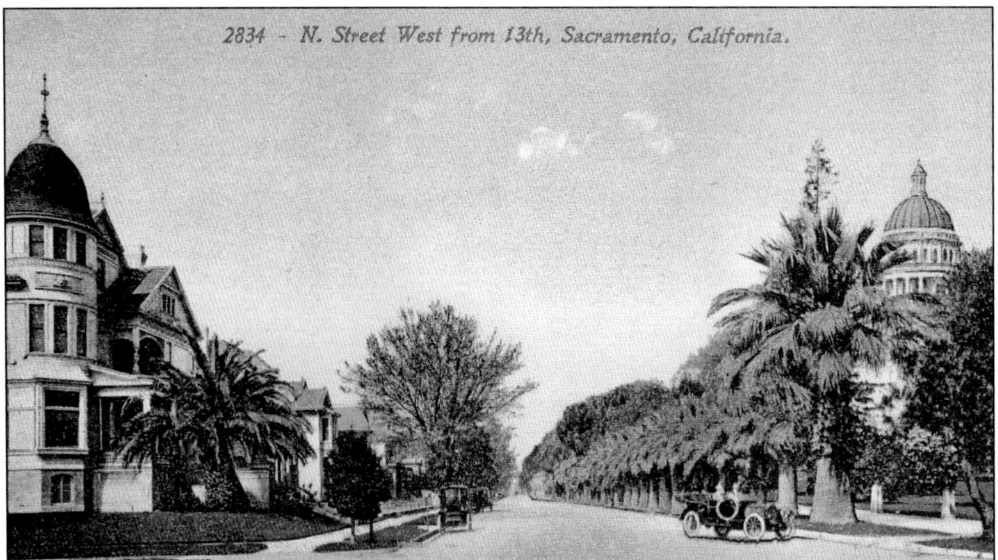

Capitol Park was flanked all along its outer perimeter by long rows of stately palm trees. Many elegant homes could be found along the adjacent streets, as seen in this early-20th-century postcard. (JA.)

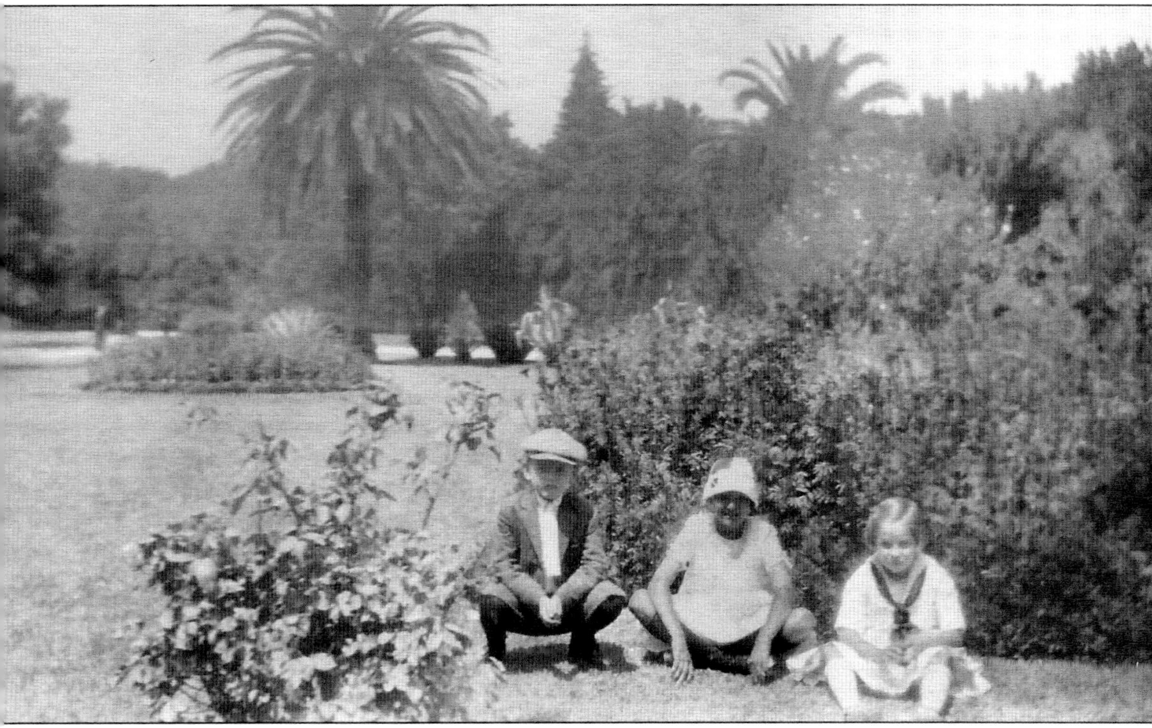

Visitors have always been attracted to the beauty of Capitol Park. Its varied flora has served as a perfect backdrop for countless snapshots, as seen here in this photograph from a family outing during the 1920s. (JA.)

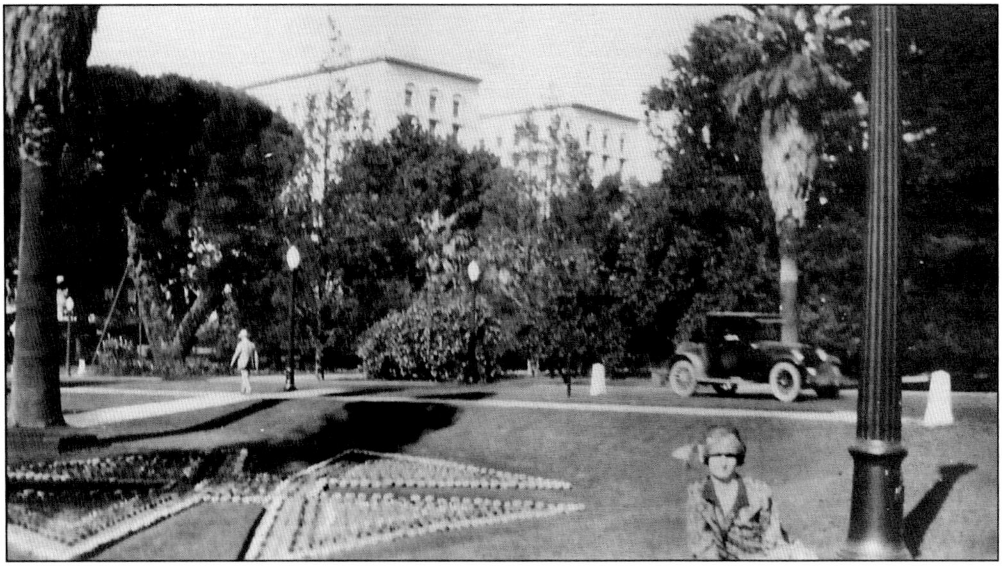

In this snapshot from the same visit, the Senator Hotel is visible in the background. At the time, people were permitted to drive automobiles through the park. (JA.)

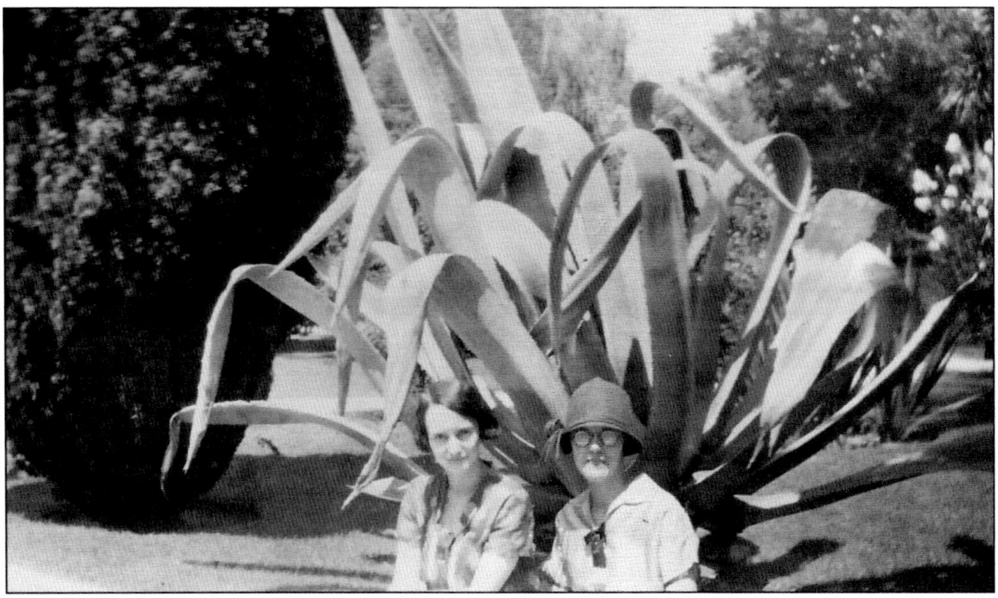

Here, two unidentified women are seated in front of a century plant. (JA.)

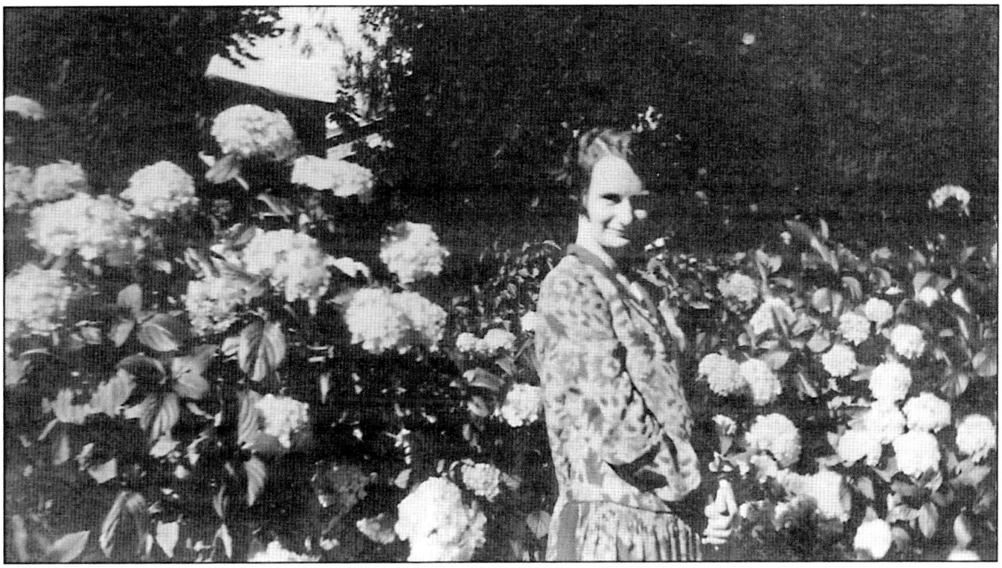

The park's numerous rose gardens have always proved to be popular attractions for visitors. (JA.)

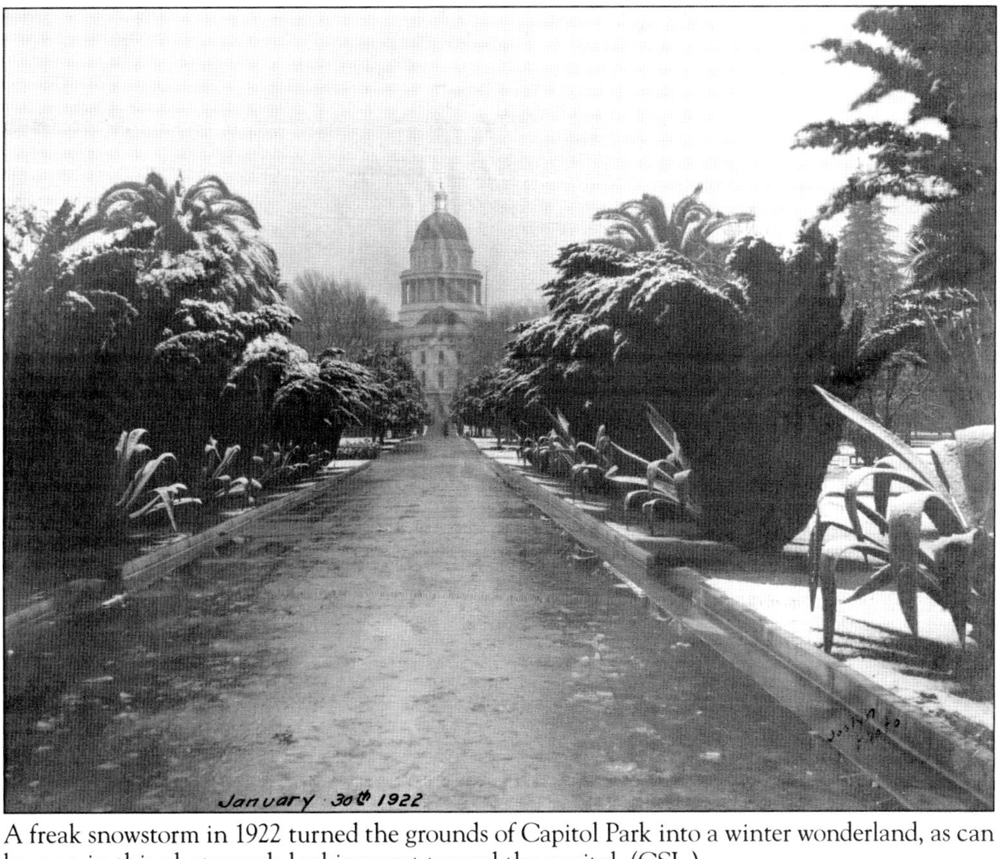

A freak snowstorm in 1922 turned the grounds of Capitol Park into a winter wonderland, as can be seen in this photograph looking west toward the capitol. (CSL.)

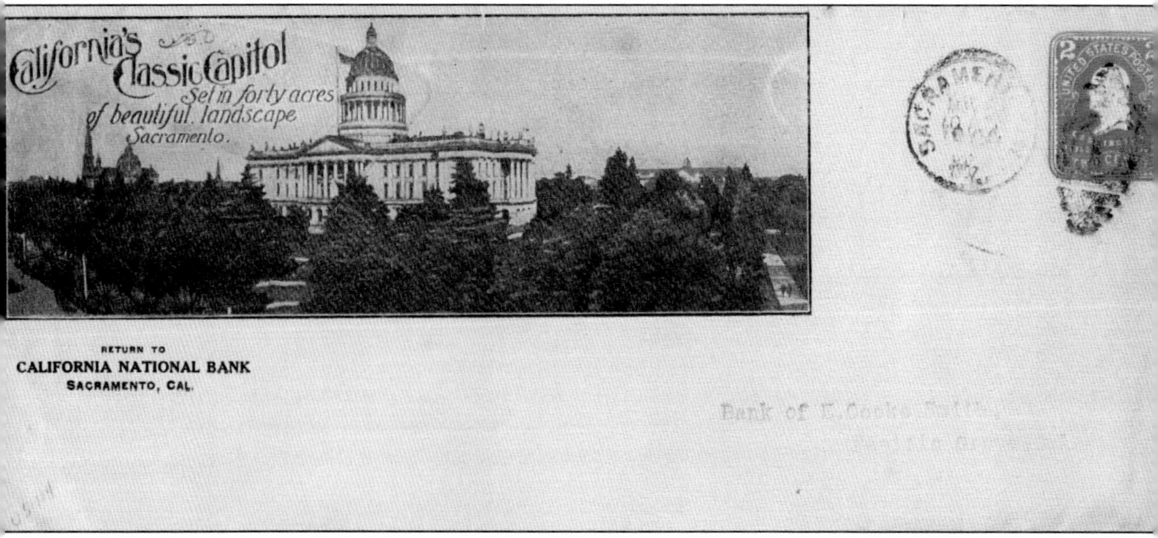

This 1907 business envelope has a bank corner card (advertisement) proudly heralding "California's Classic Park, Set in forty acres of beautiful landscape." (JA.)

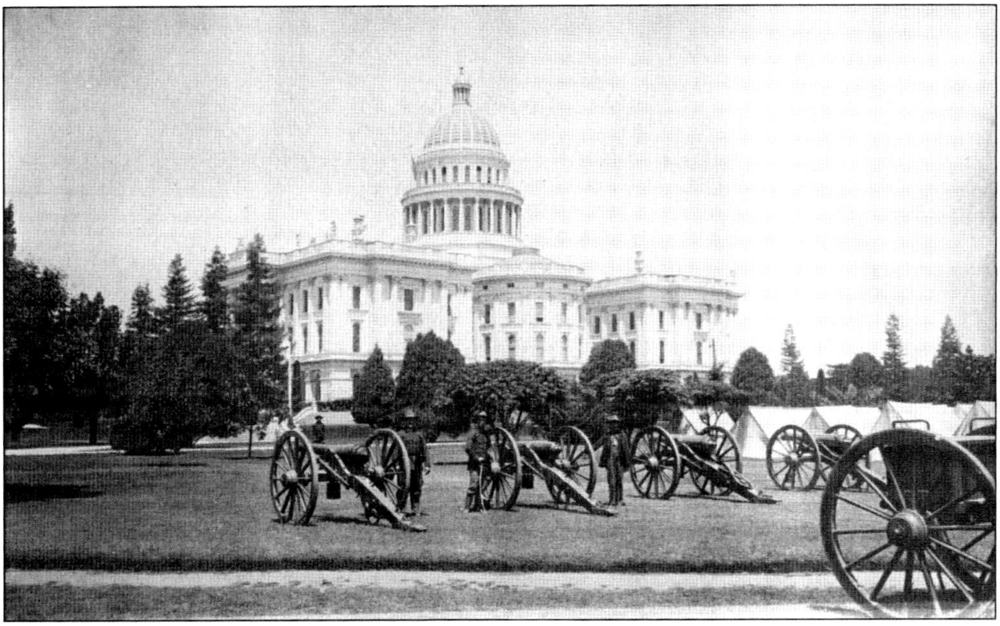

A rare cyanotype from 1900 shows an artillery battery in the park. The state militia often set up bivouac in the park grounds when conducting military exercises. (CSH.)

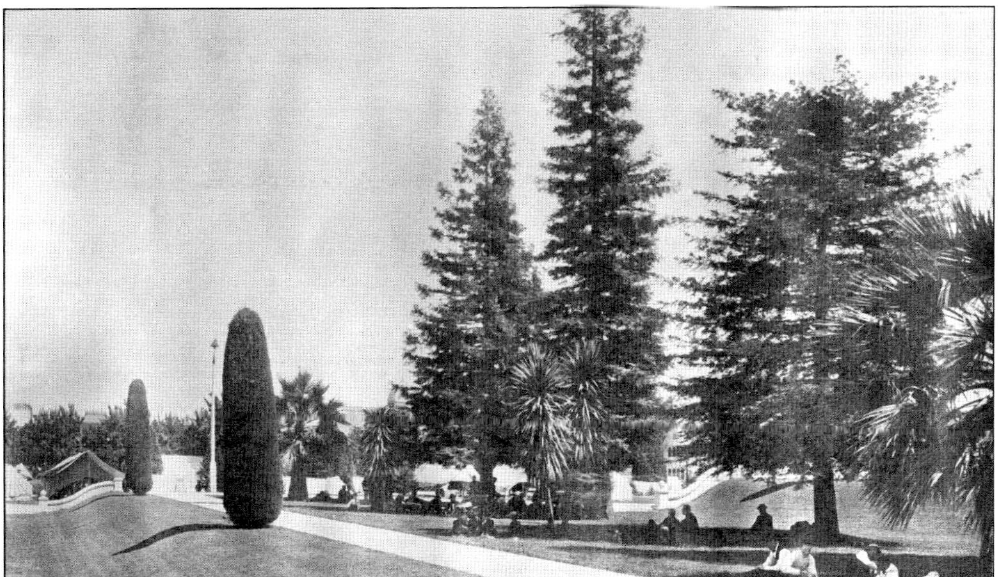

Another rare cyanotype shows visitors seeking out shade on the northeast side of the capitol on a hot summer day. More tents from the state militia encampment can be seen in the background. (CSH.)

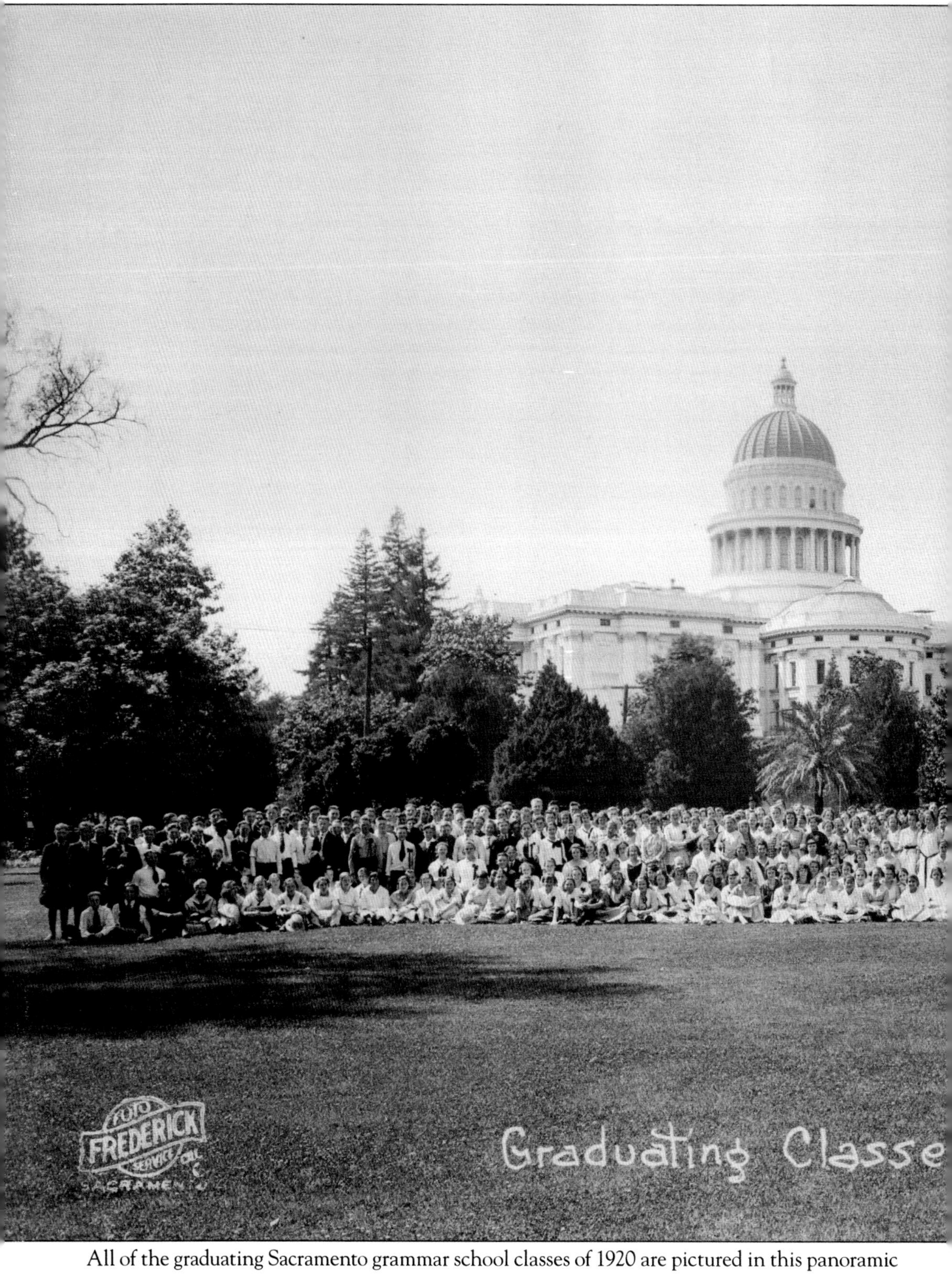

All of the graduating Sacramento grammar school classes of 1920 are pictured in this panoramic

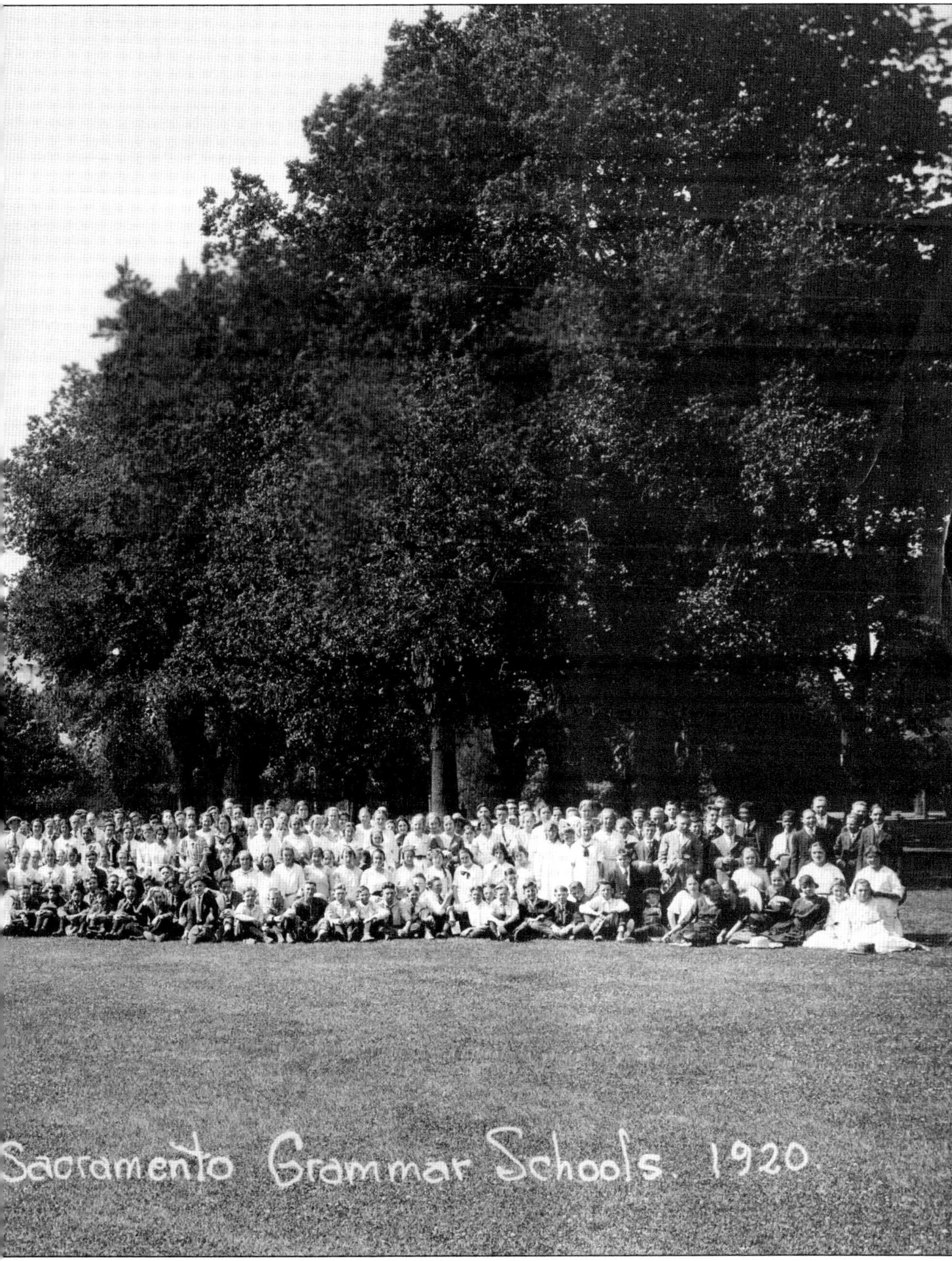

image made at Capitol Park. (CSH.)

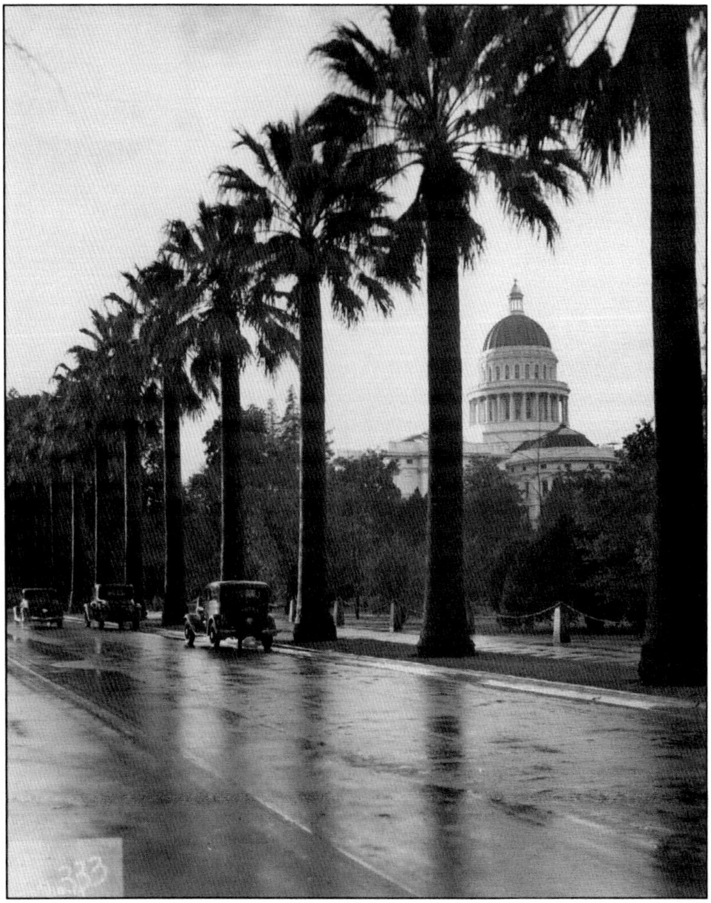

The advent of the automobile ushered in the need to provide for convenient parking for legislators, staff members, and visitors. (CSL.)

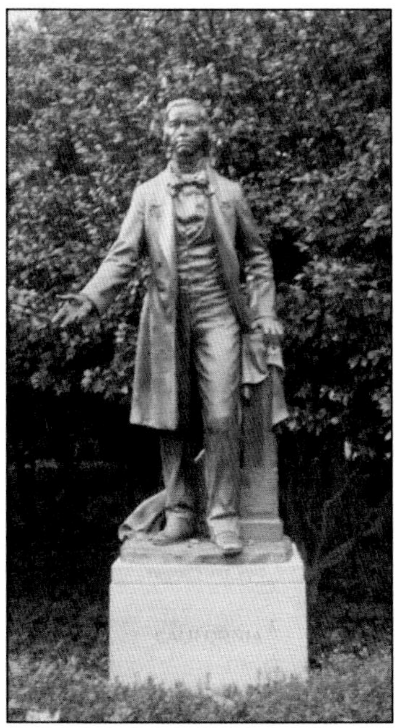

Capitol Park is home to many monuments. One of them is the bronze statue of Thomas Starr King, the famed Civil War minister who helped to rally California support for the Union. The sculpture by Haig Patigan was originally dedicated in 1931 to stand in National Statuary Hall in the Capitol in Washington, DC. It was later removed to make way for another statue and was rededicated in 2011 and now stands proudly near the Civil War Memorial Grove. (SCM.)

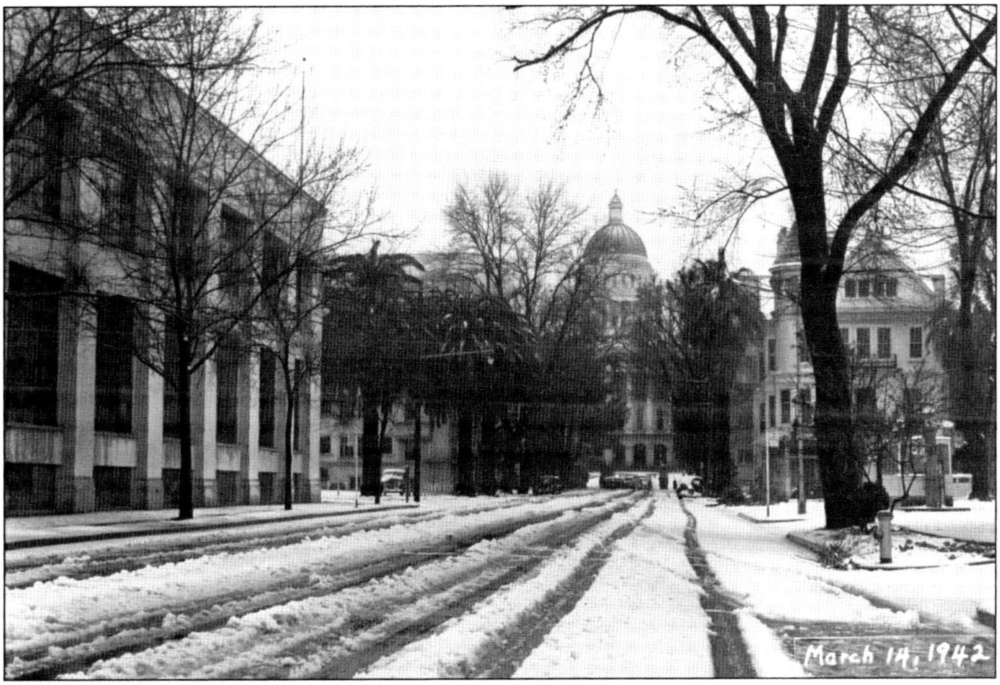

Here is a view from Eleventh and N Streets looking toward the south entrance to the capitol after another snowstorm, in 1942. The second State Printing Office is to the left. (CSL.)

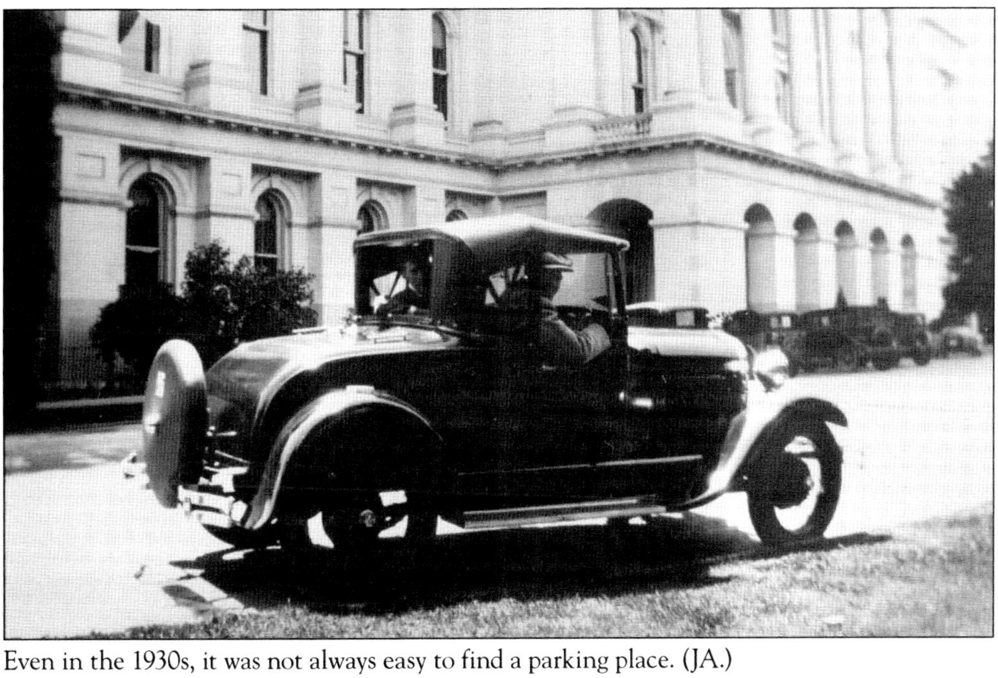

Even in the 1930s, it was not always easy to find a parking place. (JA.)

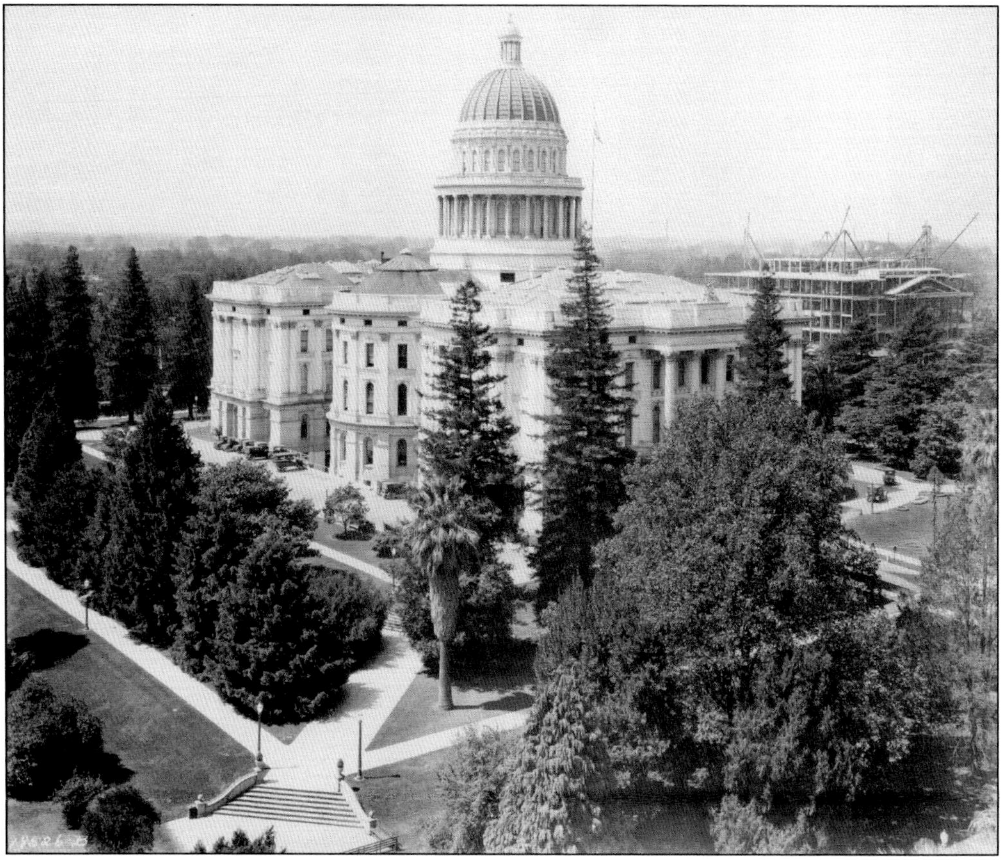

As seen in this aerial view, the area immediately next to the building became a parking lot up until the 1950s. (CSL.)

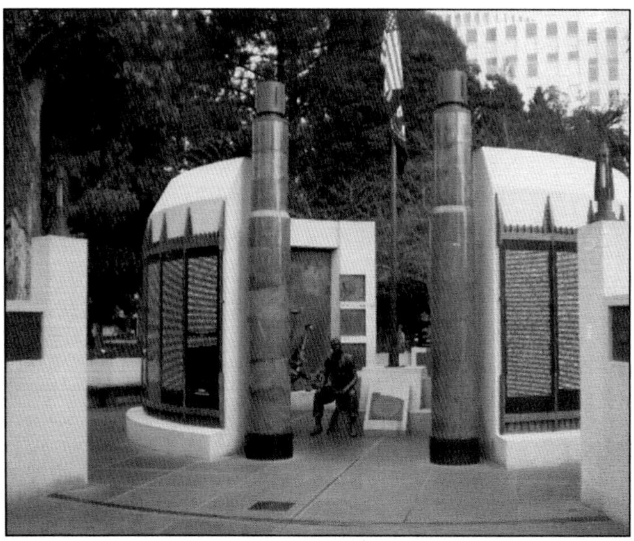

The Vietnam War Memorial was constructed after $2.2 million in private donations was raised for its construction. Completed in 1988, the 3,750-square-foot memorial honors the 350,000 Californians who served during the war and lists the 5,822 names of those killed or still listed as missing in action. Thousands visit this circular structure each year to find comfort, remember a lost family member or fallen comrade, or take part in one of the numerous ceremonies held in their honor. (SCM.)

Five

People and Events

The California State Capitol has provided space—though often under cramped conditions—for numerous government officials and employees. As the structure grew, so too did the building's staff. While employees may have only numbered in the dozens during the 19th century, thousands call the capitol their workplace today. Many prominent individuals, ranging from politicians to visiting dignitaries and film stars, have come and gone over the years, as well.

The state capitol has also been witness to many events over the last 150 years—some tragic and others joyful. The California State Capitol continues to serve as the backdrop and stage for major political dramas, protests, rallies, national and international media events, concerts, jog-a-thons, religious services, advertising campaigns, weddings, and so on. A million visitors enter the building every year.

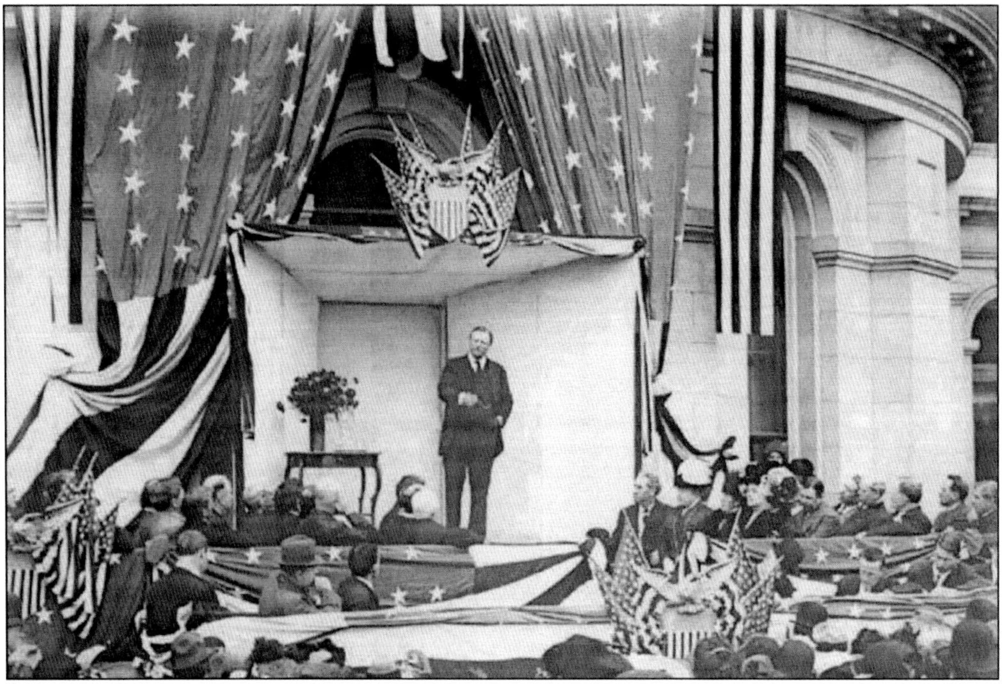

Pres. Theodore Roosevelt visited California in 1903. Shown during his stop in Sacramento, he gives a speech outside the capitol next to the rotunda. (CSL.)

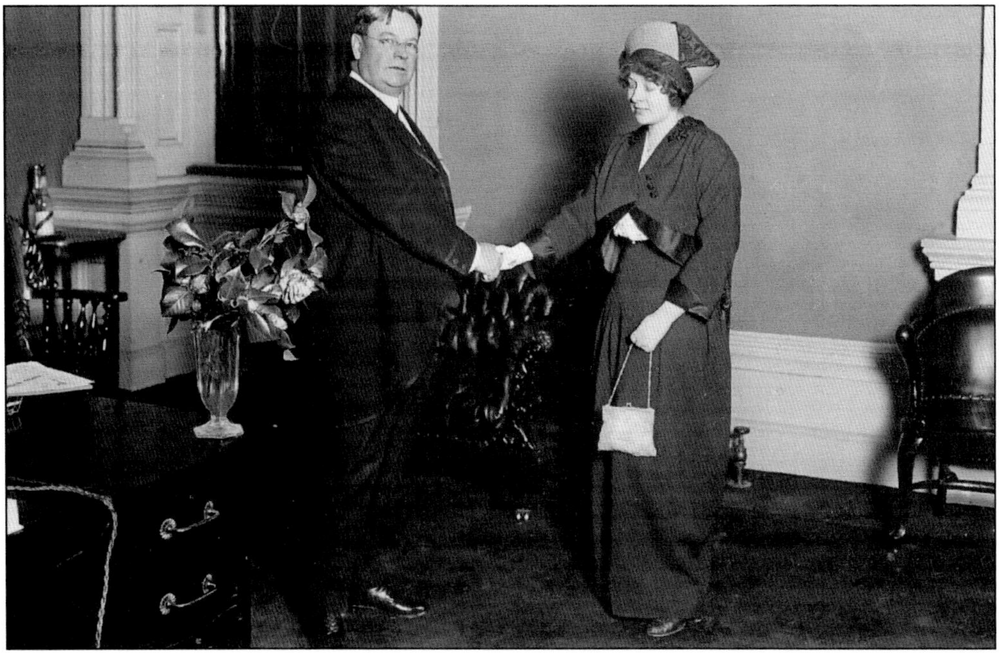

Hiram Johnson was the great Progressive reformer who was elected Republican governor (1911–1917). His election ushered in major political changes for the state of California. The former attorney was the only Sacramentan to become governor. He later ran unsuccessfully as vice president with Theodore Roosevelt in 1914. This is an undated real-photo postcard of Johnson greeting an unidentified visitor in his office. (JA.)

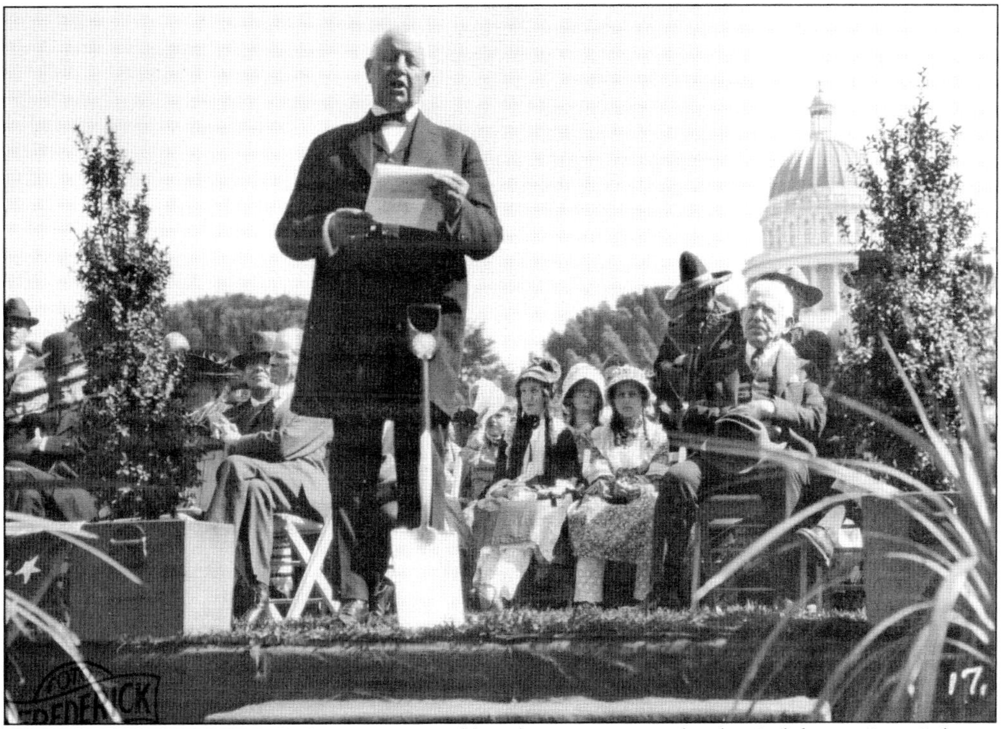

Gov. William Stephens is at the 1922 ground-breaking ceremony for the California State Library and Courts Building. The former lieutenant governor became governor when Governor Johnson assumed the US Senate seat for California in 1923. (CSL.)

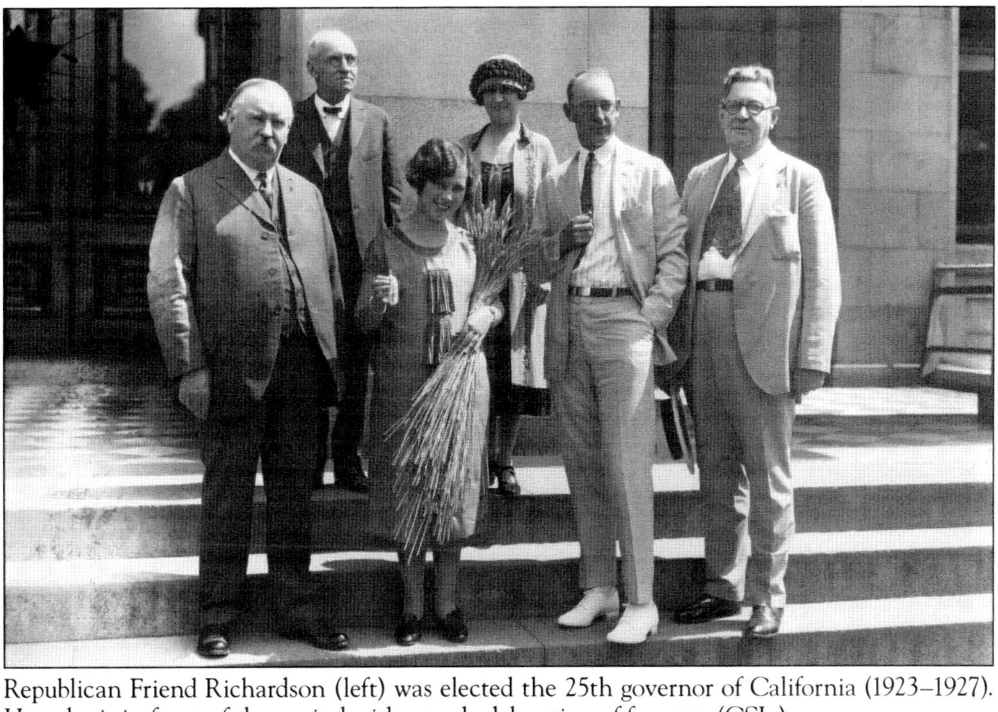

Republican Friend Richardson (left) was elected the 25th governor of California (1923–1927). Here, he is in front of the capitol with a trade delegation of farmers. (CSL.)

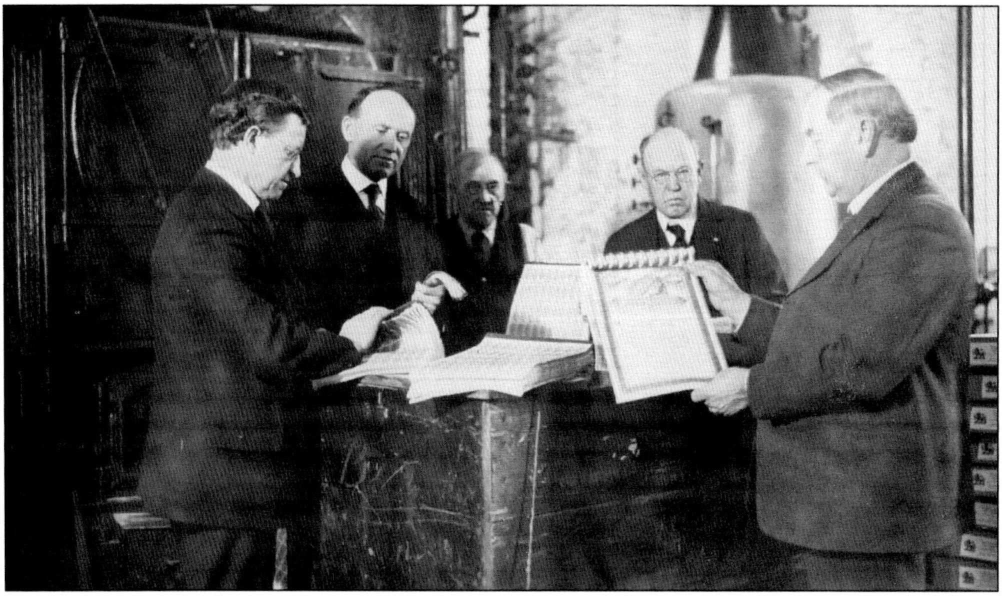

Governor Richardson and state treasury officials are shown burning cancelled state bonds in the basement furnace of the capitol. The state treasurer had a separate vault below the first-floor office. (CSL.)

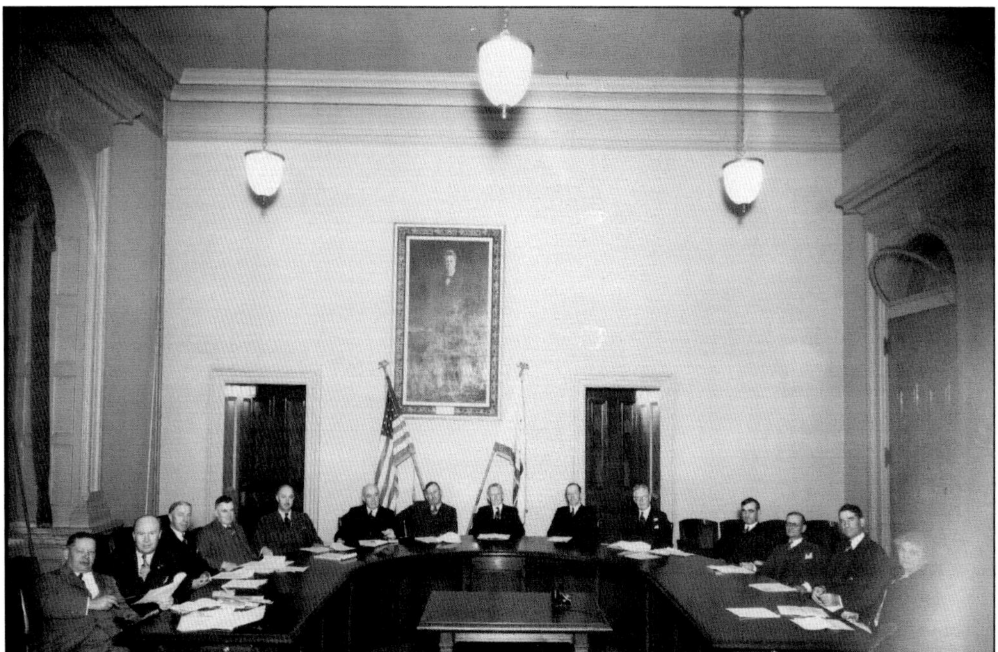

Gov. Clement Young (1927–1931), a former high school teacher and legislator, is shown seated in the center in one of the legislative committee rooms. (CSL.)

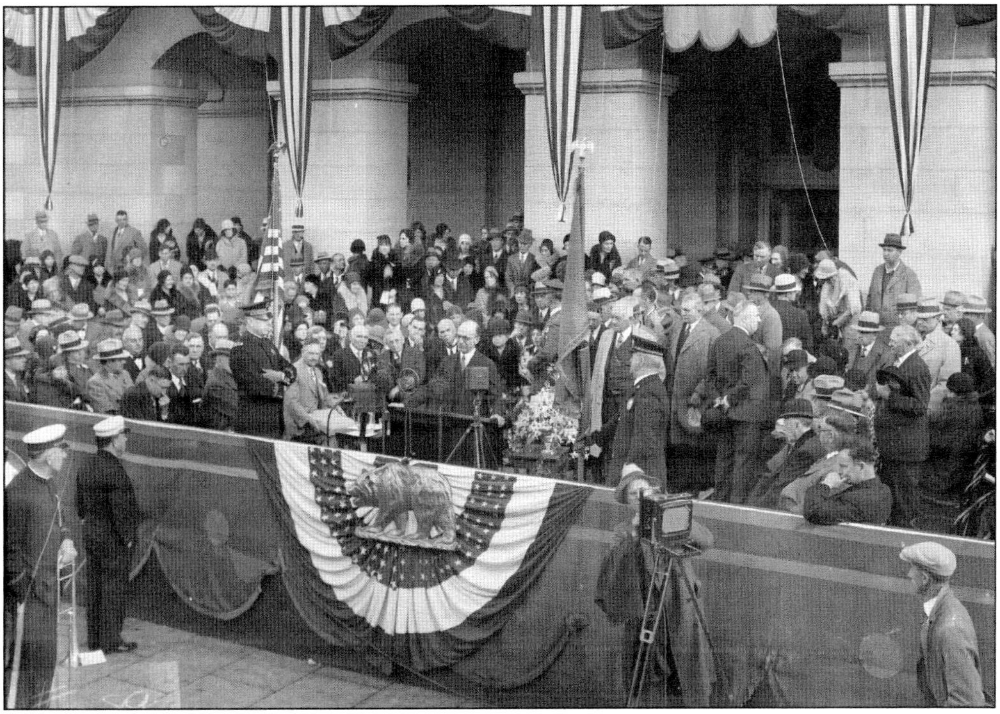

Gov. James "Sunny Jim" Rolph (1931–1935) is being sworn in at his inauguration ceremony in front of the capitol. The former San Francisco mayor was elected Republican governor in 1930. (CSL.)

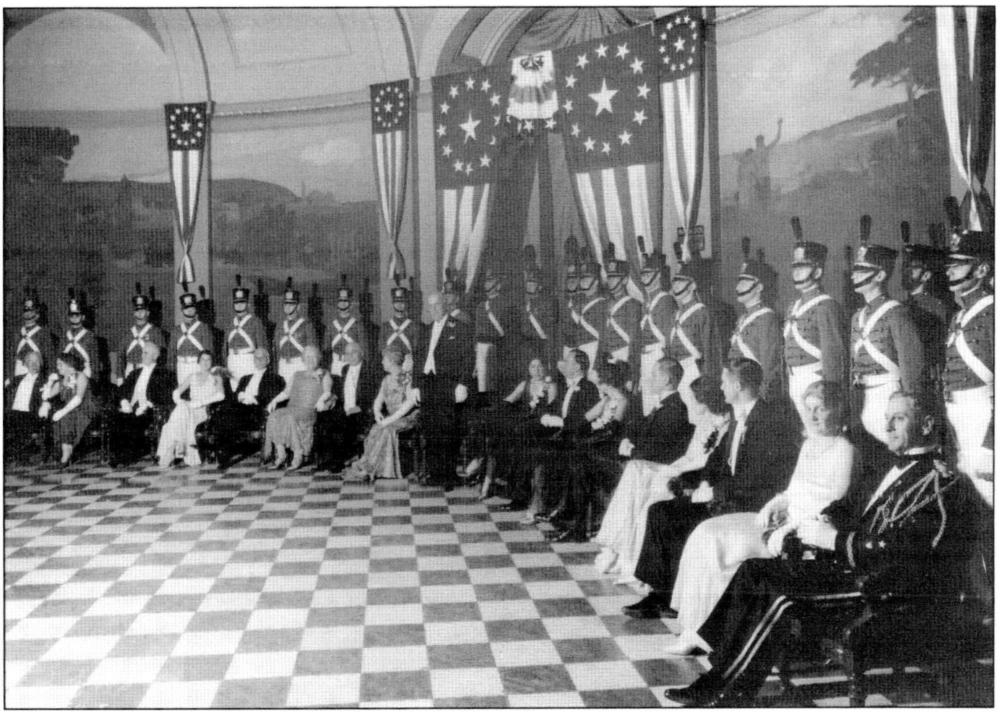

Pictured are the governor and First Lady Annie Rolph at the official inaugural ball held in the capitol rotunda. (CSL.)

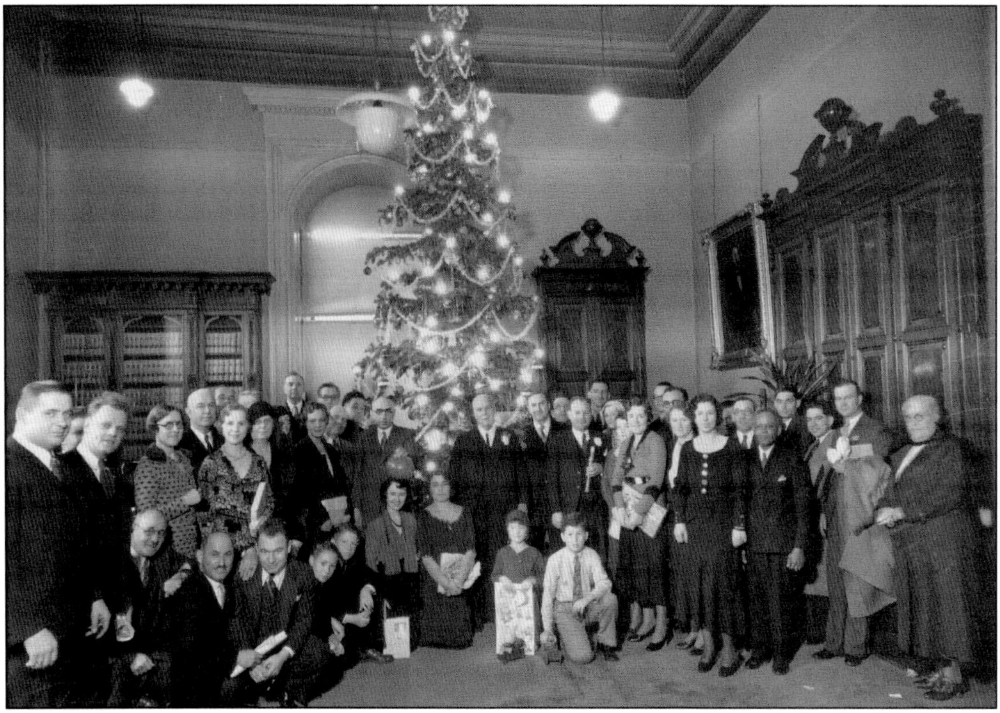

This 1931 interior scene in the Governor's Office shows Rolph (center), staff, and family members in front of the capitol Christmas tree. (CSL.)

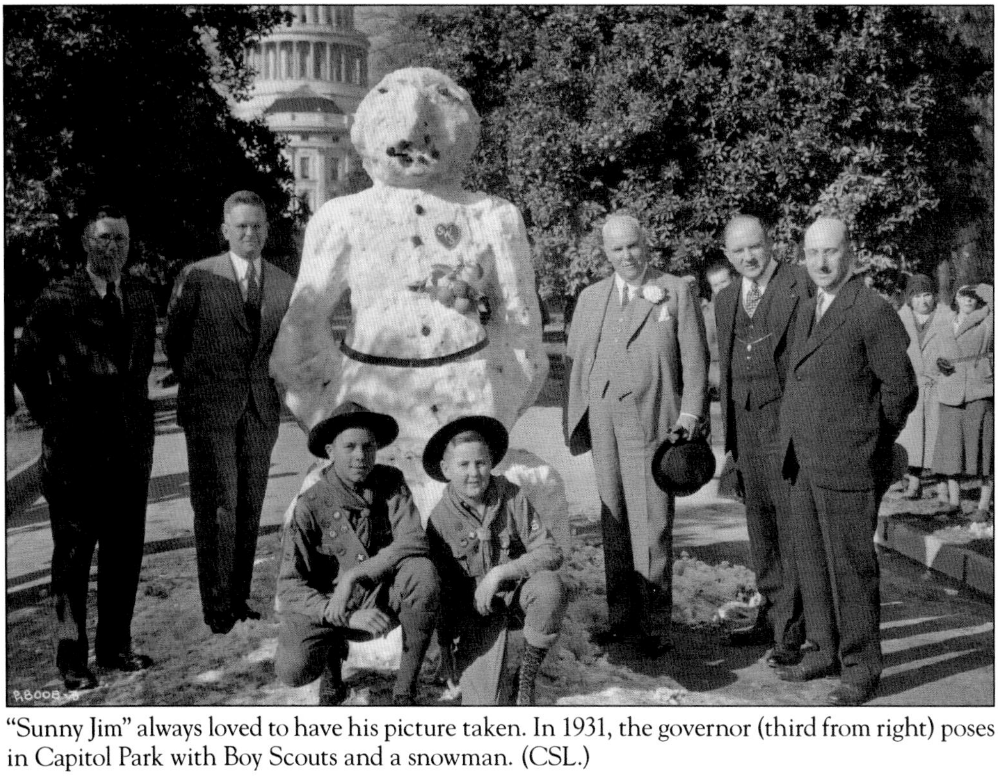

"Sunny Jim" always loved to have his picture taken. In 1931, the governor (third from right) poses in Capitol Park with Boy Scouts and a snowman. (CSL.)

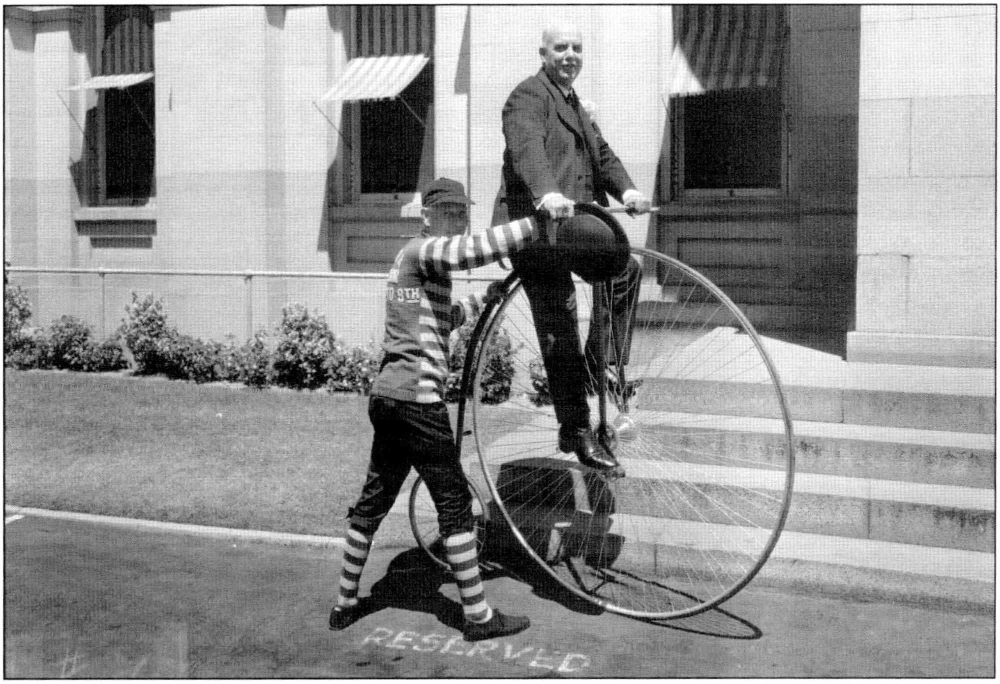

Here is an undated photograph of Governor Rolph on a "penny dollar" bicycle in front of the capitol. He was famous for wearing cowboy boots while on the job. He was perhaps one of the most colorful figures to occupy the governor's office. (CSL.)

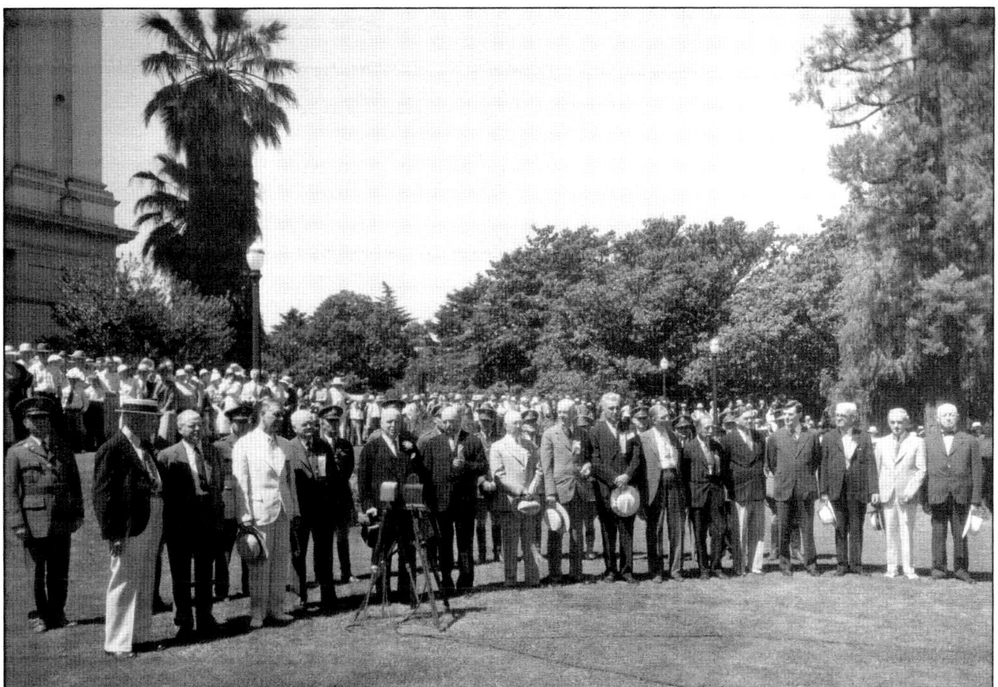

Governor Rolph in the center of a gathering before the southwest side of the state capitol for a 1933 governor's conference held by Rolph. (CSL.)

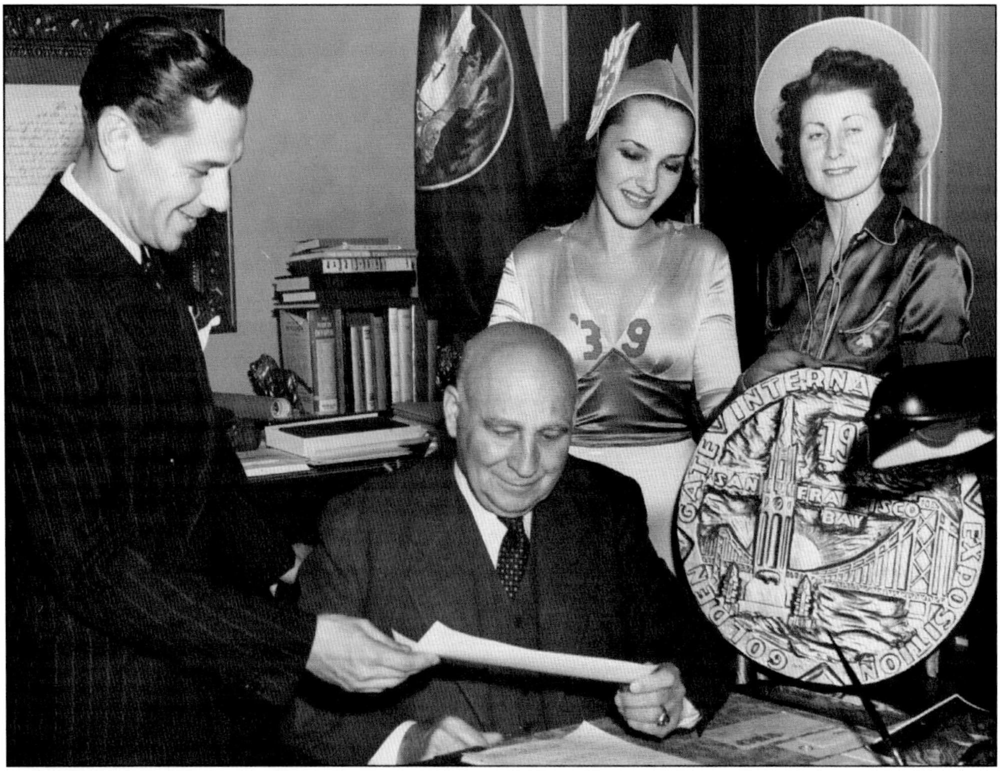

At his office, Gov. Frank Merriam (1934–1939) is in the company of two costumed women being presented with mementos for the 1939 World's Fair in San Francisco. (CSL.)

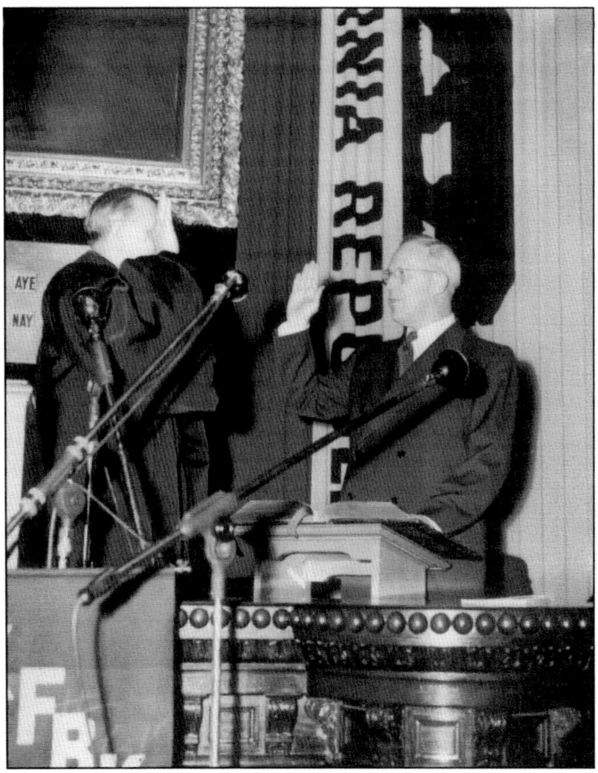

In the assembly chamber, Earl Warren is being sworn in as California's 30th governor (1943–1953). Warren was the only governor to serve three consecutive terms in the state's history. He would also be the last governor to occupy the old Governor's Office in the original building and the first to be in the new one in the East Annex. In 1954, Pres. Dwight Eisenhower named him as chief justice to the US Supreme Court. (CSL.)

The park and capitol were often used as a backdrop for promotional photographs. Gov. Earl Warren is seen here with an American Automobile Association delegation and two law enforcement officers. (CSL.)

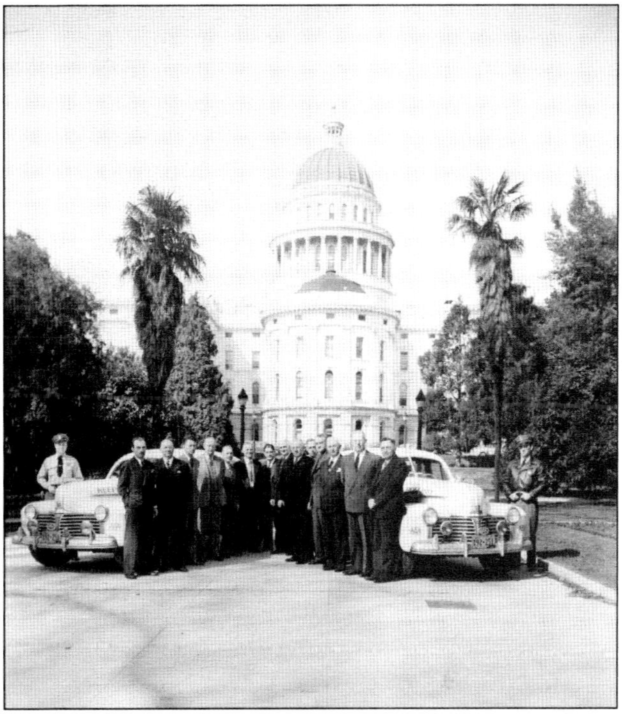

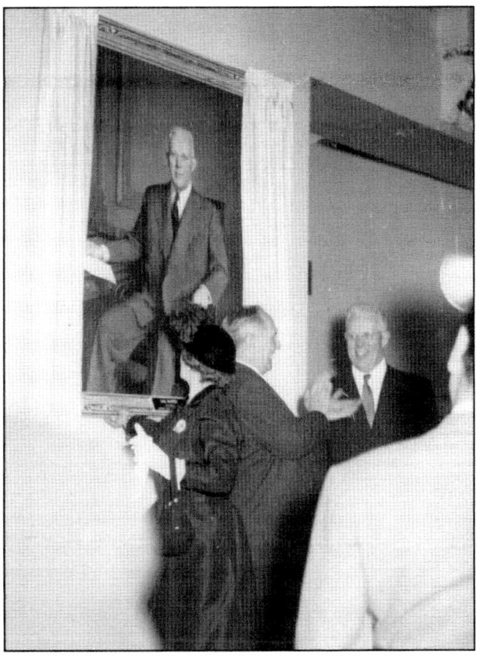

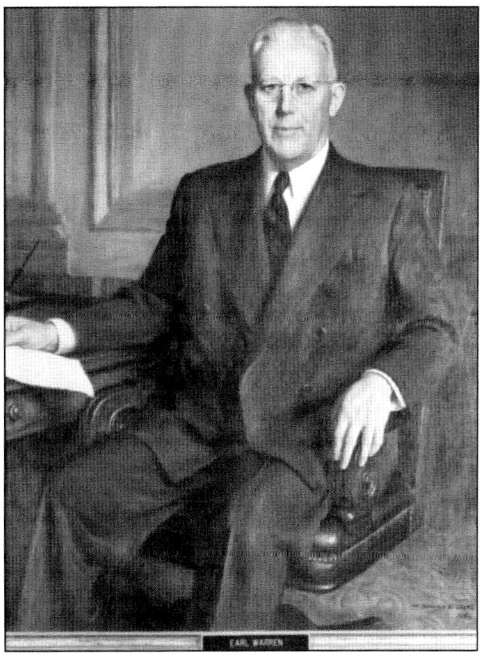

At left is the official unveiling ceremony for former governor Earl Warren's portrait in 1954. Pictured are, from right to left, former first lady Nina Warren, then governor Goodwin "Goodie" Knight, and former governor Warren. At right is the official portrait of Warren, painted by Howard E. Smith. Upon leaving office, each governor is now allowed to select an artist to paint his or her official portrait. Despite a popular misconception, private funding pays for the paintings. (Left, CSL; right, DGS.)

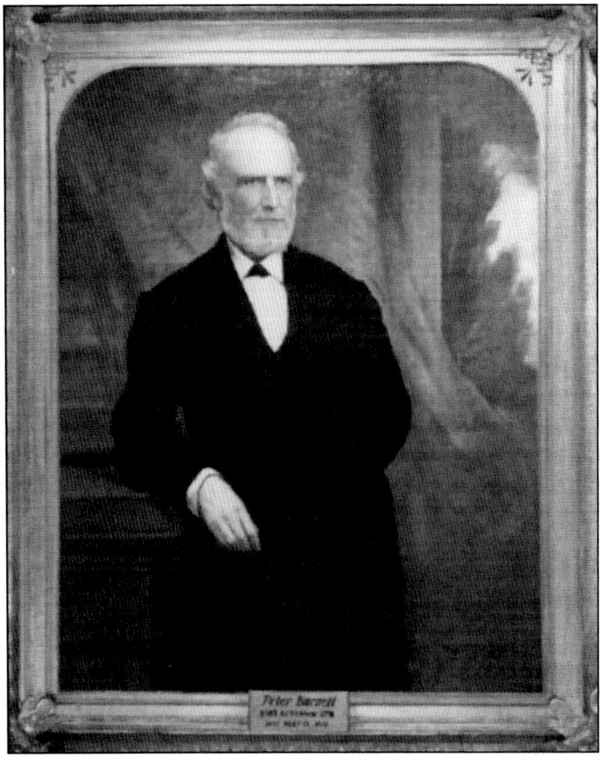

Here is an oil portrait of Peter Burnett (1849–1851), California's first governor. This portrait was done posthumously by William Cogswell and is one of the 37 portraits that currently grace the California State Capitol. It is one of many of the governors' portraits to be found in the capitol that were done in a more traditional and formal manner. (DGS.)

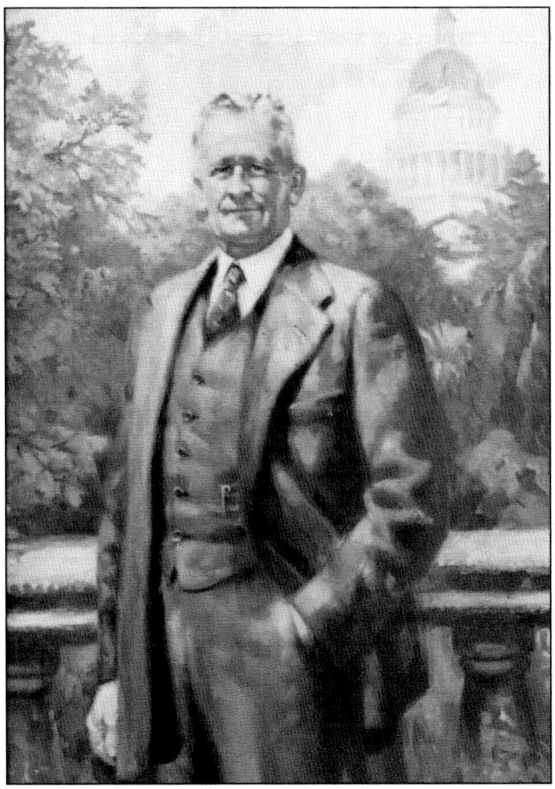

This is the second official portrait of Gov. Clement C. Young (1927–1931), the first being replaced with this more bright and attractive one. This portrait, painted by Hans Meyer Kassel, was the first to show the governor in an outdoor setting with the capitol as a backdrop. At the time, it provoked a public outcry because it had broken with the more staid tradition of the earlier portraits. (DGS.)

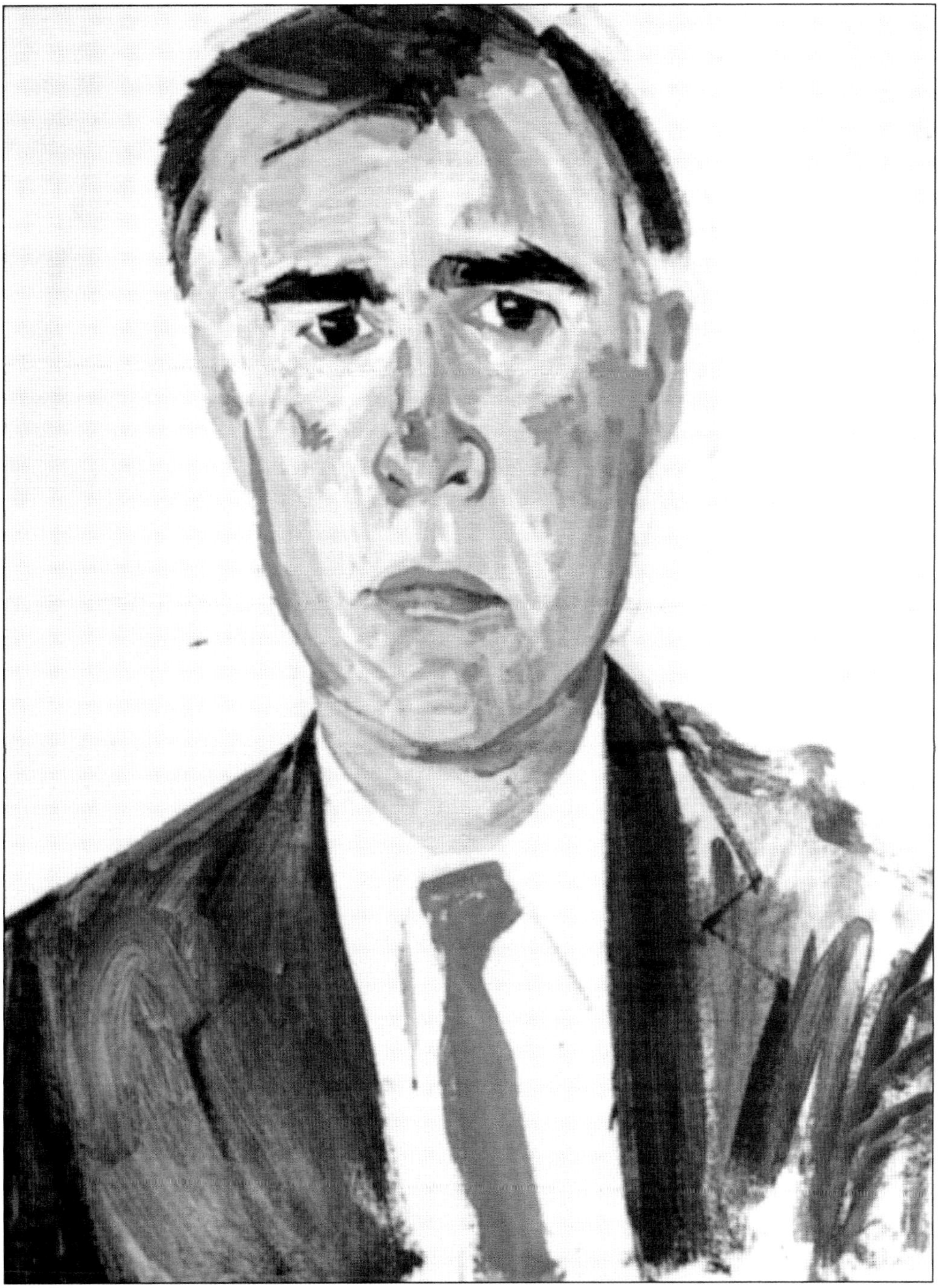

Love it or hate it, visitors continually ask to see "the portrait." Don Barcardy's modernist depiction of Gov. Edmund "Jerry" Brown Jr. (1972–1980) is probably the most noteworthy painting of all of the governors' portraits and was the subject of much controversy. Like the earlier Young portrait, it too has gained overall public acceptance. (DGS.)

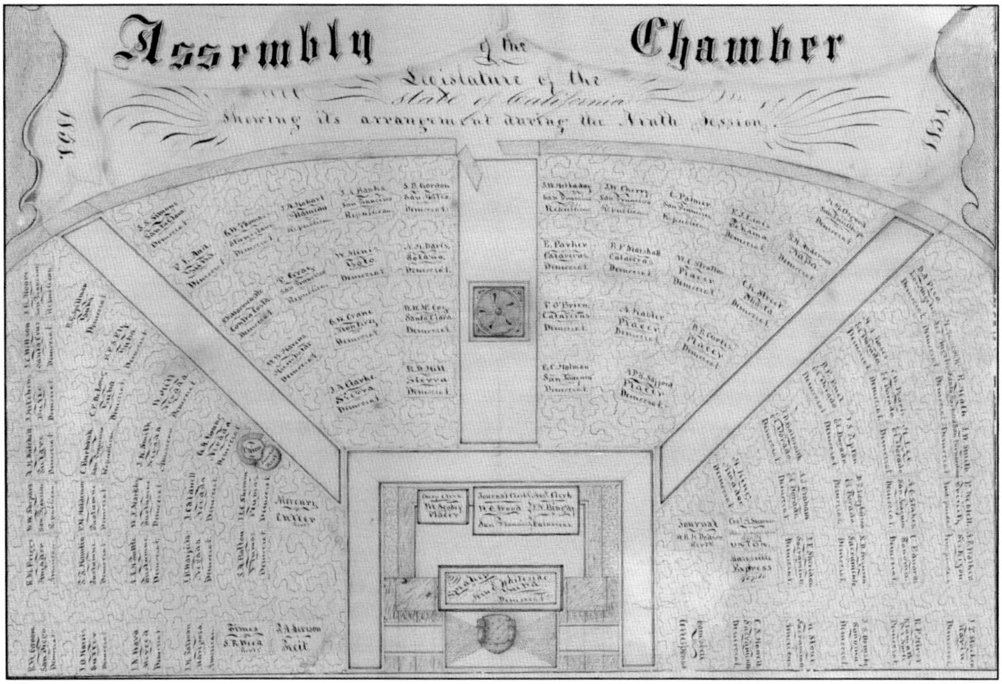

Before the advent of photography, one way to identify members of the legislature was by name, as seen in this floor plan. Here is an 1858 drawing of the seating chart for the assembly, with each member's name. (CSL.)

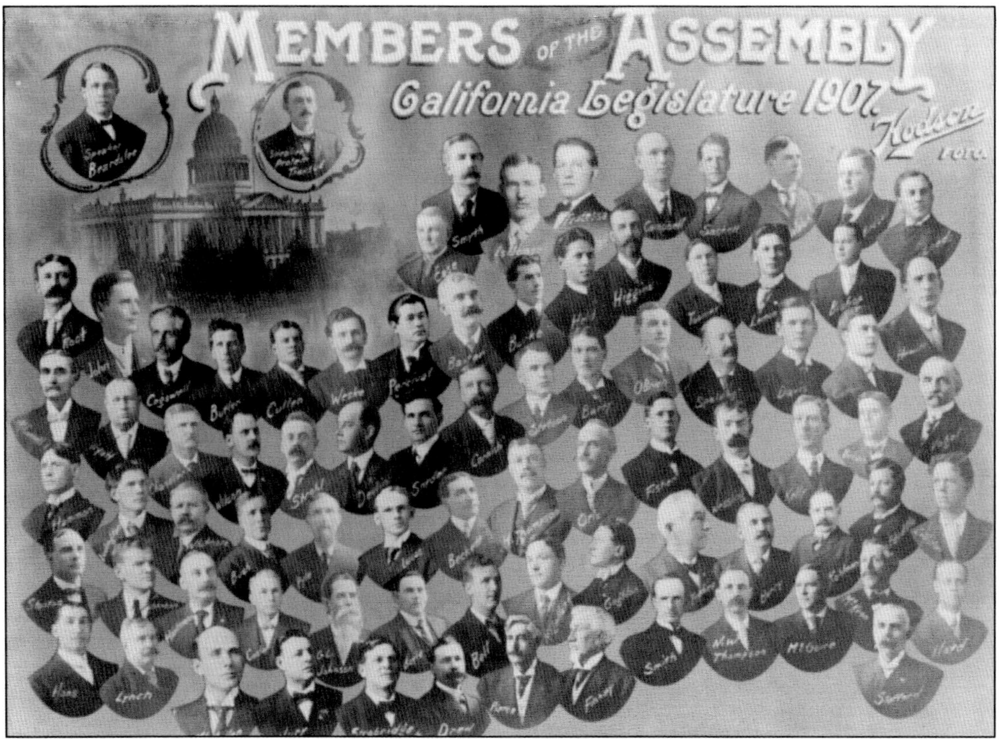

Here is a 1907 montage of "mug shots" of members of the California State Assembly. (CSL.)

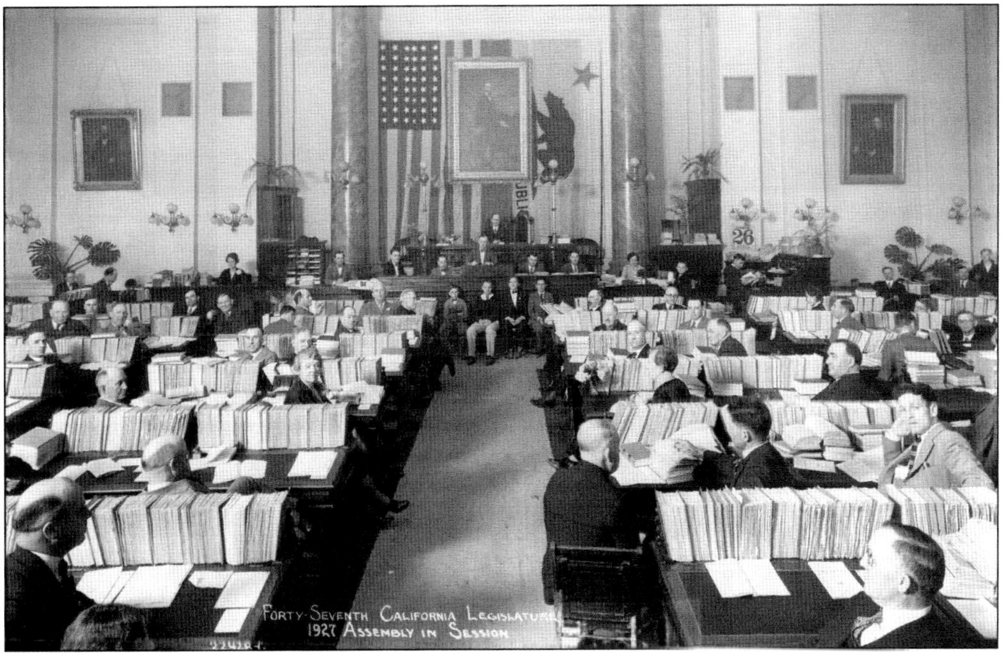

Pictured here is a very crowded and cluttered California State Assembly chamber in 1927. The members had to use their desks as office space. Electronic voting was introduced in 1933. (CSL.)

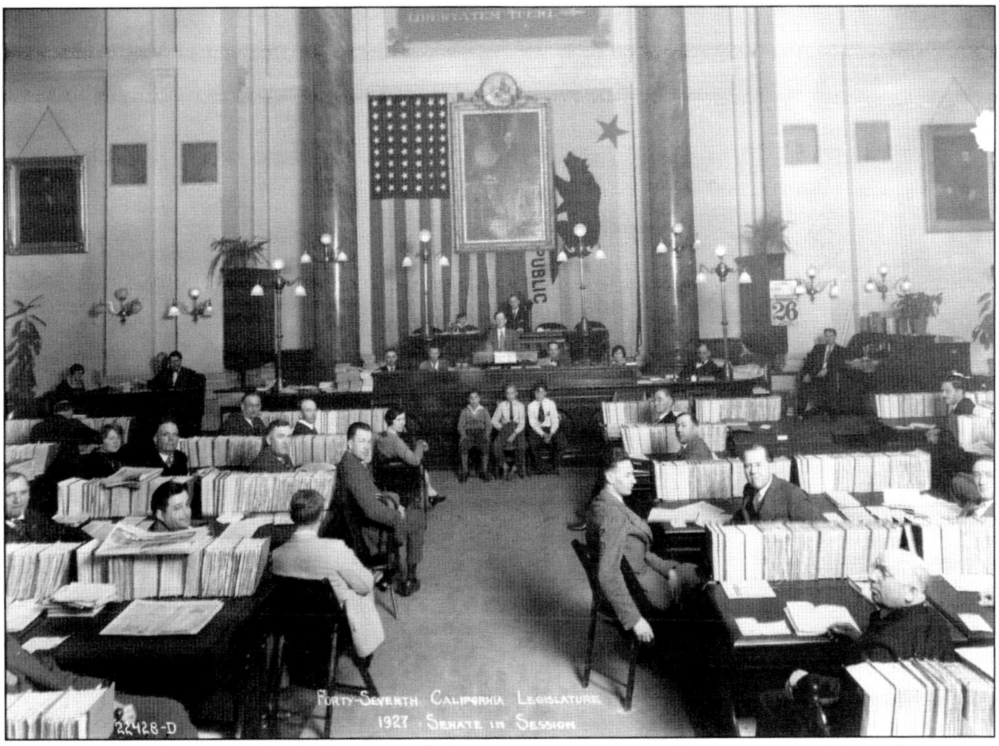

And here can be seen a little less crowded senate chamber in the same year. Note the senate clerks and pages by the dais. (CSL.)

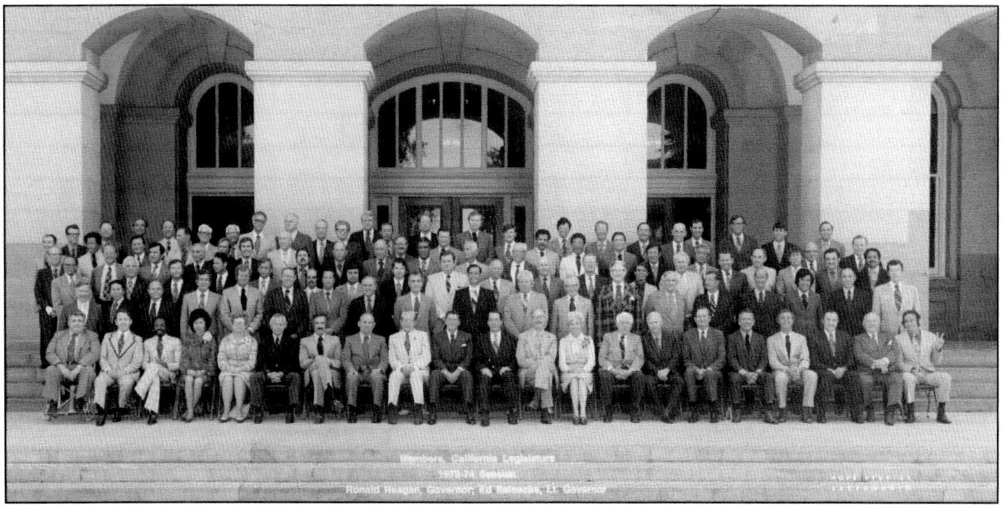

This is a 1974 photograph of Gov. Ronald Reagan (front row, tenth from left), other state constitutional officers, and the legislature. In 1966, the legislature began to meet on a full-time basis. Reagan served as governor from 1967 to 1975. (CSL.)

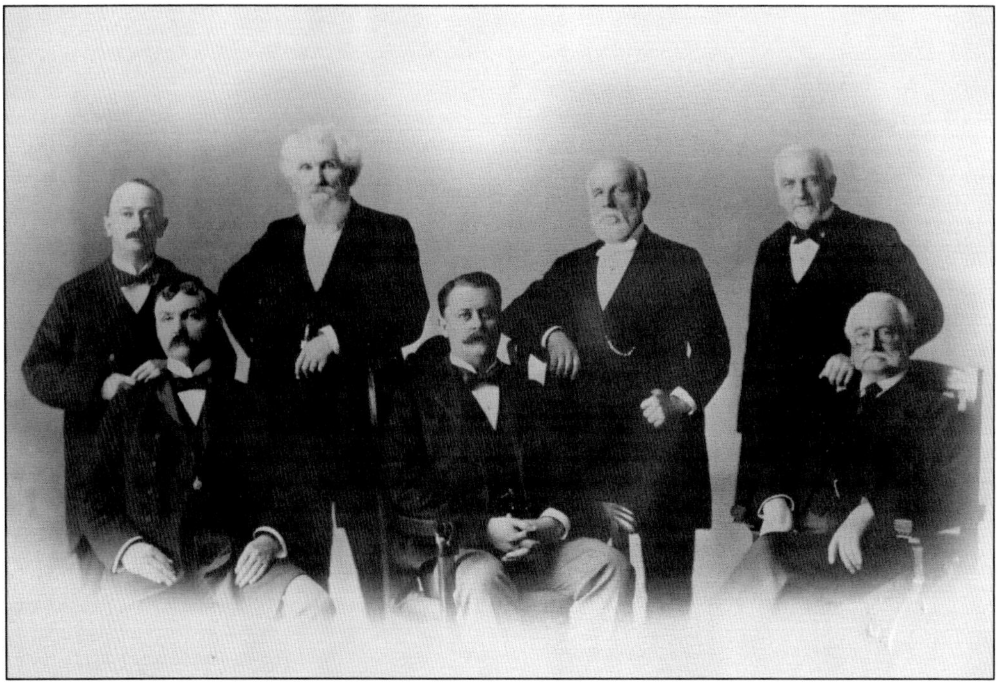

This photograph is of the 1897 California Supreme Court. After moving into the capitol, the court met on the first floor in the apse of the original structure. (CSL.)

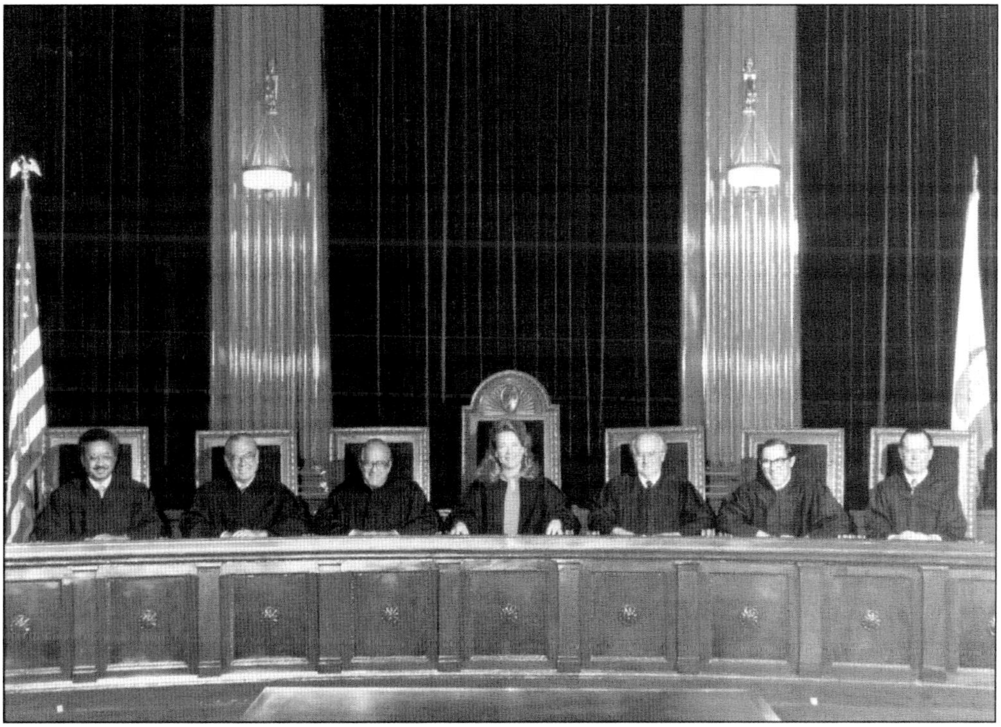

When this official photograph was taken in 1982, the Supreme Court of California had already been meeting in the courtroom in the California State Library and Courts Building for over 50 years. Seated in the center is Chief Justice Rose Bird. (CSL.)

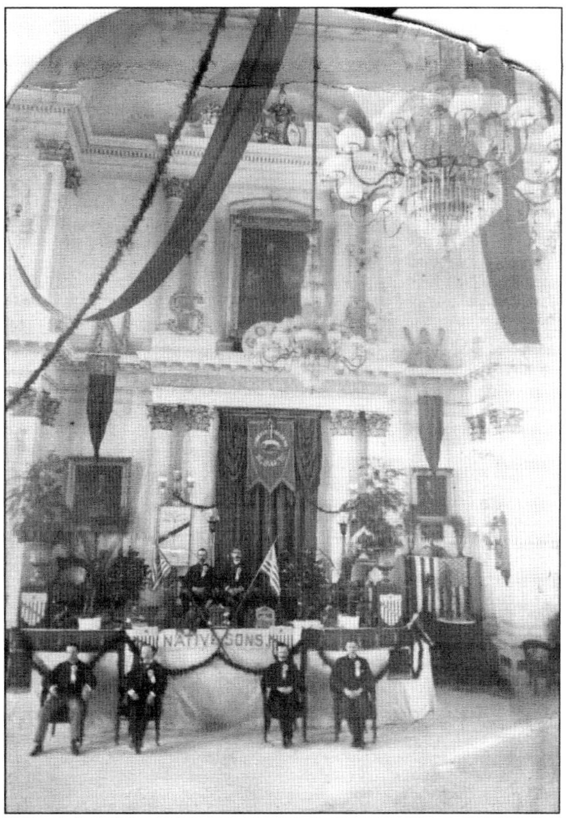

Since California only had a part-time legislature for more than a century, the legislative chambers were often used for other events. Among them were the Second State Constitutional Convention held in 1878–1879; numerous political party conventions; and various conferences and other gatherings. In this late-19th-century photograph, the assembly chamber is decked out for a meeting of the Native Sons of the Golden West. (JA.)

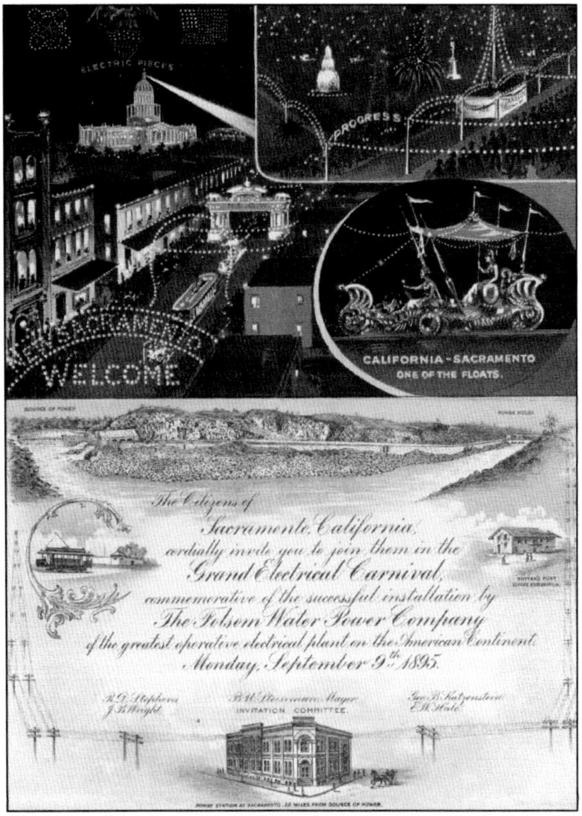

A Grand Electric Carnival was held on September 9, 1895, to celebrate the completion of a 22-mile-long electric line from the Folsom powerhouse to a Sacramento substation. At the time, this was the longest electrical transmission in the world. (JA.)

As part of the Grand Electric Carnival celebration, the capitol building was lit up with hundreds of lightbulbs. It was said that the dome could be seen for miles around the city. Electricity had originally been introduced into the capitol in 1892. (CSL.)

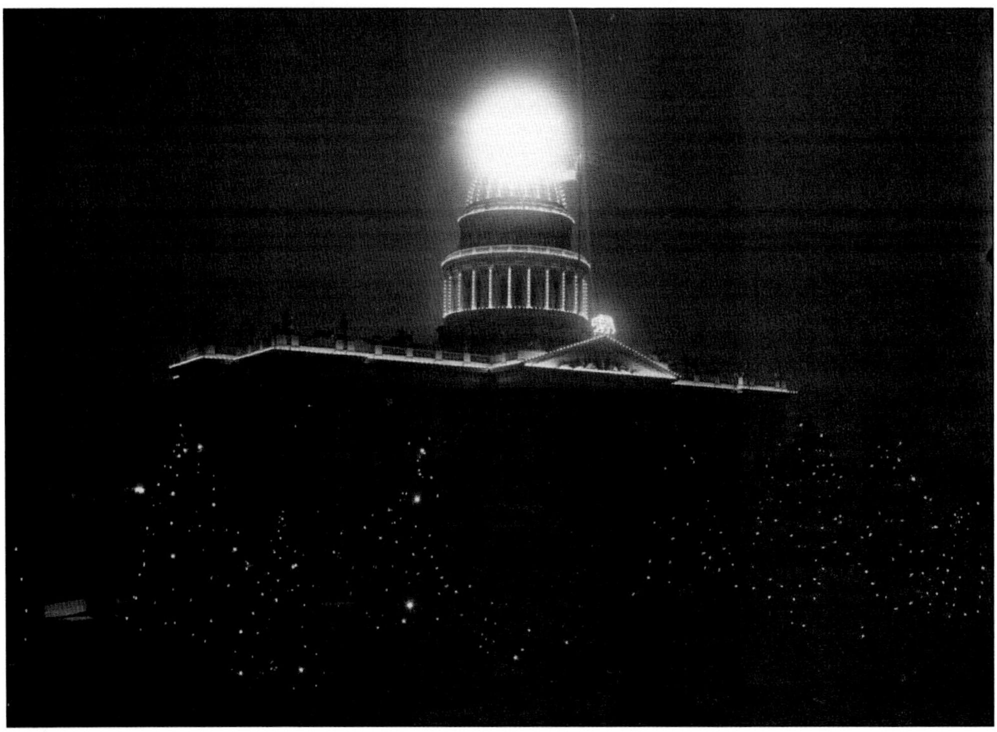

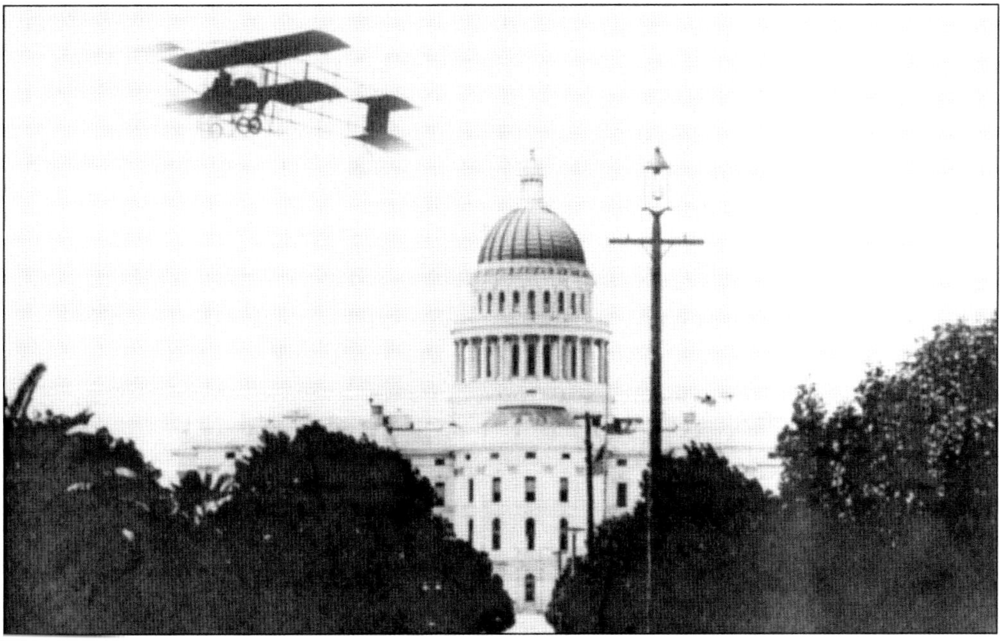

Here is an early-20th-century real-photo postcard. It is quite possible that the airplane was added to the original photograph as a way to "modernize" the scene. (CSL.)

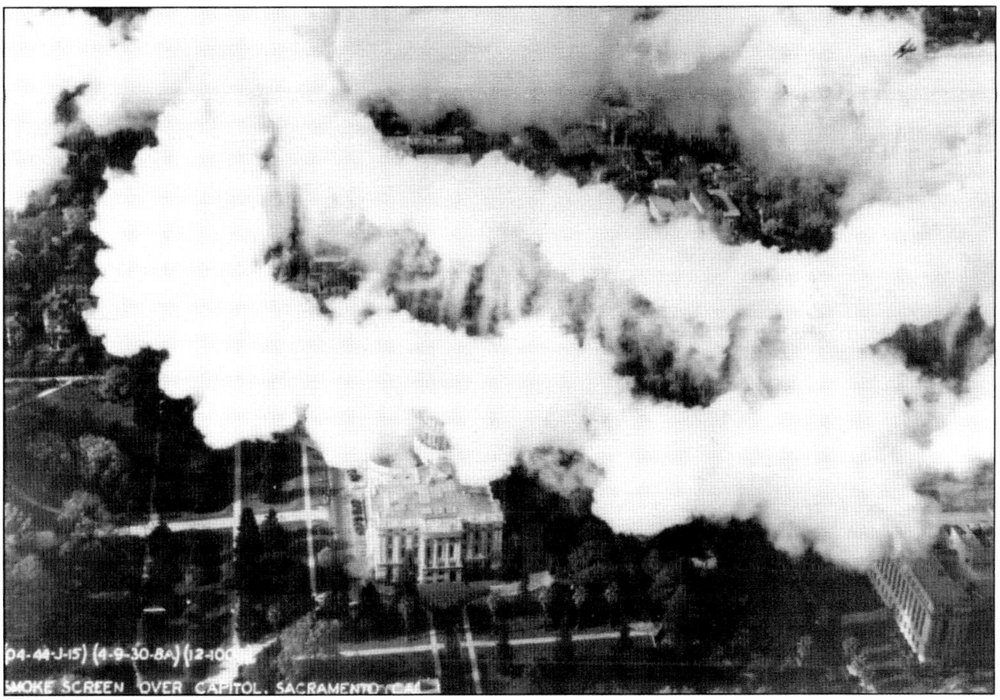

In 1930, dozens of planes from the US Army Air Corps took part in a major military exercise in the western United States. Massed formations of bombers temporarily based at nearby Mather Field could be seen in the sky above Sacramento. The capitol can be seen though the smoke screen that had been released during one of their flyovers in this aerial photograph taken over Capitol Park on April 30. (CSH.)

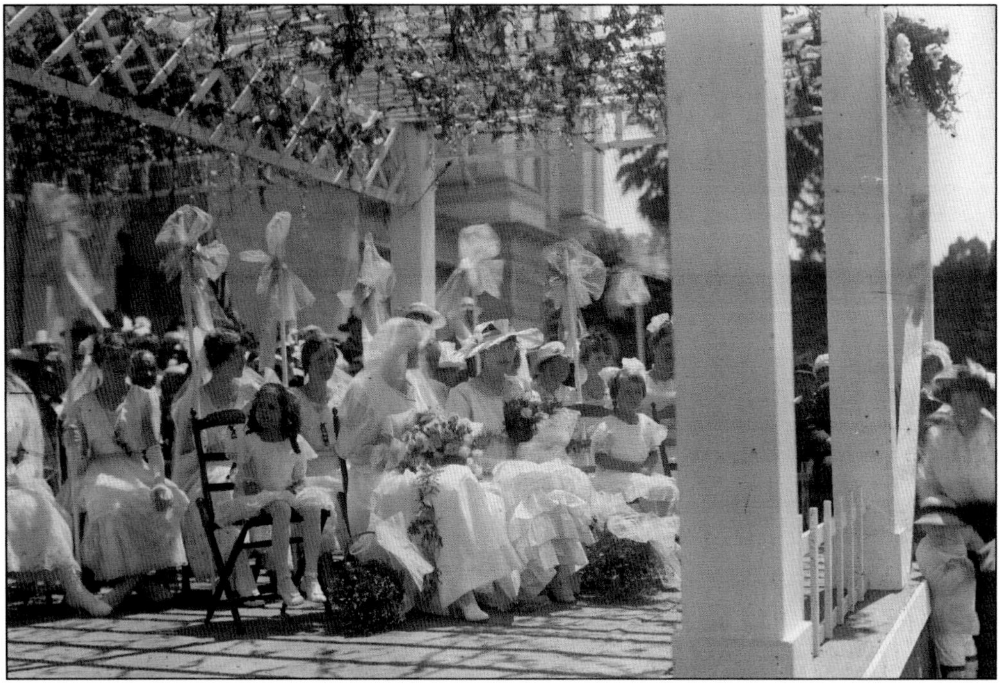

This ceremony was conducted in front of the capitol after the completion of the Yolo Causeway in 1916. A symbolic "wedding" was staged to commemorate the union of the eastern and western halves of the Sacramento Valley by the new auto causeway. (CSH.)

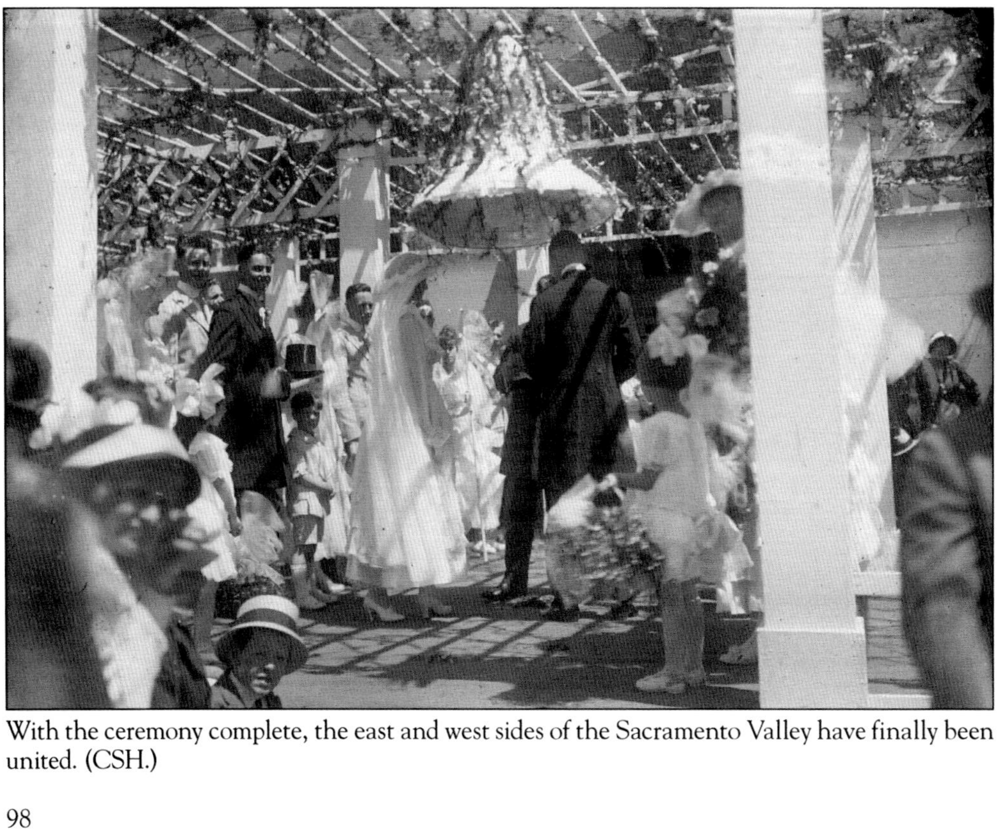

With the ceremony complete, the east and west sides of the Sacramento Valley have finally been united. (CSH.)

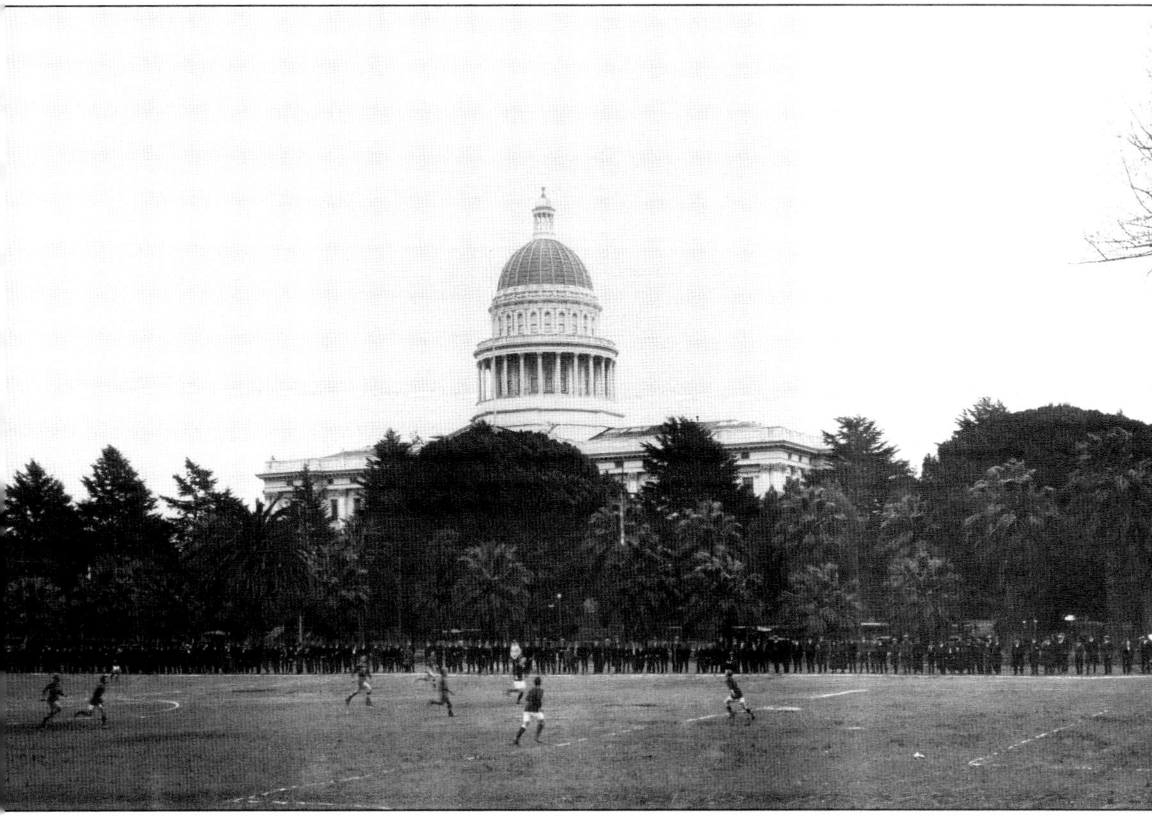

Here is a World War I–era view of the capitol and the park. A game in the foreground is being played on the land that will become the site for the future California State Library and Courts Building. (CSL.)

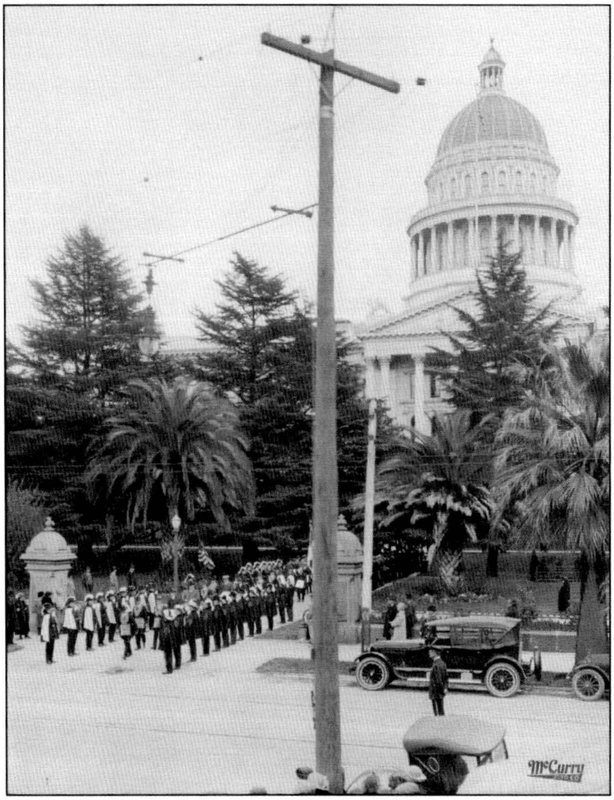

A Masonic procession is leaving the capitol grounds to cross M Street. Many fraternal organizations held ceremonies inside or outside the capitol. (CSL.)

Here is an interior scene on the upper floor of the capitol apse showing a library typing class in 1919. The introduction of the typewriter at the end of the 19th century helped to revolutionize the workplace for women, enabling them to enter the ranks of the civil service for the first time. (CSL.)

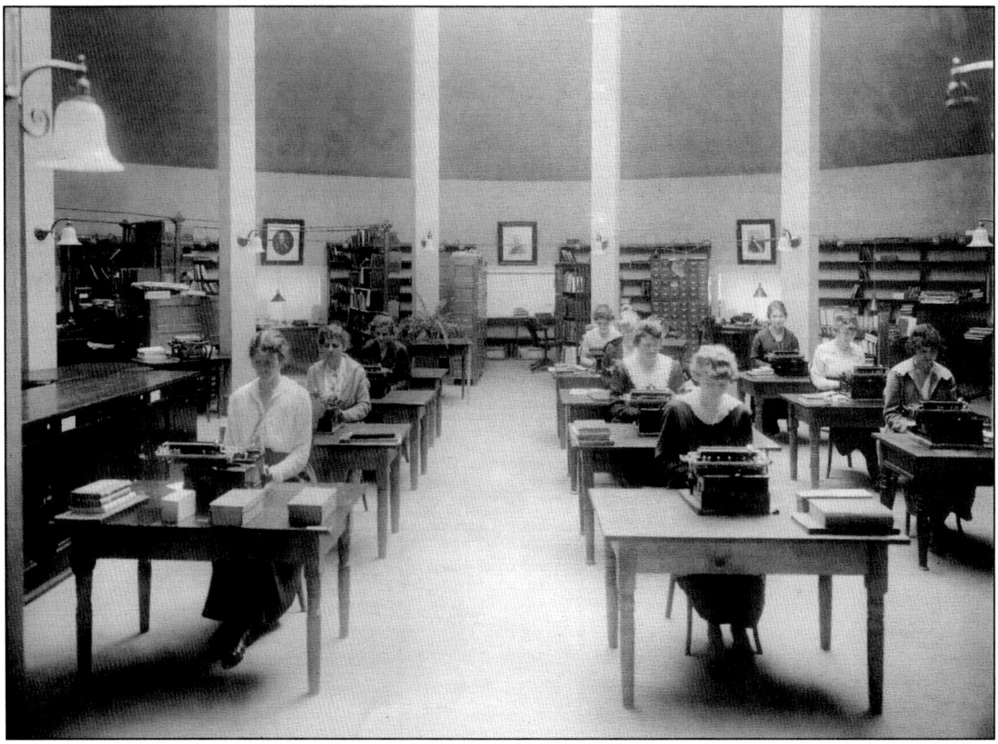

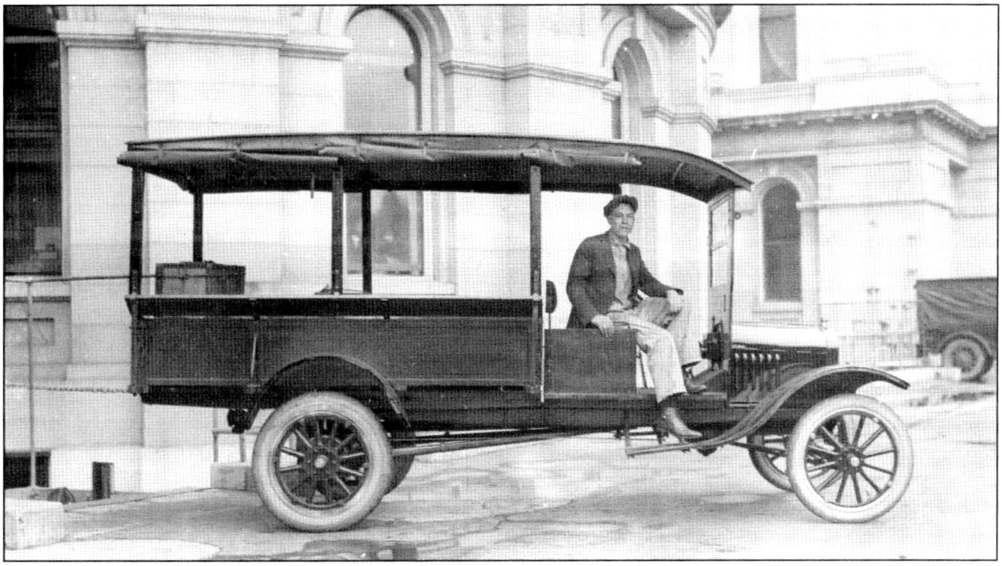

Here is a library delivery truck in front of the apse where the California State Library had its home. The staff had the responsibility of delivering thousands of books on loan from the library's collection each year to local libraries throughout the state. (CSL.)

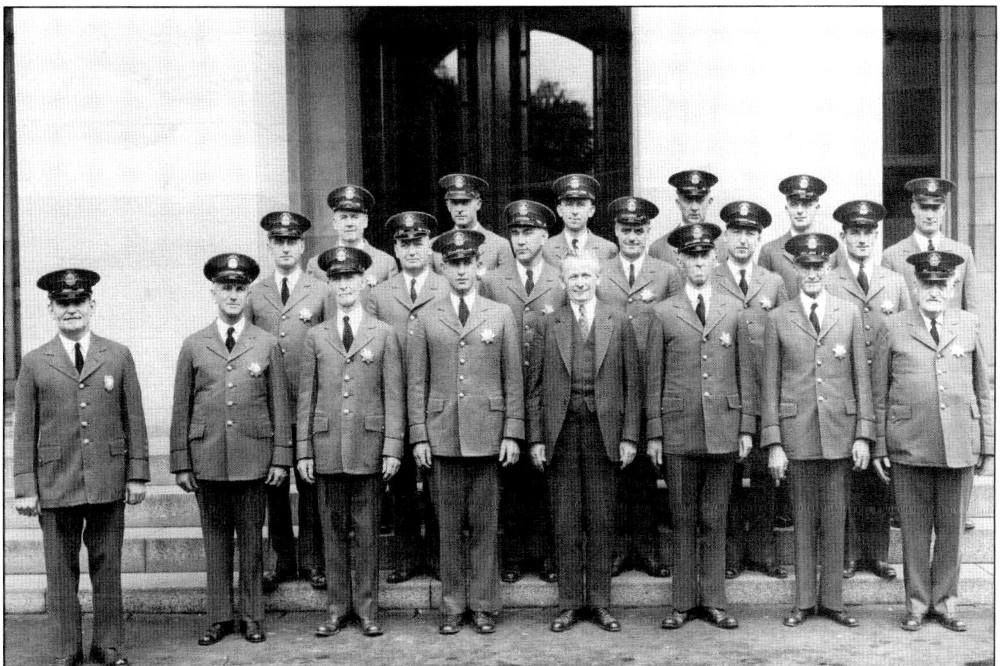

Gov. Clement Young (1927–1931), a former high school teacher and legislator, is shown with the capitol police in front of the capitol. The century-long history of the state police ended when it was absorbed into the California Highway Patrol. (CSL.)

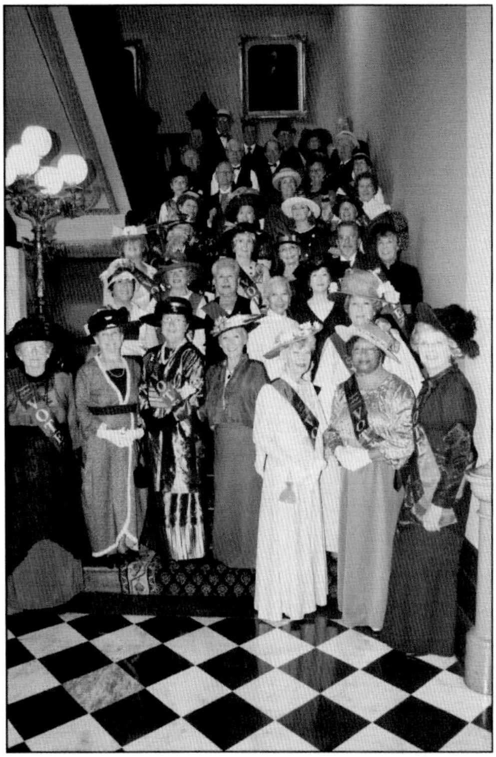

Here is a group photograph of the State Capitol Museum docents in period costumes on one of the capitol's restored grand staircases. The State Capitol Museum has been well served by a coterie of loyal and dedicated volunteers. Besides staging many living history events throughout the year, the volunteer association helps to raise much-needed funding for the museum's excellent interpretation programs and maintenance of the capitol's historic rooms. (SRC.)

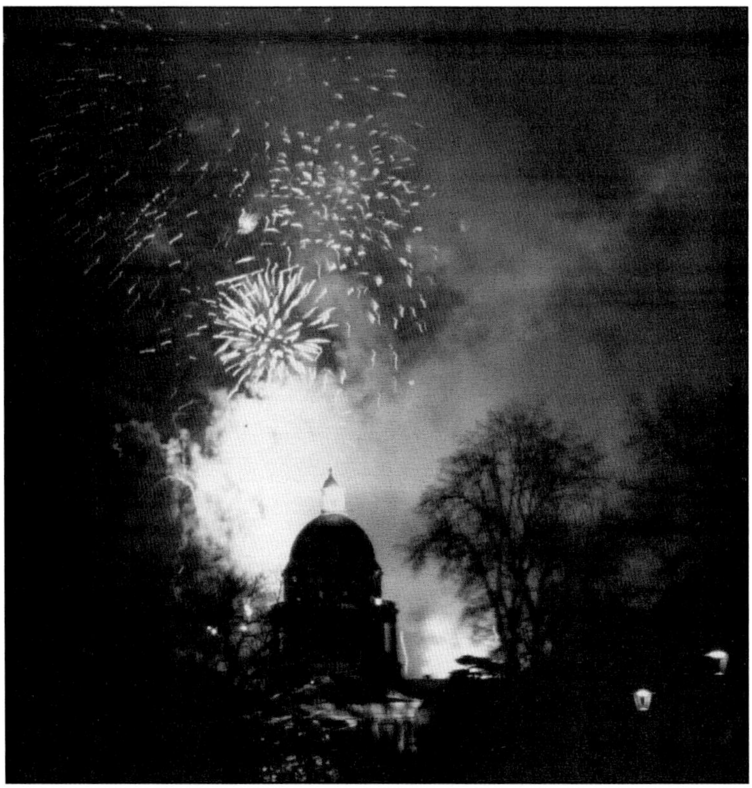

The grand fireworks and light display celebrating the grand opening of the newly restored California State Capitol was a major milestone for Sacramento. Today, over a million people visit the capitol and its park each year. (CSH.)

Six

Governors' Mansions

The residence itself is one of those good old-fashioned, roomy homes.

– from a description of the Governor's Mansion, *Sacramento Union*, 1903

At the time of the writing of this book (2012), California does not have an official governor's mansion. Many homes—some humble and common, others magnificent and stately—have provided shelter for California's chief executive officers during the 160-plus years of its history. California, for a third of that time, has had only one official governor's mansion. An attempt was made in the early 1870s to build a governor's mansion on the park grounds. The building, however, was never completed or occupied. Other proposals to build or buy a residence have also failed to gain acceptance. Over the years, most of California's governors have called their Sacramento home, apartment, or hotel an "official residence" while in office.

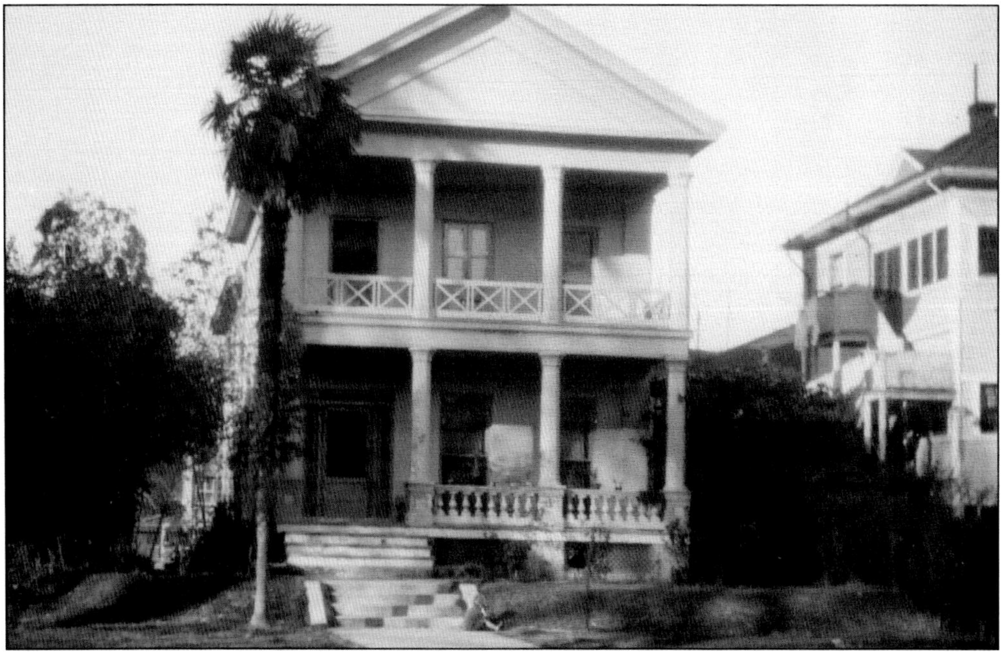

The J. Neely Johnson home at 1029 F Street was built in the mid-1850s. Johnson was elected governor in 1856, as the "Know-Nothing" party candidate. This house was also the residence of the notorious California Supreme Court justice David Terry, who killed US senator David Broderick in a duel in 1859. (CSL.)

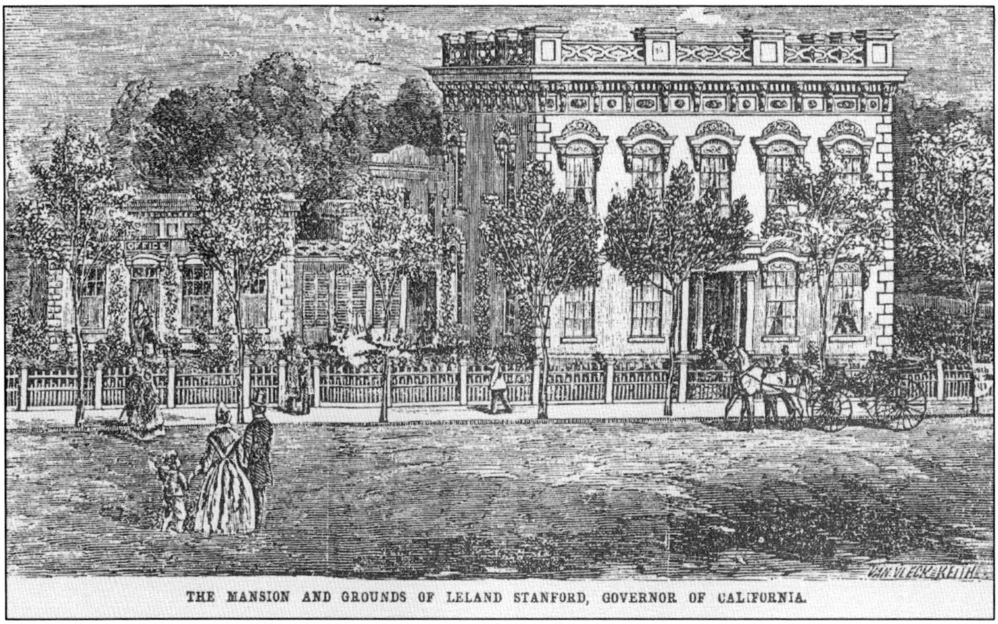

This 1862 engraving is of the original Stanford Mansion at Eighth and N Streets. Constructed in 1857, the two-story brick structure was considered at the time "the handsomest house in Sacramento." It was purchased in 1861 by Leland Stanford, the first Republican governor of California. It would serve as the residence of two governors—Stanford (1862–1863) and Frederick Low (1863–1867). The wing to the left was used as a Governor's Office between 1862 and 1869. (CSL.)

After suffering flood damage in 1861–1862, the Stanford Mansion went through a major remodeling a decade later. The original structure was elevated another story, and a fourth floor with a Mansard roof was added. These changes, along with the addition of extensive wings, helped to add over 15,000 square feet of floor space. An all-night grand ball was held on February 6, 1872, to celebrate its completion. (CSL.)

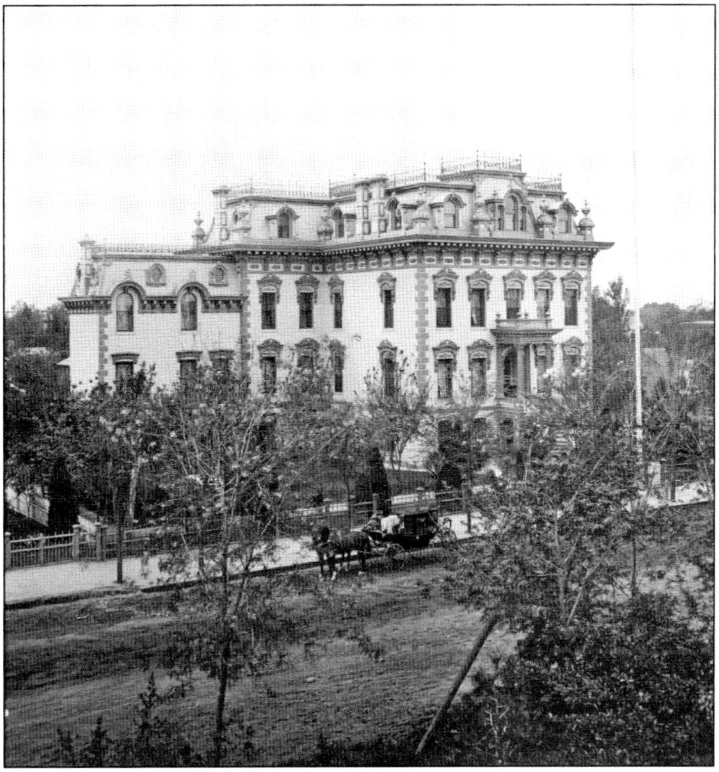

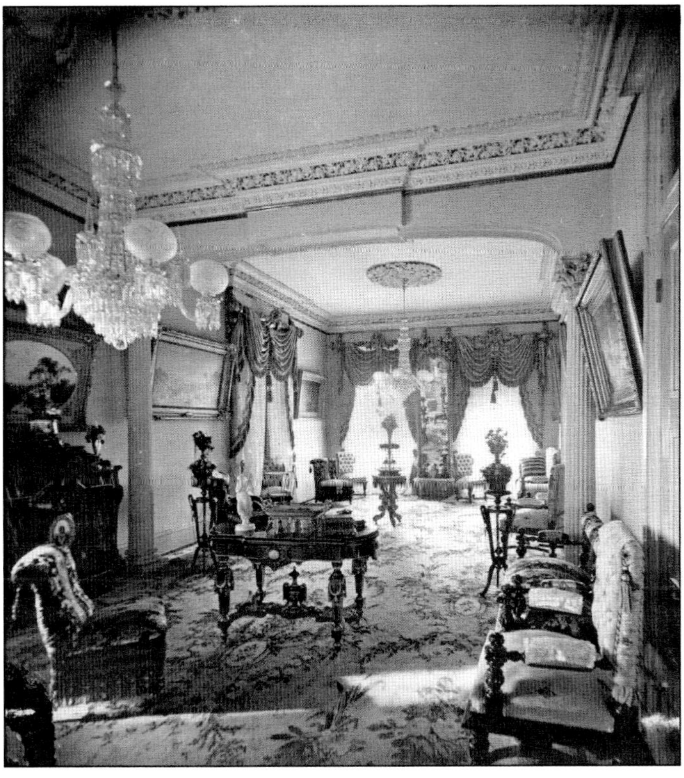

The formal parlor was just one of 44 rooms in the newly remodeled Stanford Mansion. The Stanfords' main home was their much more luxurious mansion in San Francisco. After the tragic death of their only son, Leland Jr., in 1884, the Stanfords only used the home on infrequent occasions. In 1900, Jane Stanford deeded the mansion to the Sacramento Catholic Diocese to serve as a home for "Friendless Children." It served in this capacity as an orphanage and group home for over half a century. (CSL.)

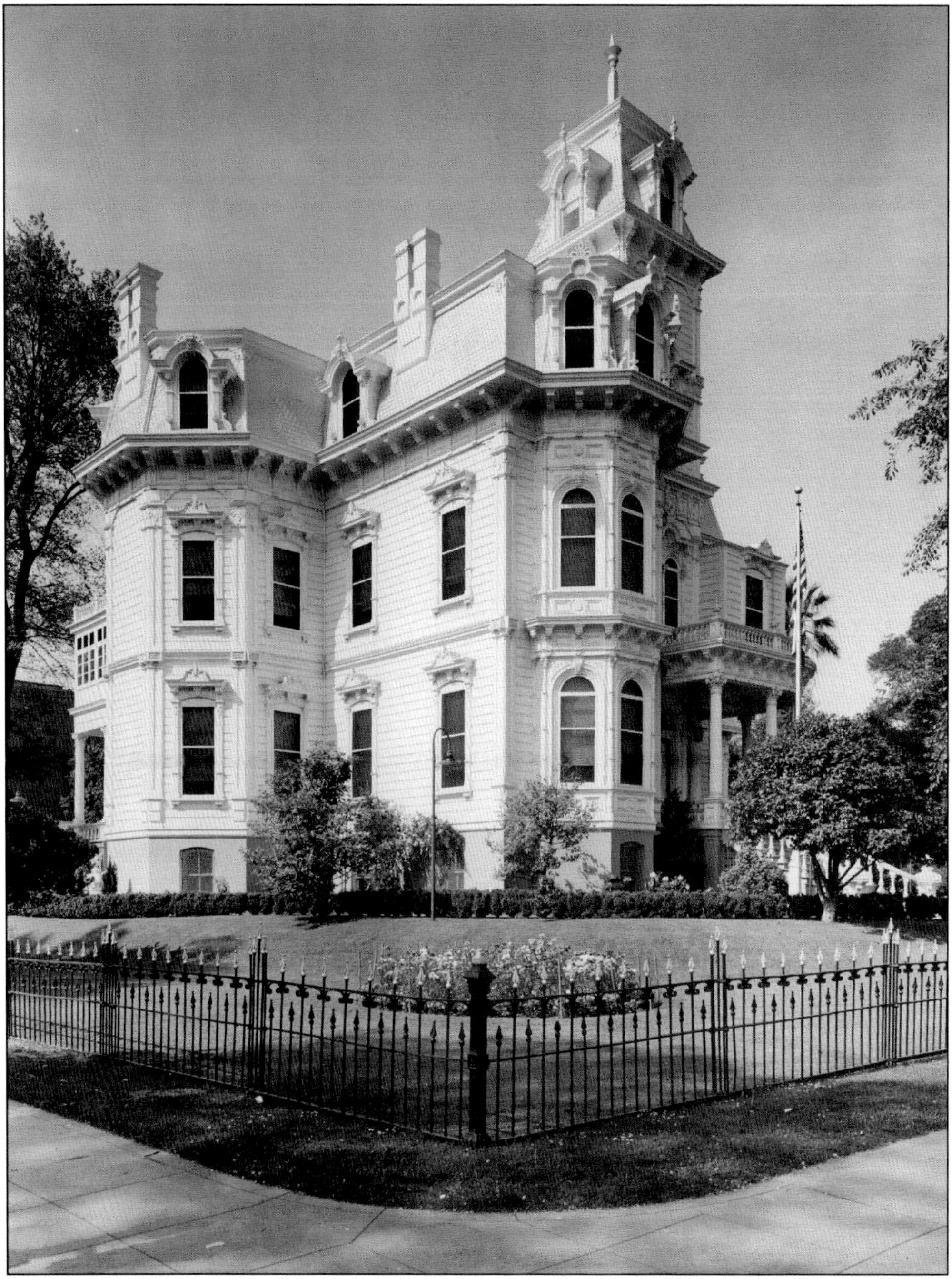

The Albert Gallatin Mansion at Sixteenth and H Streets was originally constructed in 1870–1871. A later owner, Joseph Steffens, father of the famous journalist Lincoln Steffens, sold the home to the state in 1903 for $32,500. The stately Victorian house became the official residence for 13 governors until 1967, when Ronald Reagan was the last governor to reside there. The Governor's Mansion is now a state historic park and is open to the public. (CSL.)

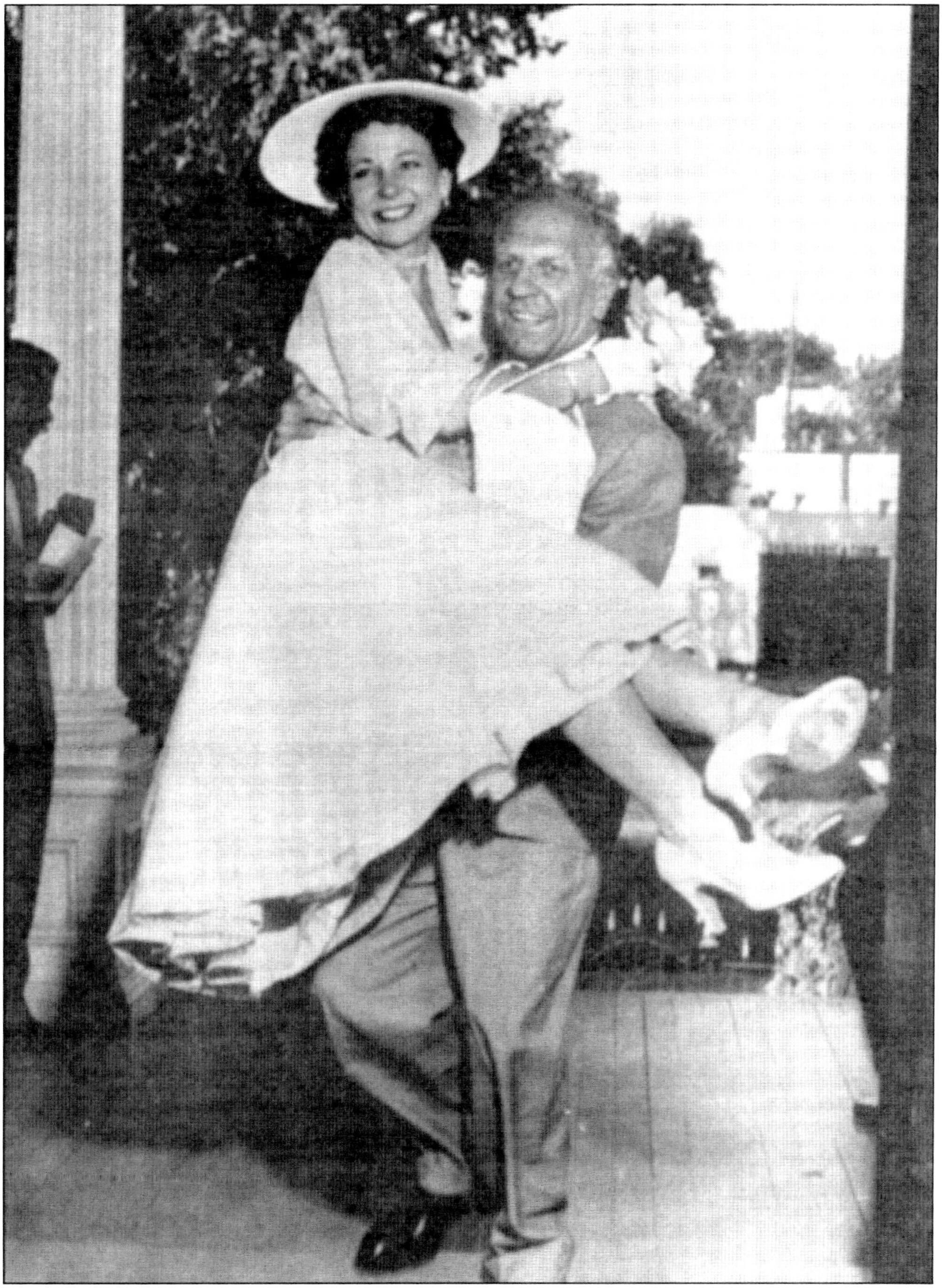

Gov. "Goodie" Goodwin Knight carries his new bride, Virginia Carlson, across the threshold of the Governor's Mansion in 1954. (CSH.)

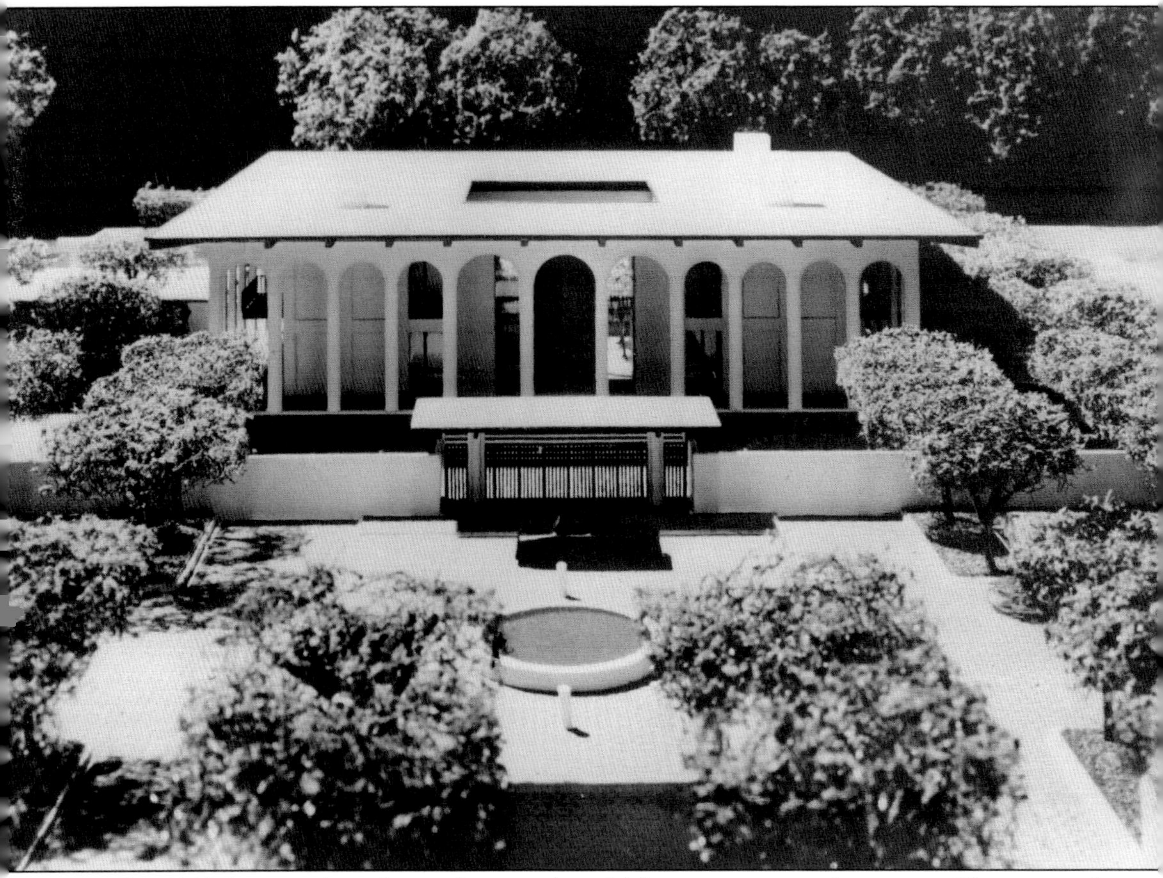

This 1966 photograph is of an architectural model for a new governor's mansion. The proposed modernistic mansion, which was to be located across from the capitol on N Street, was never built. There is still no official governor's residence even at the time of the writing of this book. (CSL.)

Seven

ADS AND IMAGES

Sacramento, the Capital City of California, has many attractions to exhibit. Chief of these is the Capitol itself, set in a beautiful park near the heart of the city.

—1915 postcard

Over the years, the capitol building has been the subject of countless artists and photographers. Its name and image have graced all manner of advertisements and publications for more than a century. It has figured in everything, including magazine covers, political cartoons, business letterheads and logos, posters, campaign ribbons, and postcards. In 2012, over 300 Sacramento businesses were listed in the city's telephone directory using either "capital" or "capitol" in their company names. In many ways, the state capitol is Sacramento, and Sacramento is its capitol—the two are, and will continue to be, inseparable. The capitol will always remain a great source of civic pride for the people of Sacramento and of California and the iconic symbol of the "city on the plains."

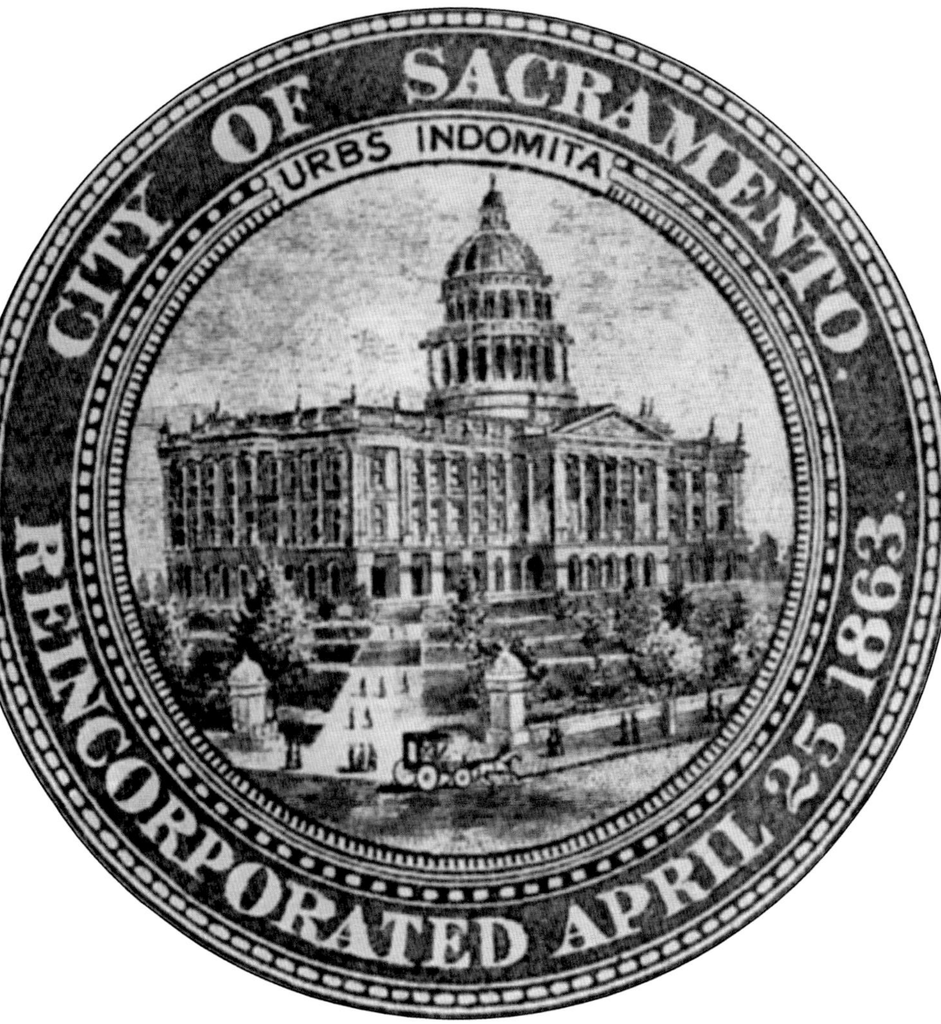

The City of Sacramento adopted the state capitol as the center design of the city seal. The city's pride in its best-known building is also reflected in its motto, *Urbs Indomita*, meaning "Indomitable City." (JA.)

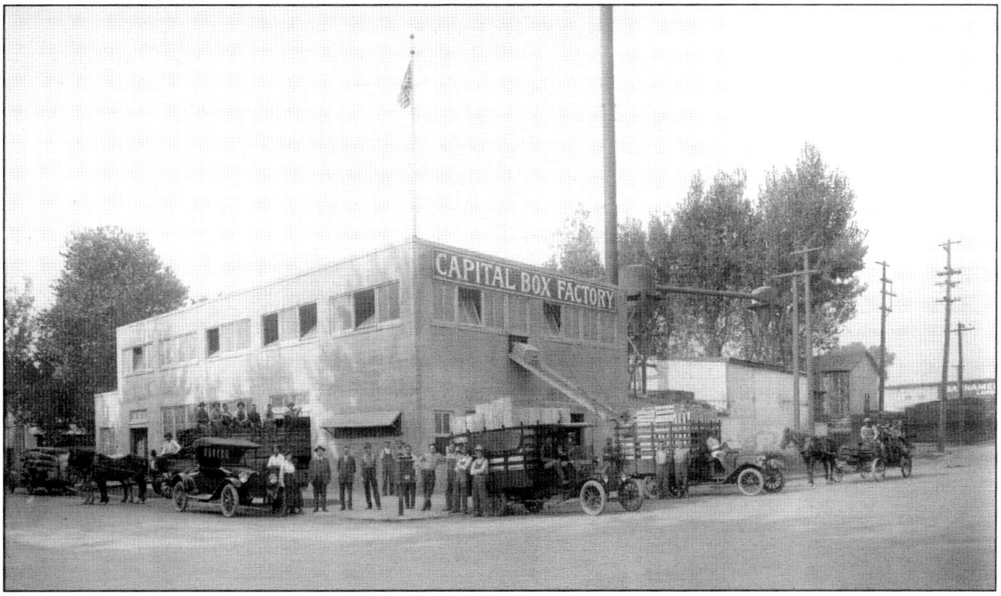

Numerous Sacramento businesses have used the name "capitol" or "capital," as seen in these photographs of the Capital Box Factory and Capital Dairy. (Both, CSL.)

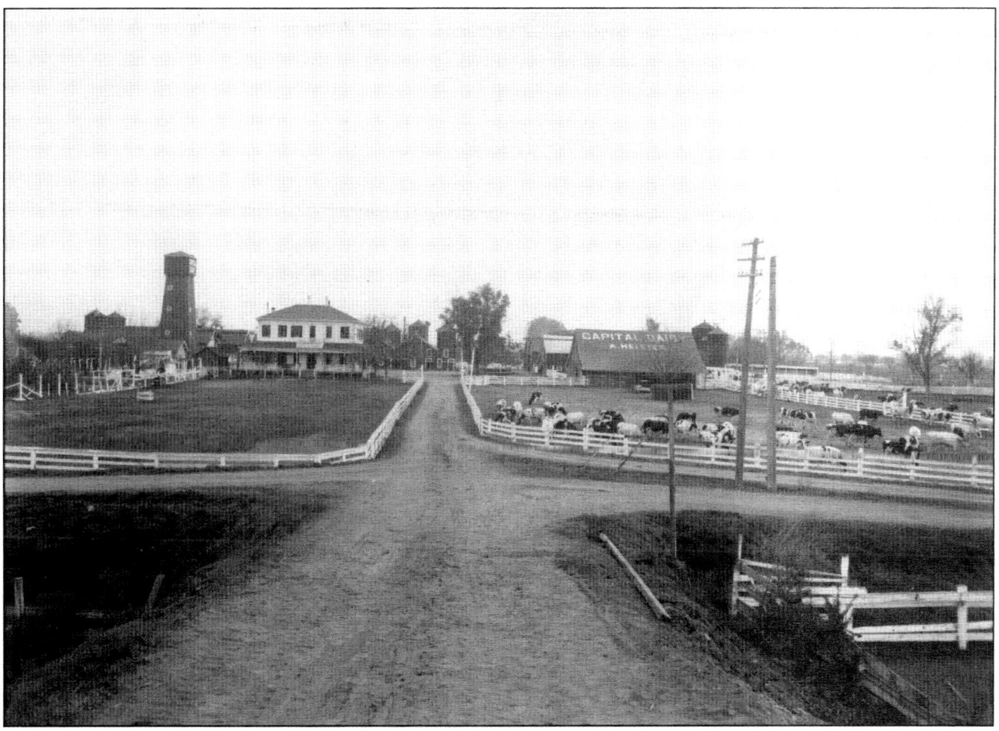

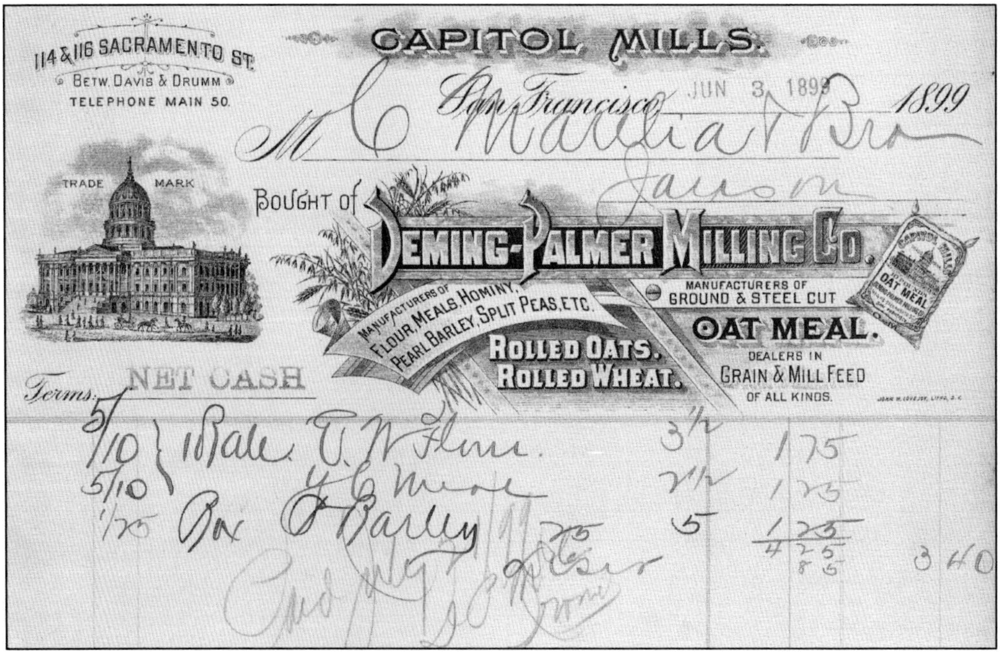

Representations of the state capitol graced bill heads, checks, and advertisements for many Sacramento businesses and government agencies, as can be seen with these two examples from Capitol Mills, and Capital Telephone and Telegraph Company. (Both, JA.)

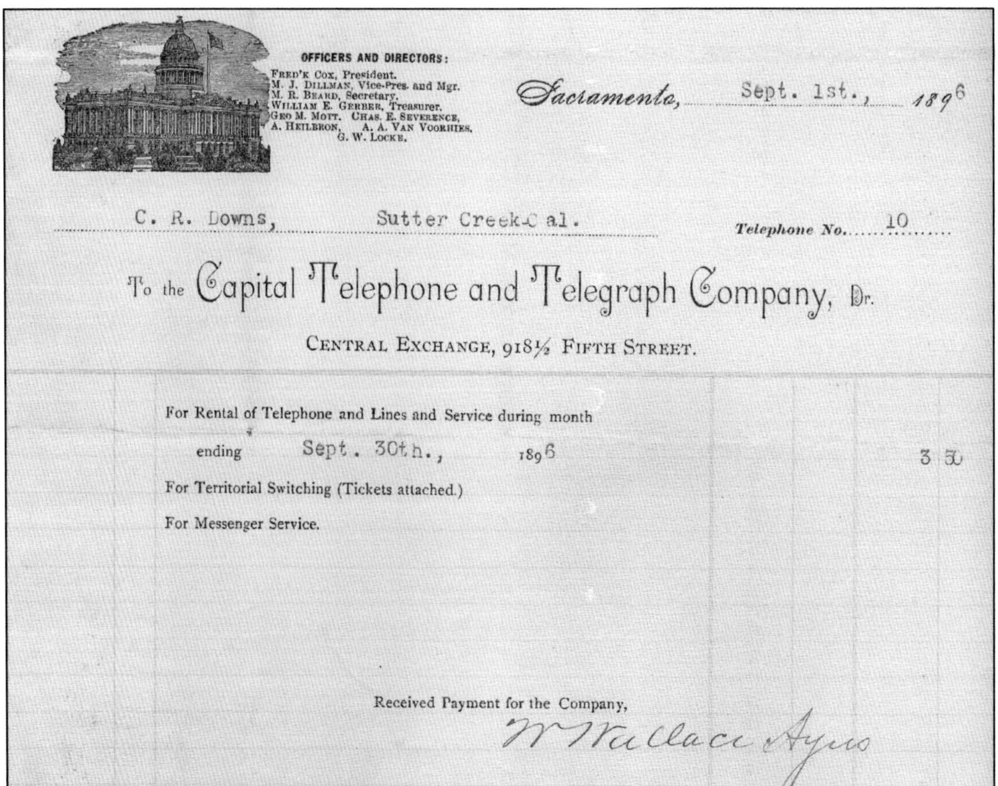

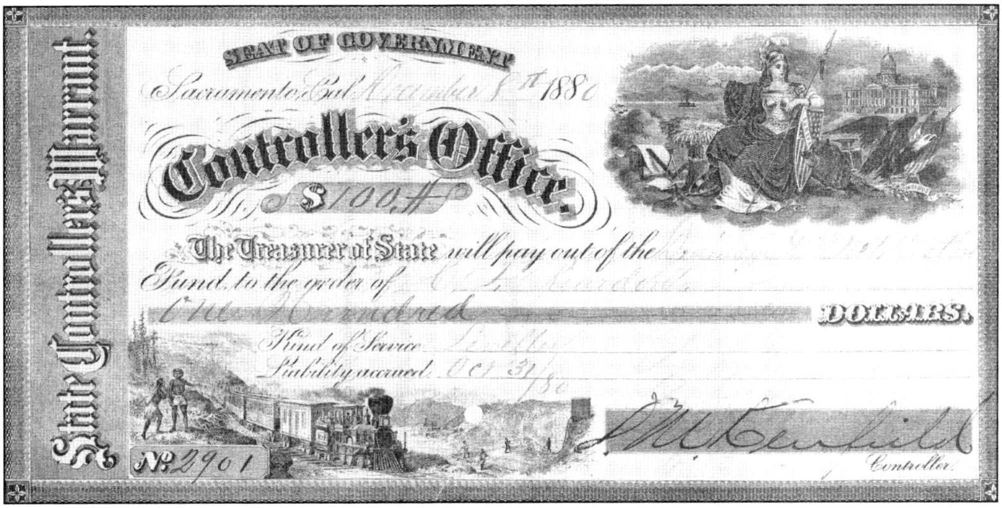

Here is an elaborately engraved state controller's warrant from 1880 with a vignette of the goddess Minerva seated in front of the capitol building. (JA.)

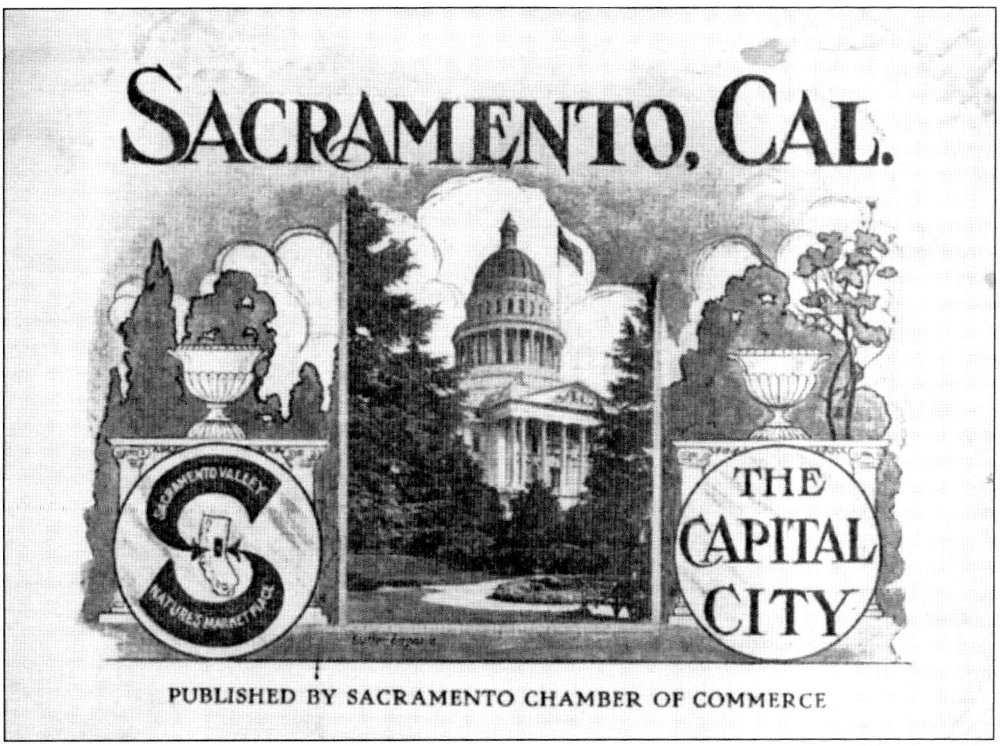

The capitol is proudly featured here on a Sacramento Chamber of Commerce pamphlet from the early 20th century. (JA.)

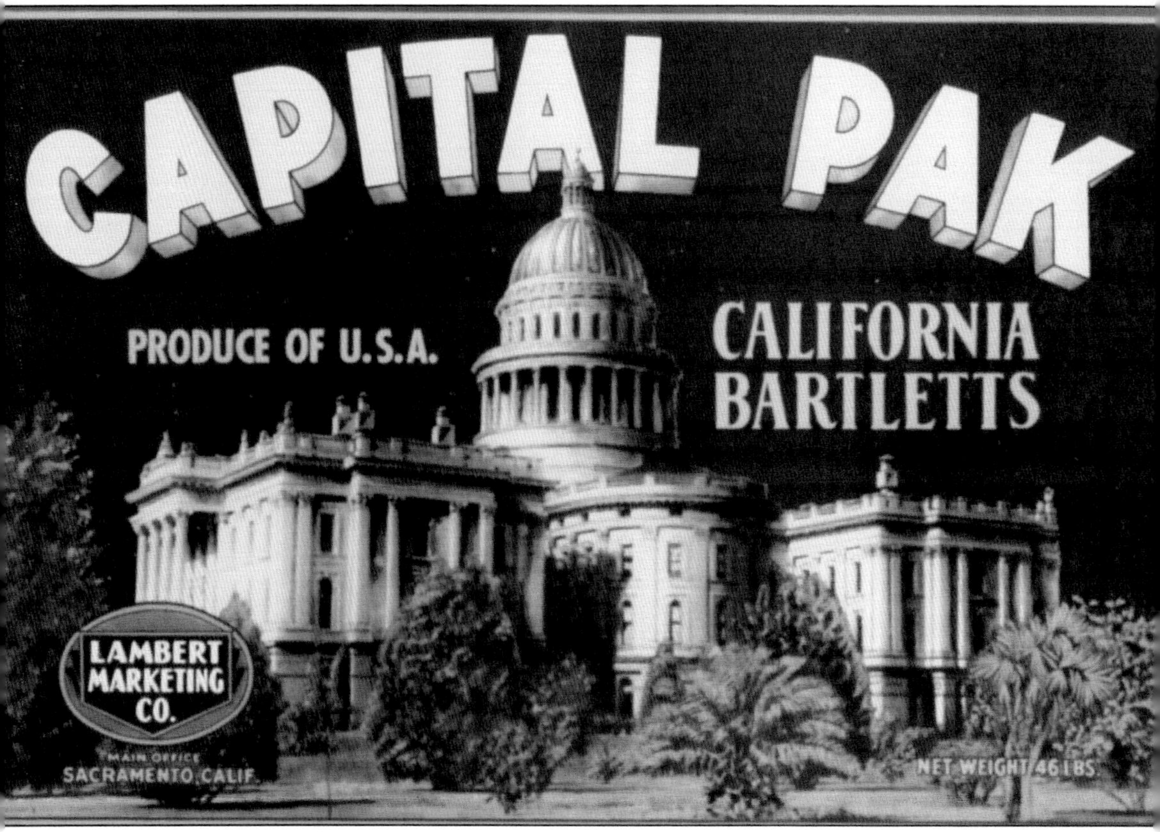

A 20th-century produce label is pictured here. The Capitol Pak pear crate label prominently features the California State Capitol. (JA.)

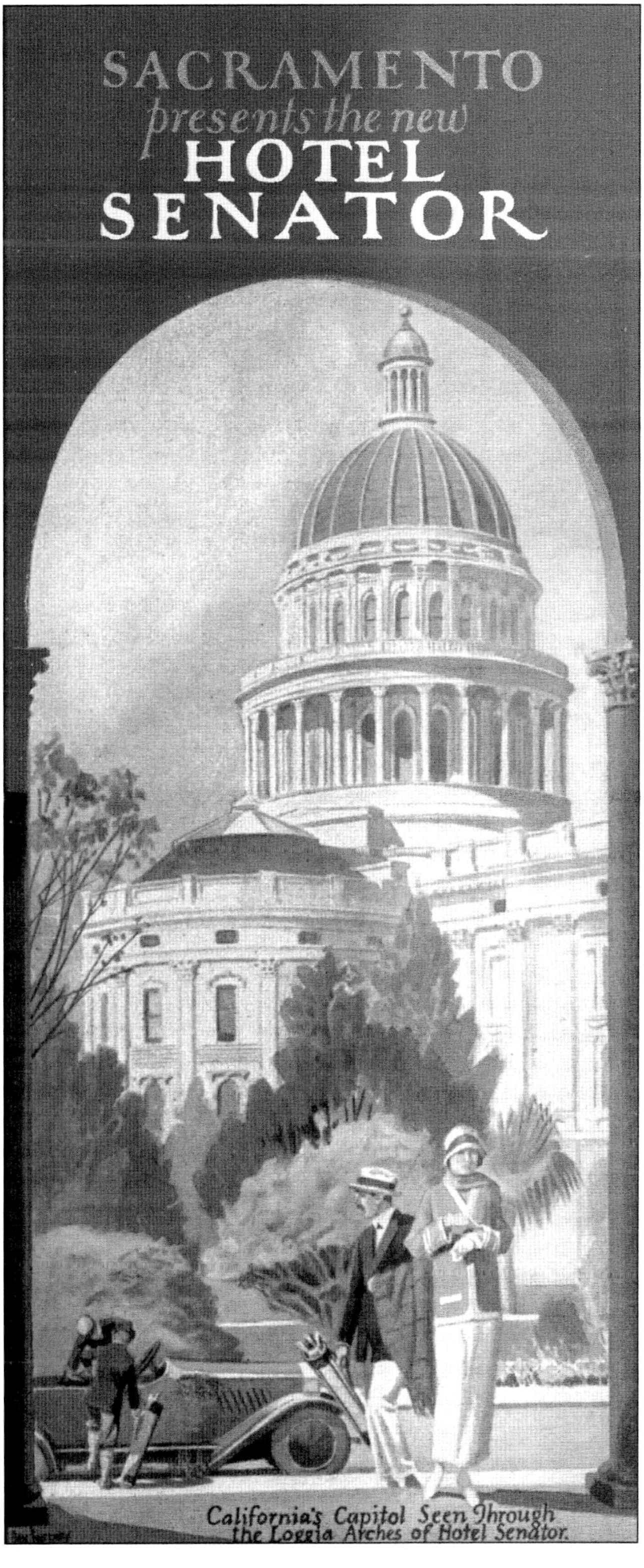

The Hotel Senator, Sacramento's premier hostelry, had a commanding view of the capitol, as can be seen in this 1920s brochure. No longer a hotel, this grand structure at Twelfth and L Streets serves as a bank and office building. (JA.)

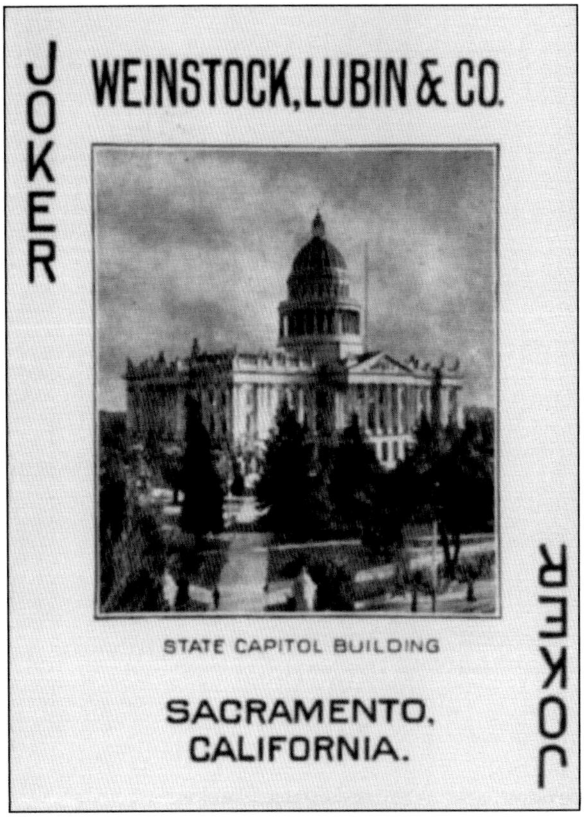

Some playing cards also had the image of the capitol, as was the case for this joker advertising Sacramento's premier department store—Weinstock, Lubin & Company. (JA.)

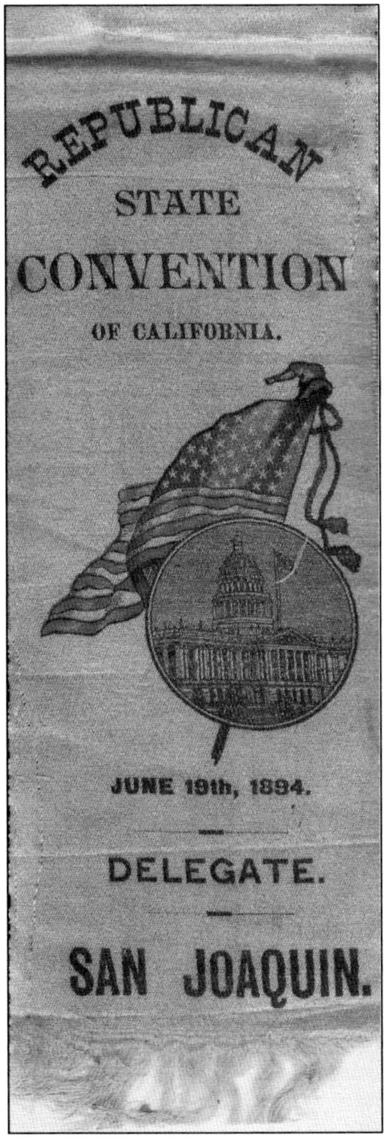

Campaign ribbons and political memorabilia also occasionally featured the capitol. (JA.)

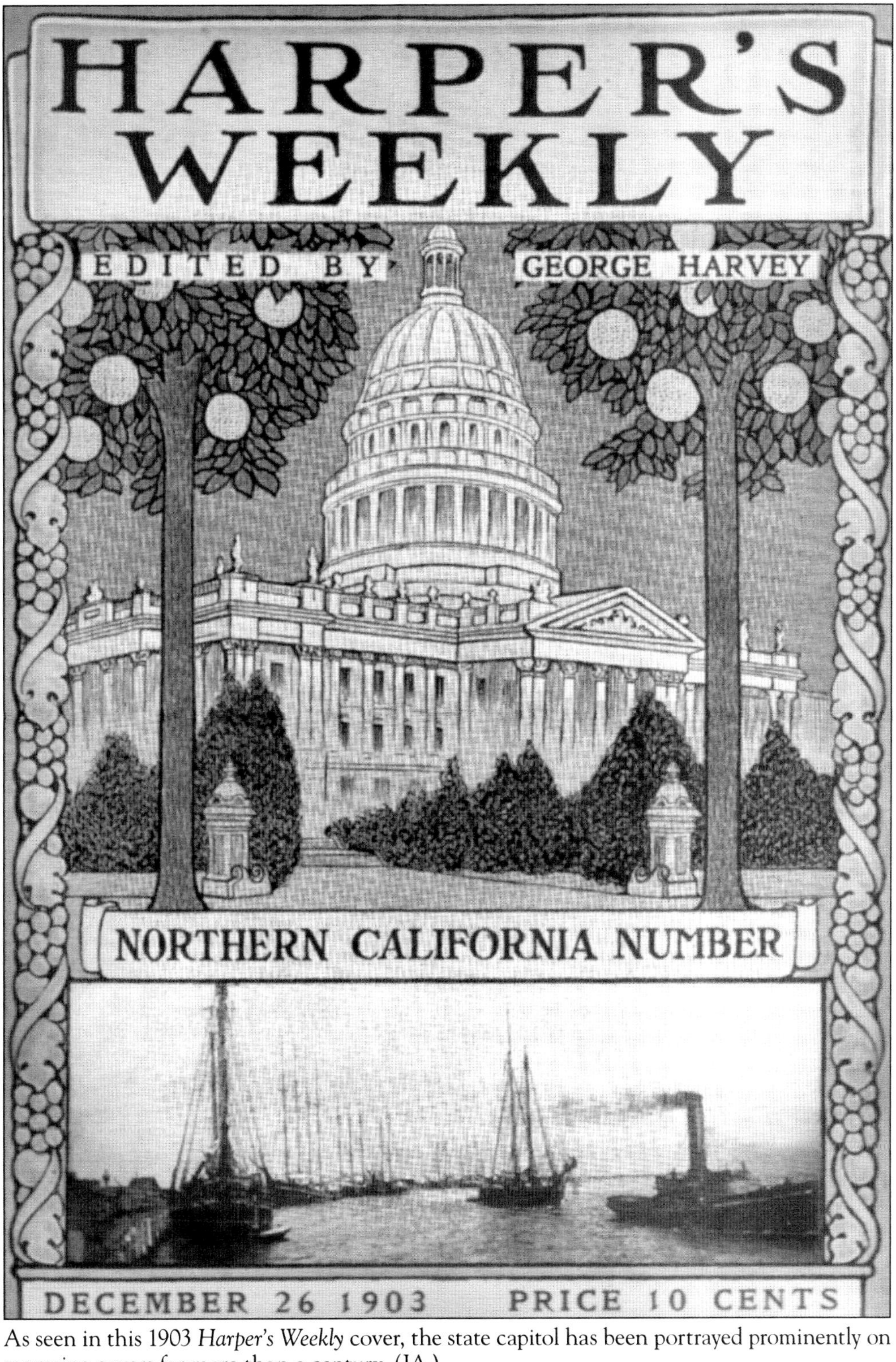

As seen in this 1903 *Harper's Weekly* cover, the state capitol has been portrayed prominently on magazine covers for more than a century. (JA.)

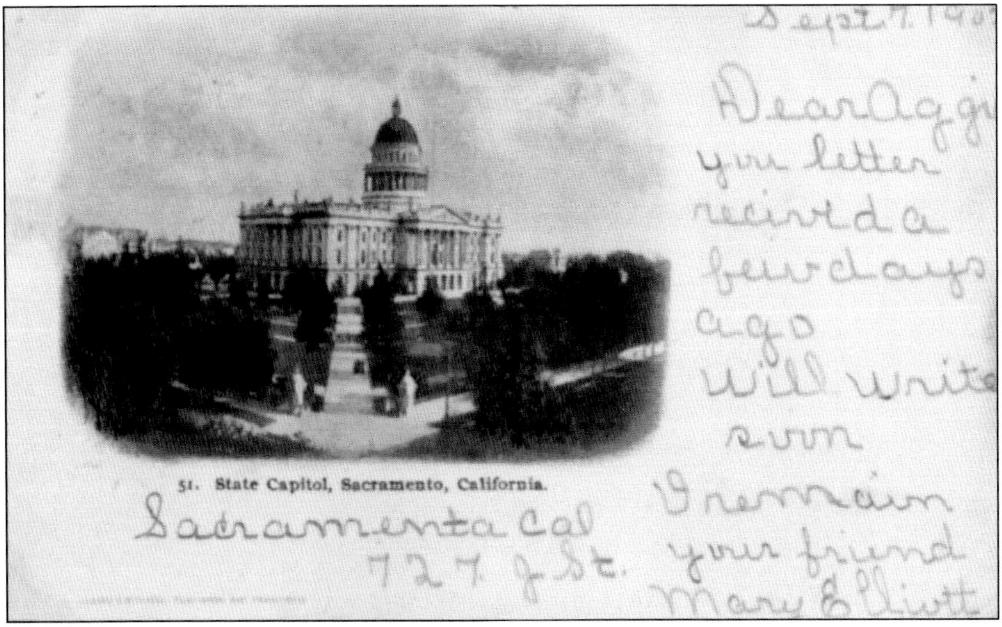

What would an attraction like the state capitol be without postcards? Here are two of the earliest known examples, one from 1902, and the other embossed in high relief. (Both, JA.)

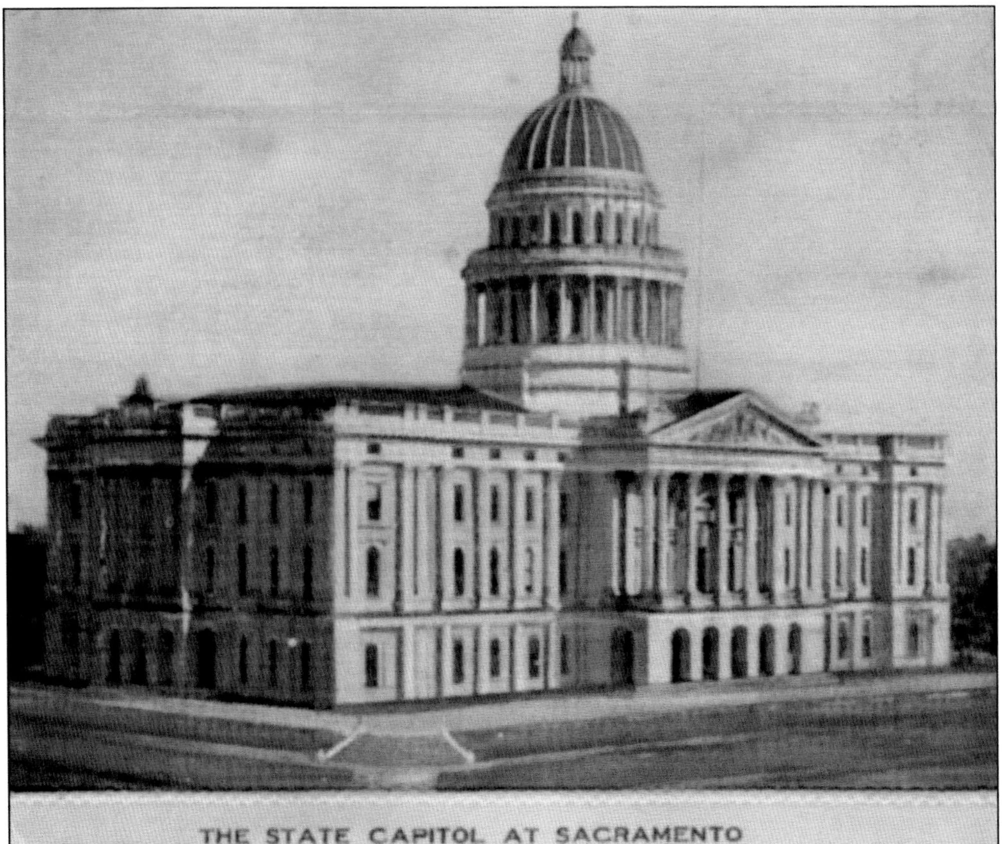

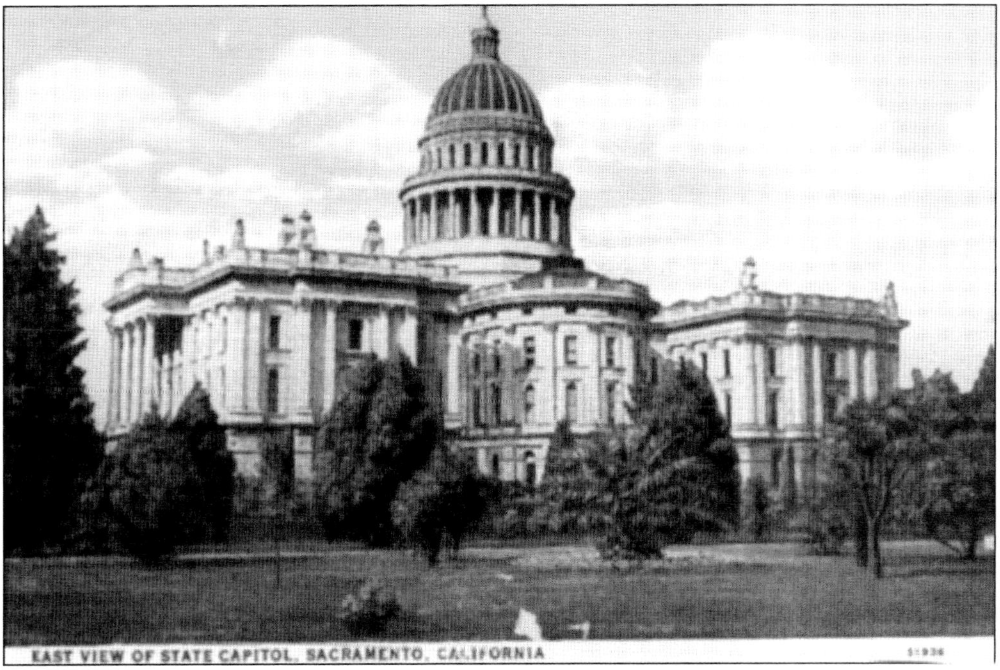

There are artistic renditions of the same view of the east side of the capitol during both daylight and nighttime. (Both, JA.)

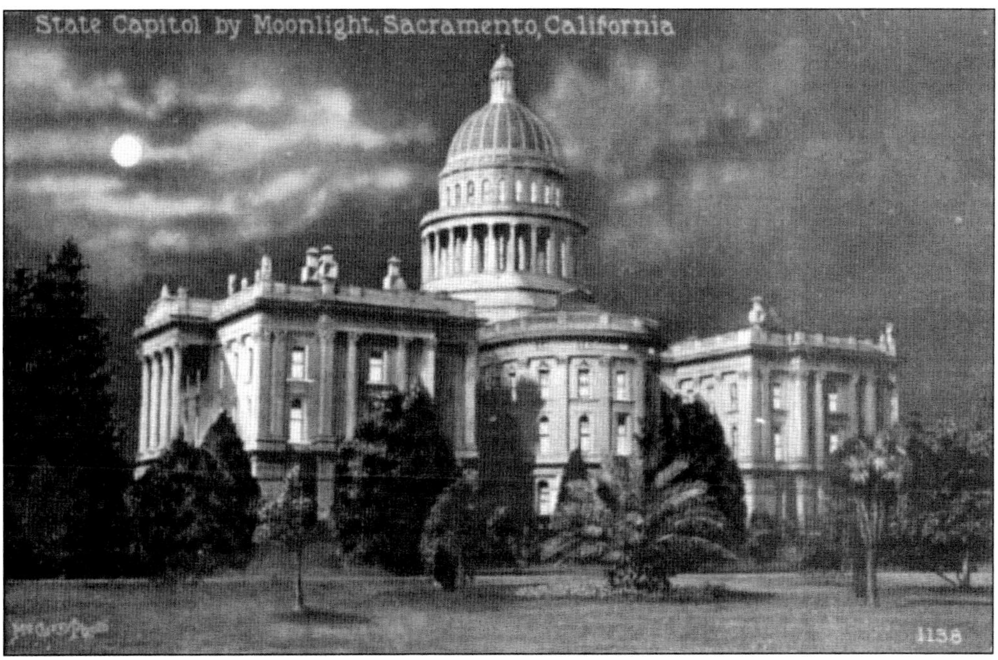

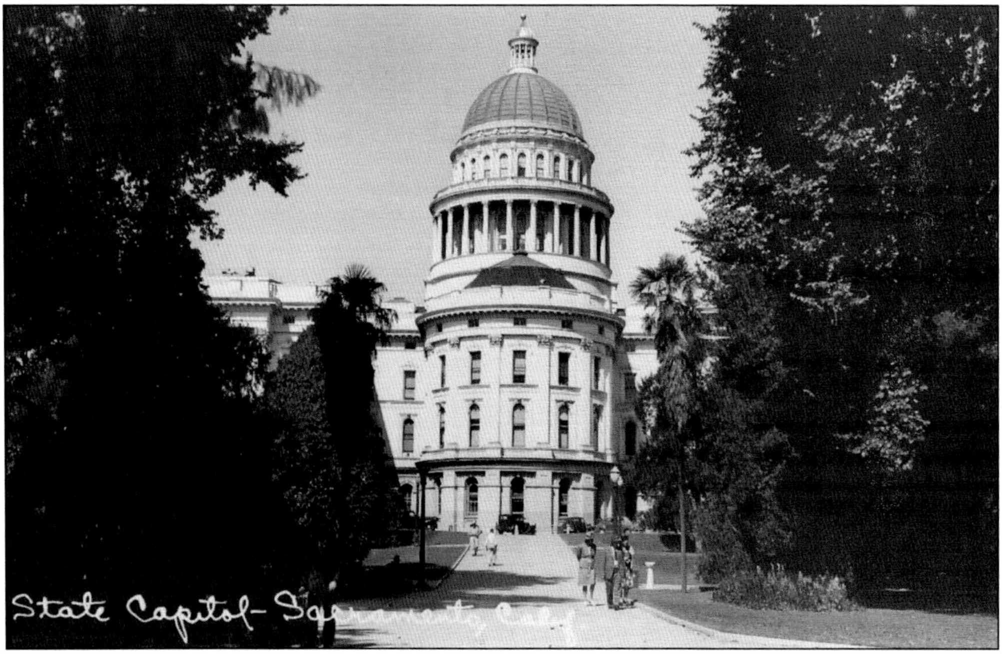

Also popular were real-photo postcards, such as this 1949 view of the apse just before its destruction. (JA.)

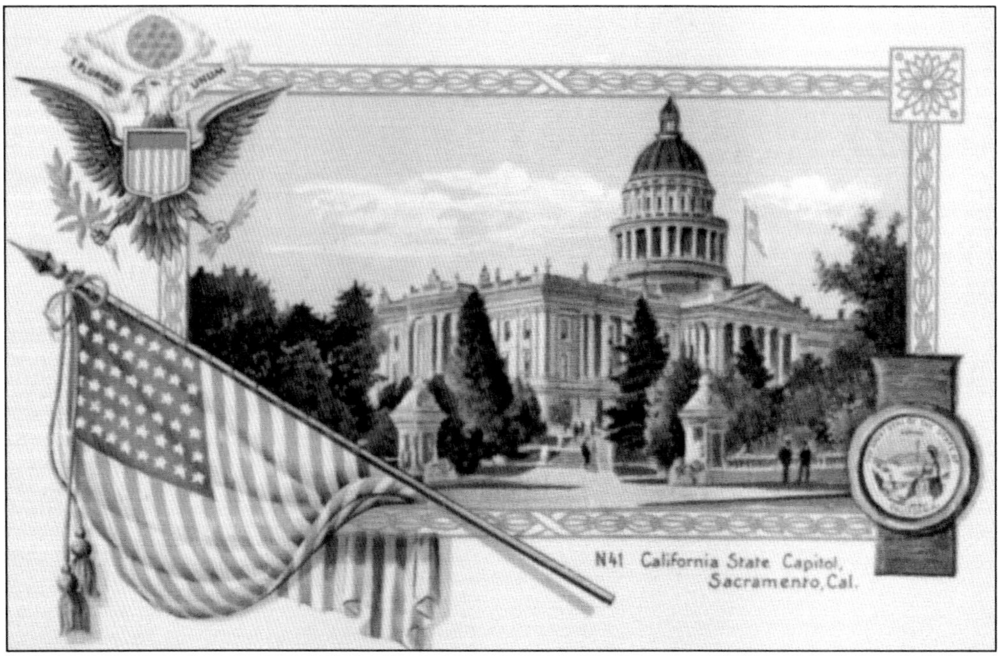

Elaborately colored chromolithograph postcards from the early 20th century celebrated various popular themes and holidays, like patriotism, New Year's, and the California, or golden, poppy. (JA.)

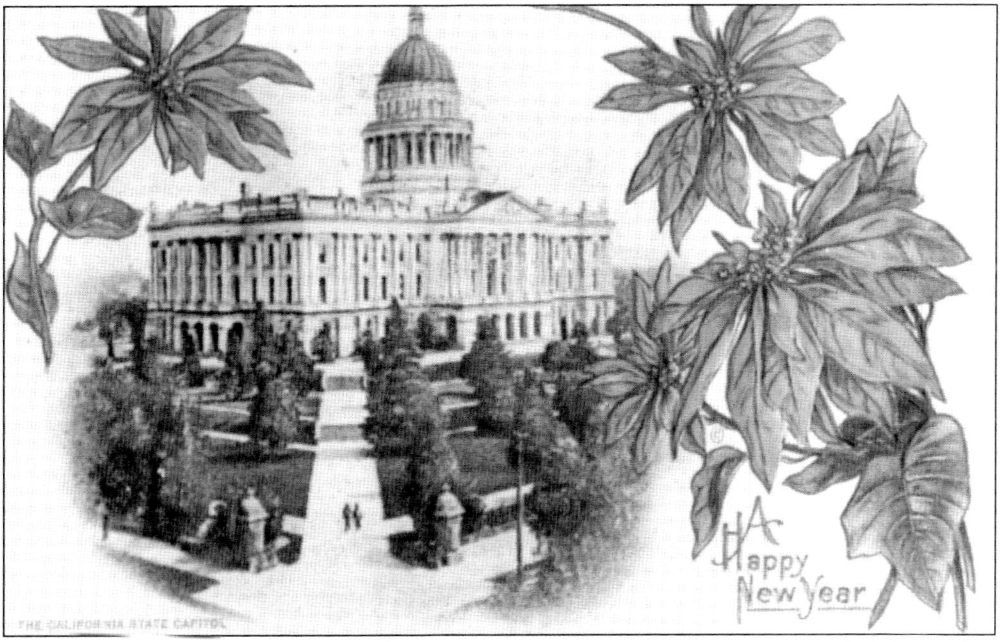

Colorful chromolithograph postcards like this 1916 one wishing the recipient holiday wishes were published. (JA.)

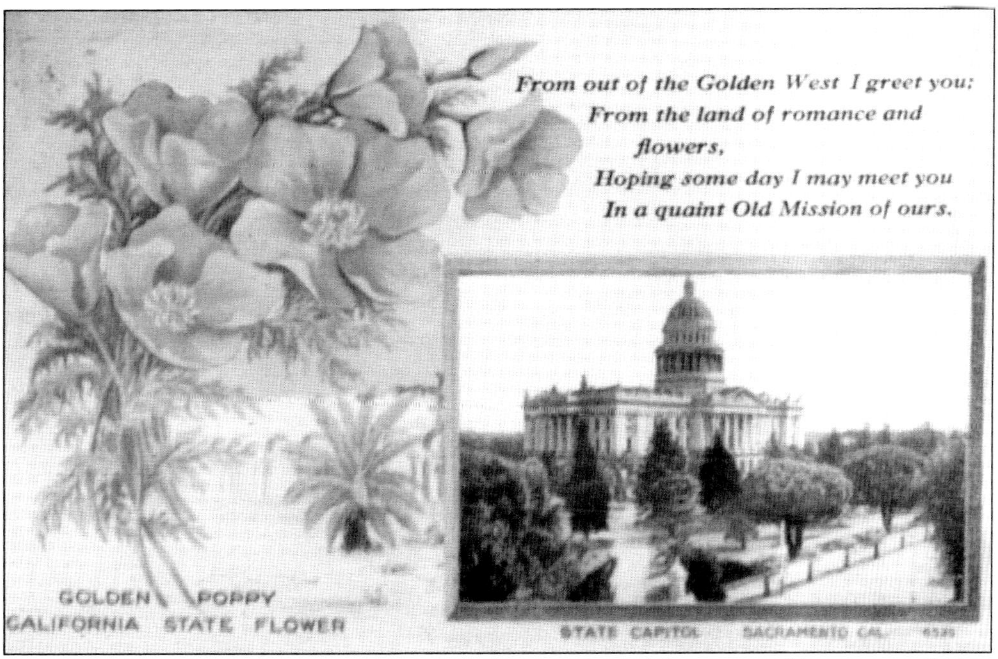

This is a c.1915 postcard celebrating the state flower—the California, or golden, poppy. (JA.)

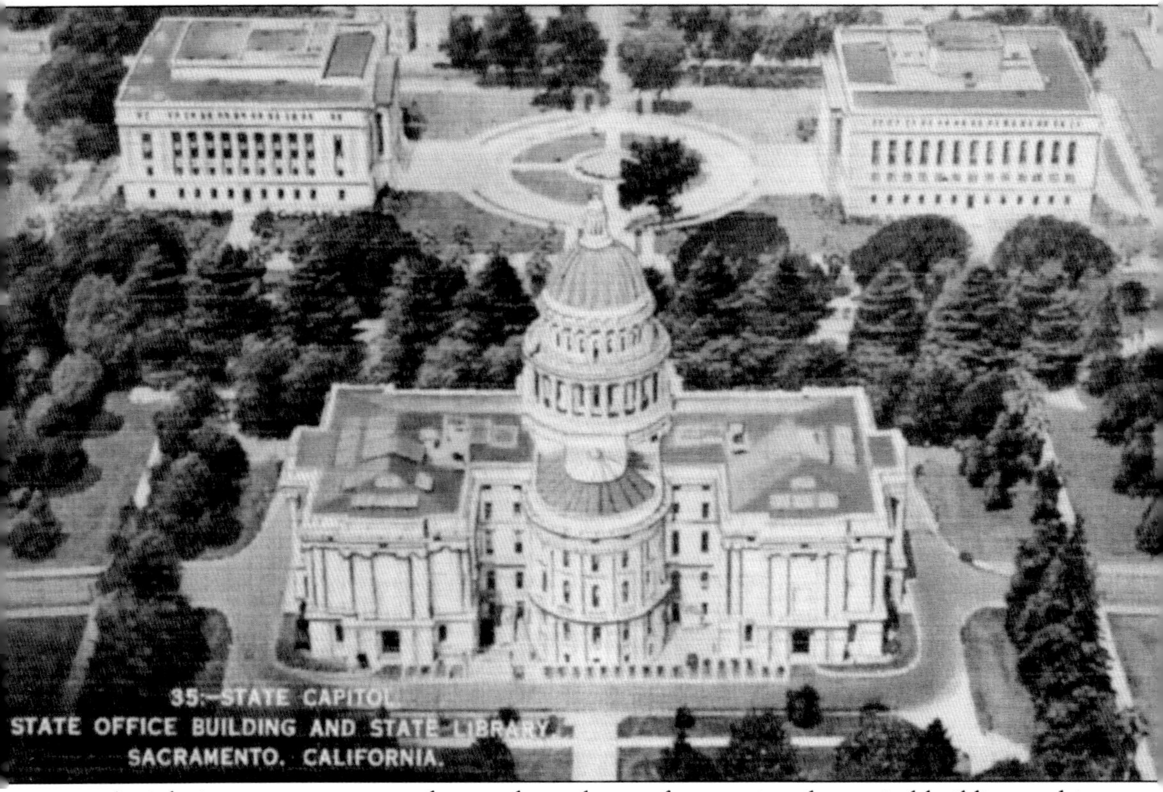

Aerial views were a more modern and novel way of portraying the capitol building and its surroundings for some postcard producers. (JA.)

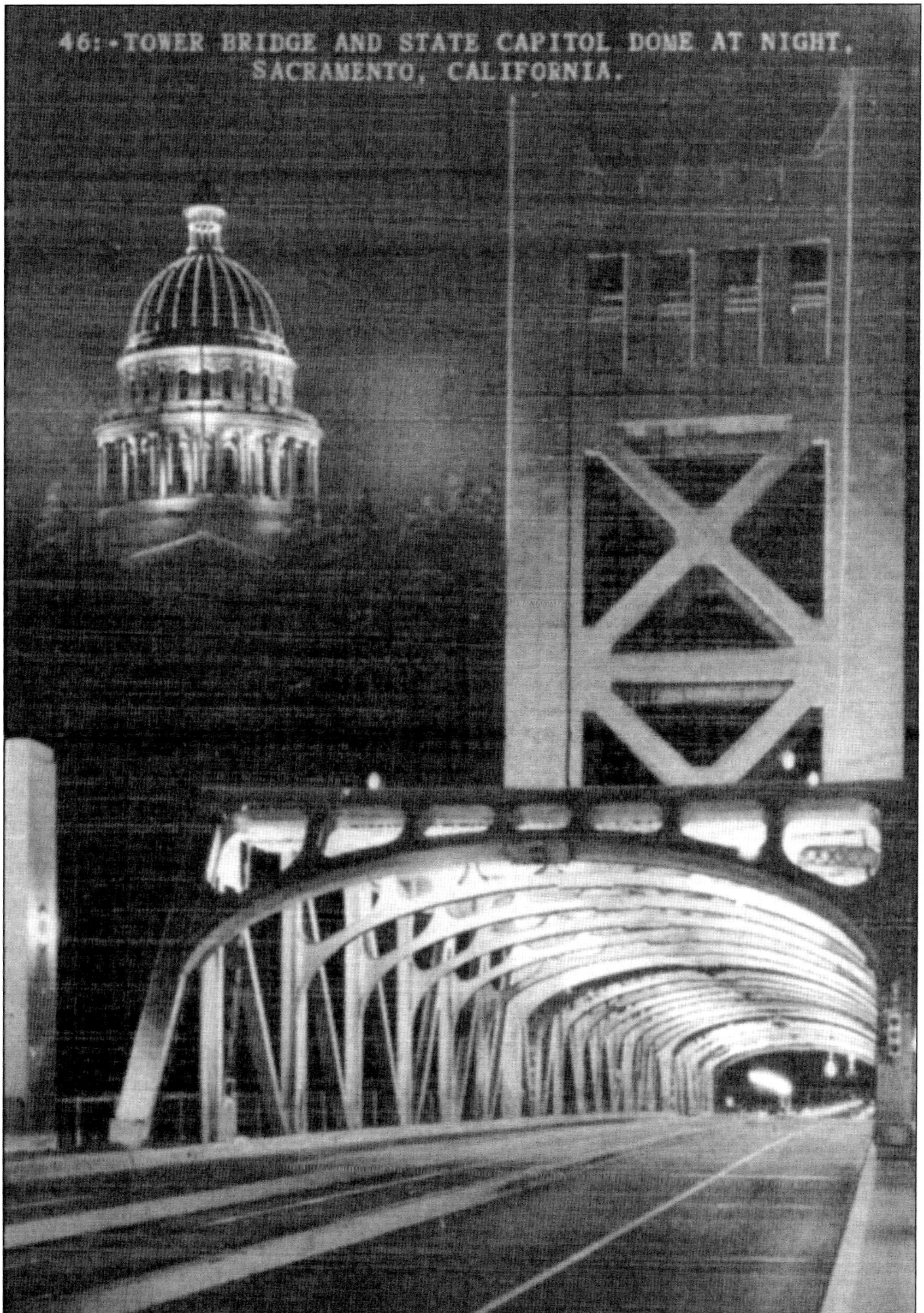

Then, there were invented views. In this 1940s postcard is another iconic symbol of the city, the Tower Bridge, combined with the dome of the capitol, which is actually more than a mile away. (JA.)

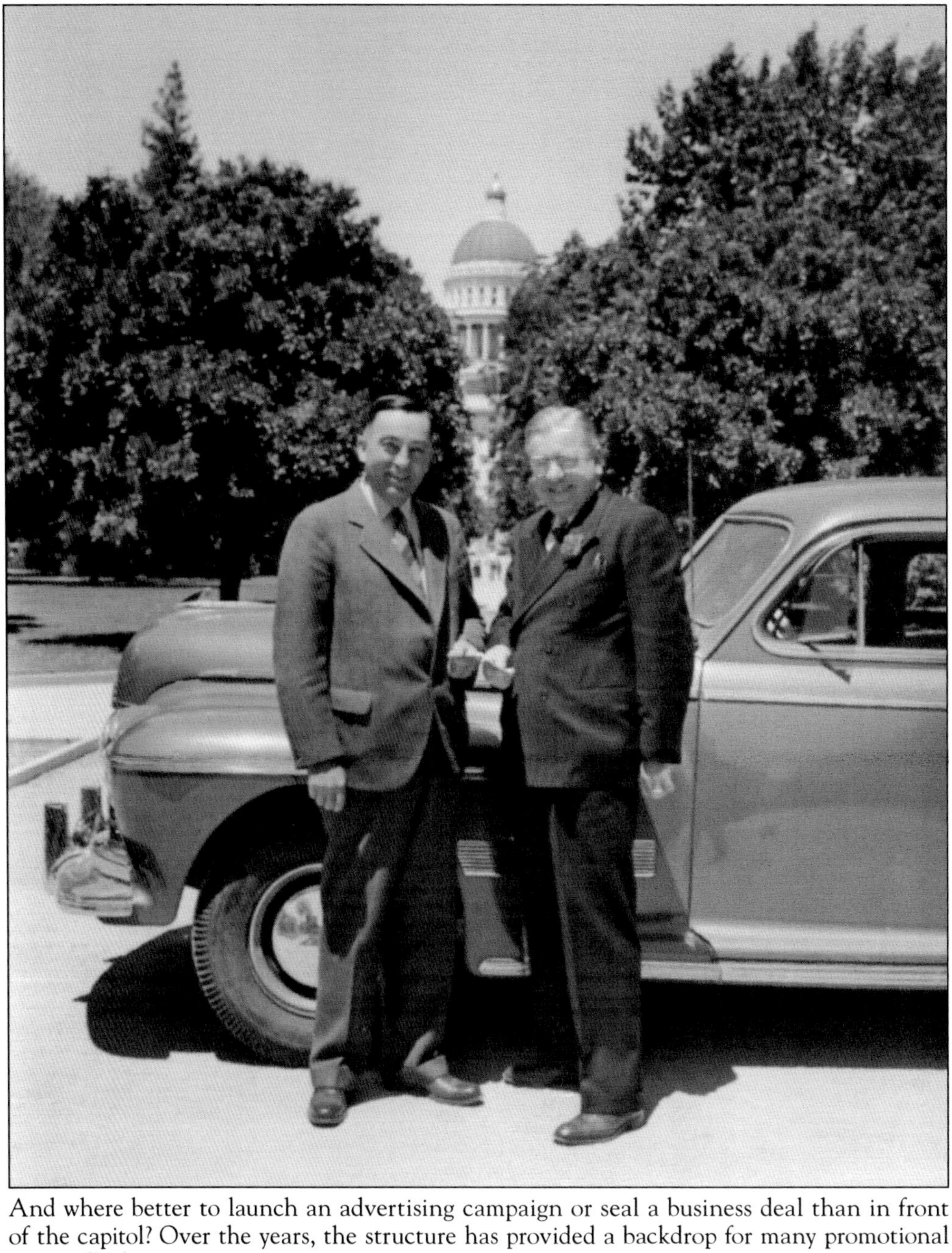

And where better to launch an advertising campaign or seal a business deal than in front of the capitol? Over the years, the structure has provided a backdrop for many promotional events. (JA.)

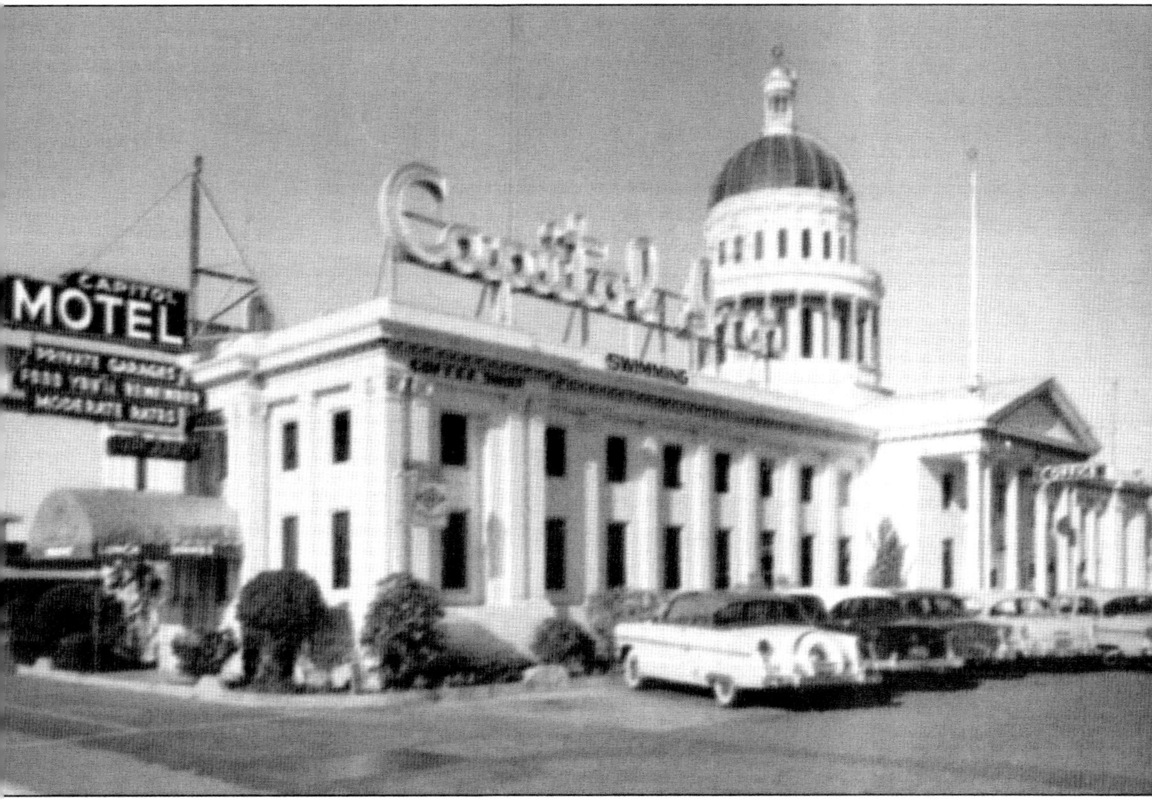

Also, what would the Sacramento region be like without its own knockoff version of the capitol building? Here is a postcard showing the Capitol Motel in nearby West Sacramento. (JA.)

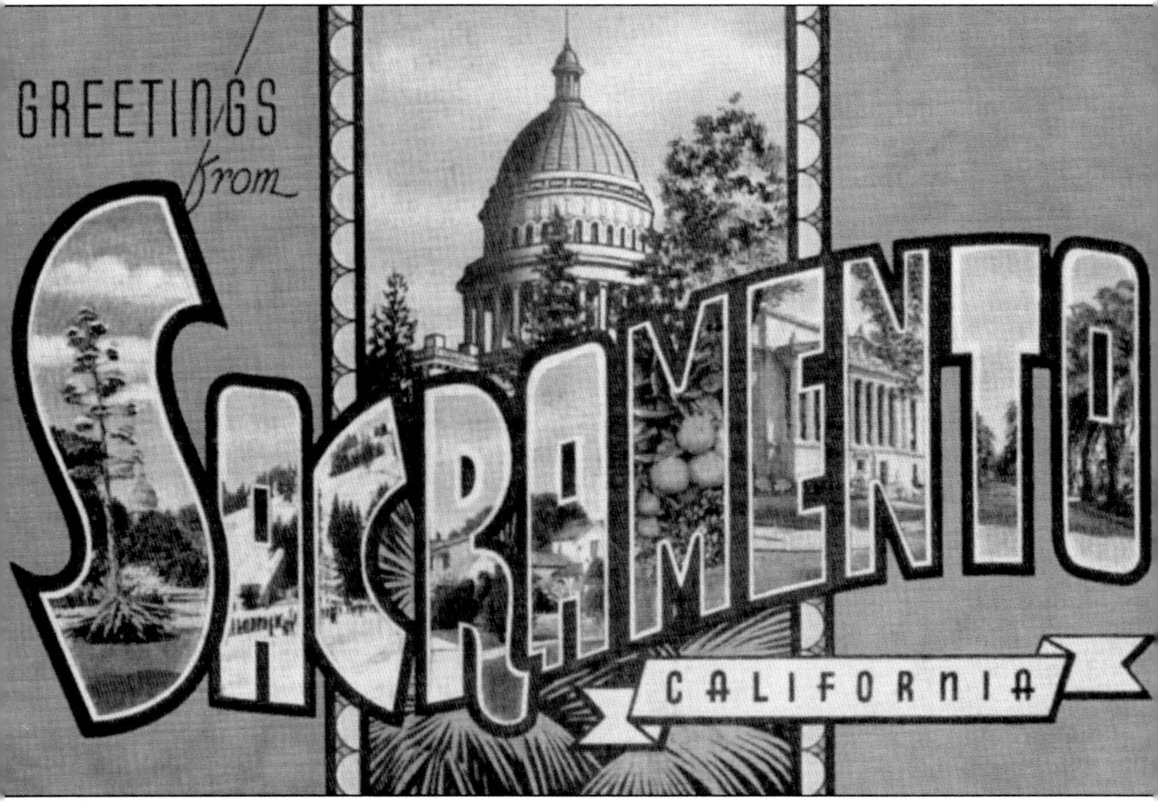

And finally, this "Greetings from Sacramento" postcard shows many of the region's many delights—Capitol Park, ski resorts, Spanish Revival homes, orange trees, the California State Library and Courts Building, palm tree–lined streets, and, of course, the dome of the California State Capitol. (JA.)

Bibliography

Arts and Antiques of the State Capitol: Sacramento, California. Sacramento, California State Legislature, Joint Committee on Rules, 1984.

California Blue Book: Sesquicentennial Edition, 2000. Sacramento, Office of the Secretary of the Senate, 2000.

California Blue Books 1891–1975. Sacramento, Office of the California Secretary of State and the California Legislature.

California State Capitol Restoration: A Pictorial History. Sacramento, California State Legislature, Joint Committee on Rules, 1983.

Capitol Collection, The: California State Capitol. Sacramento, Capitol Art Program, California State Legislature, May 2006.

Heisch, Edward Joseph. *California's Capitol Park at Sacramento: an illustrated manual of the flora of Capitol Park with detailed planting maps and scientific botanical classification of the flora.* Sacramento: Anderson Printing, 1936.

Helmich, Mary A. "The Railroad King's Party: Sacramento's Event of the Season, February 6, 1872." *Golden Notes* (Winter 1989).

Hendricks, Carson. *California State Fair.* Charleston, SC: Arcadia Publishing, 2010.

Leland Stanford Mansion State Historic Park: Historic Structures Report. Sacramento, California State Parks, April 1996.

Melendy, H. Brett and Benjamin F. Gilbert. *The Governors of California: From Peter H. Burnett to Edmund G. Brown.* Georgetown, CA: Talisman Press, 1965.

Munizich, Joseph M. "The Governor's Mansion: A Sacramento Landmark." Special issue, *Golden Notes* (July 1989).

Oxford, June. *The Capital That Couldn't Stay Put: The Complete Book of California's Capitols.* Fairfield, CA: James Stevenson, 1983.

Restoration and Development of the Capitol for the Committee of the California State Legislature. Vols. I & II. No publisher. Sacramento, 1975.

Wood, Robert M. *Past into Present: The Documentation of the California State Capitol House Museum.* Sacramento: California Department of Parks and Recreation, 1983.

Woodward, Lucinda. *A Documentary History of California's State Capitol.* Sacramento: California State Capitol Restoration Project, 1981.